UNVEILING THE MASK

The Ultimate Guide to Rebound From A Financial Disaster

Printed in the United States of America
First Printing, 2018

ISBN 13: 978-0-9991837-6-2
ISBN-10: 0-9991837-6-1

SBG Media Group
ATLANTA

DR. COZETTE M. WHITE

Bestselling Author of "*Attracting The Best*"

Cozette M. White

DEDICATION

To my grandmother, Dorothy M. Bethel for continuously encouraging me to fly towards my dreams – Let's Soar!

To my daughter and son, Briana and Roderick, I pray that I have been a great role model for you to soar to greatest heights.

To Jerome, thanks for believing in me and your endless support. I am genuinely thankful to have you in my life.

To those women who have suffered in silence seeking healing rituals for a new profound financial wellness.

For those that have trusted me to mentor, coach, and empower them to gain clarity and focus on their finances.

To those that will learn about me firsthand through this book. I am with you along the journey to financial success. It is my greatest prayer that this book will make a positive impact on your life.

ACKNOWLEDGEMENTS

This book started with a vision to set out and help women improve their finances. I thank God for giving me the insight, guidance, and fortitude to turn the idea into a reality.

Over the years I have had the esteemed pleasure of mentoring, coach, consulting and guiding thousands on their journey to gaining clarity and focus on their finances. However, I remained in silence about my struggle for financial freedom. For years, I was the "quiet storm" – keeping my trials and tribulations to myself. It was not until I began to globally empower, educate and inspire others with my "financial literacy" messages, that I felt the need to reveal how I was able to make it through the storms after years of suffering through a marriage filled with domestic violence and substance abuse, which nearly left me penniless.

I thank everyone that encouraged me to step out on faith and share my story knowing it would help someone else break their silence.

It is a story about RESILENCE!

Why I Wrote the Book for YOU

This book is for anyone who has ever been in a bad situation or who is currently in a wrong place. It is a tribute to my past experiences, the acknowledgment of the fact that the horrible circumstances individuals may find themselves in, do not have to last nor do they define a person. It must be an emotional rollercoaster all the way through, reliving what most would prefer to be locked in an irretrievable, unreachable mental place. However, my past marital issues are my past.

This book is neither a guide nor a detailed step-by-step process on how to overcome the crippling effects of domestic violence. It does not suggest how to deal with post-traumatic disorder, anxiety or depression. However, I make referrals at the end of the book and share resources to organizations that have invested time in people's lives and have served as a beacon, allowing for that liberating experience, the longed-for "light at the end of the tunnel."

This book is about a young woman and her experiences after falling in love with the wrong man. It detailed the domestic violence, psychological trauma, and verbal abuse she suffered.

More importantly, it tells us about her courage in the face of fear, financial liberation, morphism and her fight against being in denial, the asphyxiating neutral place, where whatever wrong was done is viewed as "All right."

It was Dale Carnegie who said "All the king's horses and all the king's men cannot put the past together again. Don't try to saw sawdust." Amidst other quotes, this has been my "moving on and letting go" anthem. I am not saying it was easy, truthfully, nothing truly liberating. Disillusionment begets rehabilitation; admittedly, no one wants to find out that a cherished individual is a monster in disguise, giving the lernaean hydra a run for its money.

"I want to share my story with you. The unvarnished truth."

Dr. Cozette M. White

TABLE OF CONTENTS

THE FOREWORD

I was delighted when I received a request from Dr. Cozette M. White to write a foreword to support her book *"Unveiling the Mask."* We first met because of our passion to ducate, empower, and inspire on financial empowerment. Subsequently, we have shared our diverse stories of esilience, perseverance, and tenacity with audience globally. The carefree and unbridled joy of adulthood is a beautiful thing. It's the enviable innocence that makes us smile. It's one's rightful, age-appropriate ignorance of the world's challenges that allows us to revel in their happiness. Every adult deserves this season of life, but as time passes, some ride with the storm. Life isn't about waiting for the storm to pass; it's about learning to dance in the rain. Learning to dance is a critical step in the process. If they continue their childhood ignorance, they will experience the full impact of life's challenges. After all, the wind can resurface and tear them down. Contrary to popular belief, ignorance is not bliss. Ignorance is a pain. And in the category of personal finance, ignorance can mean poverty.

Unfortunately, financial setbacks are common in our society and more prevalent when domestic violence is a contributing factor. When it comes to personal finances I often hear stories such as "I am not good with money," or "I am not a numbers person," or "money is evil," or "money is not a worthwhile area to focus on." Stories like these are from limited thinkers. When people want to make a change in their financial situation, they must first uncover the damaging stories and limited beliefs they keep telling themselves. Without shifting your story and embracing new opportunities your story won't change.

In the pages ahead, Dr. White has done an outstanding job of sharing her story of thriving through the storm. She shares her incredible journey of survival and recovery from domestic abuse, divorce, and living on public assistance, to a life of financial healing, success, and joy. She follows by laying the groundwork for anyone willing to embark on the journey for a new financial future after hitting rock bottom.

If you pick up this book it might be because you have been down the path that Dr. White walked at one point in her life, or maybe you are sick of the story you've been telling yourself about money and the time has come to make a shift. That's a great place to be, as frustration can be the launch pad to change. Or perhaps you are at a place in life where the pages are blank, and you need to unveil your own mask. Either way, this book is a great place to start your journey to financial success.

So, as you turn to the next page consider what new story you will write for yourself that will empower you and propel you on the road to financial freedom!

Dr. George C. Fraser
Author, Speaker, Entrepreneur

I N T R O D U C T I O N

T he fear of being hit with a miserable incident that could change your financial condition, like losing your job, impoverishment, or a sudden medical emergency, can be a nightmare for anyone. Such miserable events require you to make significant changes in your life and the revitalization period is incredibly stressful. When that moment comes you realize that you need to make major changes in your life. Often, it's the culmination of a lot of minor stresses building up to one significant breaking point, and then suddenly everything rushes through, creating a tidal wave of worry, fear, and anxiety.

It can feel like everything you've worked for in your whole life is slipping right through your fingers. When you finally look your financial mistakes in the eye, what you see can shake you to your core. The truth is, much of the early success you might see from your turnaround occurs because of your ability to handle that wave of stress. It can hit hard and it can cause you to take your eye off the ball.

For many Americans, financial concerns are a regular source of anxiety, which is understandable given the uncertainties of today's economy. It is important to remember that worry doesn't solve much, but answering the question of how to overcome financial problems does. However, your financial disaster can be remedied by regaining your self-control and taking solid actions. The financial benefits of dealing with financial disaster; saving more, paying down expensive debt - will improve not just your self-confidence, but your overall mood as well. The less you worry about dealing with finances and money issues, the more you can enjoy life.

You may consider your circumstances as unique, but many people around the world have walked this path before you. The road to financial revival is shabby but the steps to return after the financial disaster are well-proven. So let's get started on some useful steps to recover from a financial catastrophe.

Let's Get Straight to Cozette's Story

I met Rod in 1987 while doing a summer internship at a company called "DCAA" in El Segundo, California.

I was young, bright, and eager to learn, and ready to deal with whatever the great, big profound world brought my way. I can remember being introduced to my co-worker at the time who later became my husband. I recall that we started out by having lunch and going out, things people do when they want to know where the camaraderie leads. Although I cannot quite recollect all the vital details and happenings during that period, there were specific peculiar and striking occurrences. One thing led to the other and in a matter of months, less than six months, he had asked me to marry him. My answer was yes! Yes, to a civil union, the joining of our bodies, minds, and souls. Yes, to forever.

However, how wrong was I? Now that I look back, it almost seemed as if I was setting myself up for a severe case of the "I told you so's." To some, marriage was too quick, a naïve move on my part, and what the hell did I expect from a marriage with such a short and brief dating period.

I now realize it was most certainly the quickness in the timing of our marriage that caused the spiral downfall. Had we stayed in the dating phase for a longer period, maybe some of the behavioral problems would have become apparent to me. It was roughly five years into our marriage that I began noticing inconsistencies. If I had courted Rod for a more extended period, maybe I would have seen the discrepancies.

At the time we got married, I was a senior in college, so we prolonged having kids. We lived a beautiful life. Financially speaking, we were at that point where we lived life as it happened. We failed to have a substantial savings of any kind because we were just living life in our late twenties. We did much traveling and many things that some of our friends chose not to because they were not able.

The domestic violence started as a result of an argument. I cannot recall what led to the discussion

– it seems almost trivial and petty now – but at the end of it all, something as little as a petty argument left me being socked in the eye. The black eye came really quick. I was punched in the jaw too. All this was while I was nurturing and breastfeeding my five-week-old daughter. At this point, I kept asking myself if I could bear this, yet so many things blindsided me. You know that period in your life where you are wondering what to do next. Do you stay and plead? Do you save your marriage? Do you become a better person? Is what's going on your fault? I knew what was going on wasn't right, but I had on blinders moreover, wasn't aware that there were things I could do to get out of this mess.

Let me say; there is no justification for violence of any kind. Victims need to learn that it is no fault of theirs that they find themselves with fractured ribs, a broken jaw or a black eye. There is no excuse or justification. If you know this, then perhaps you can take it easy on yourself and demand better.

In abusive relationships, there may be a cycle of abuse during which tensions rise, and an act of violence is committed, followed by a period of reconciliation and calm. I call it the cycle of chaos. Domestic violence victims often dismiss or excuse the first acts of violence directed at them. Most often, they look for reasons to justify the first hit, barrage, psychopathic outburst.

Approximately 5.6 million women and 2.4 million men are estimated to be physically assaulted by an intimate partner annually in the United States.[1] In the United States, domestic violence is the leading cause of injury to women between the ages of 15 and 44.[2]

Most often, individuals have their definition of domestic violence skewed. Some restrict their understanding of it to physical abuse. (Battery, acid throwing and all things physical). Domestic violence indeed does not preclude that. However, it could be psychological, (child's play to a psychopath), verbal, economic, sexual, religious as well as, reproductive. It is not restricted to heterosexual couples; it can also take place against children, the elderly, former spouses or partners.[3]

It can range from subtle, coercive forms to marital rape and to violent physical abuse such as choking, beating, female genital mutilation and acid throwing that result in disfigurement or death. Domestic murders include stoning, bride burning, honor killings, dowry deaths and is not restricted to a particular gender. Domestic violence can also affect the fetus and can have lingering effects on the child after birth. Physical abuse is associated with neonatal death (1.5% versus 0.2%), and verbal abuse is associated with low birth weight (7.6% versus 5.1%).[4]

Six months after having my second child, I reaffirmed what I already knew. It was then I discovered that substance abuse was there and that he had begun to use marijuana. I remember this particular incident that happened on November 17, 1993. I can recall we were in a confrontation over who was to pick up the kids from daycare or why I did not pick them up. I remember we began to exchange words and the exact words out of his mouth were "Shut up before I throw this boiling hot water on you." Who says that to a wife? Someone you promised to uphold, cherish and protect? The bone of your bone and the flesh of your flesh? Unfortunately, the boiling hot water did land on me, and I ended up in the emergency room with second and third-degree burns on my right arm.

I was embarrassed, ashamed and in denial because I did not share this information with anyone, not even my family members. No one knew what was going on. I noticed this was the trend among domestic violence victims. There is this shame that cloaks you, and you end up hiding all these problems because you are embarrassed, and you do not want people to see you in that state. That is what a mask does. It protects your real face, making it hard for you to shine forth.

In my case, I discovered this hindrance almost a little too late. I kept hiding and hoping it would all go away, but it did not. Nothing will unless you use the last strength left in your body to break the barriers. You need to take charge, cross that hurdle yourself, and let go of the shame. It is a decision every victim must make.

On Thanksgiving, we decided to show up to our family gathering. This particular fall day was a hot day here in California. However, I showed up in a sweater that covered my entire wound. Of course, my warm attire looked ridiculous. However, I could not let my family in on my struggles.

Now I am not talking about random people here. I am talking about those who have your interests at heart. I am talking about family and support. Numerous people asked me why I had the sweater on, but I covered it up and told them "Oh, it was cold when we left home" when in fact I was hiding my wound. Multiple bruises, to be exact! Injuries, burns, and fractures. I had an ace bandage on me from permanent second and third-degree burns in which I was going to the doctor every other day to have the skin peeled and removed, and the ace bandages changed.

Again, I was afraid, and in denial so I just stayed in the marriage. During a victim's years of abuse, they may want to do everything they can to accept the situation. That is because they do not know better. I am telling you today, the only way to live is by unveiling that mask and walking out of that situation. Shortly after that, I discovered that my husband was using crack cocaine. The discovery came when I got in one day from work, and he was in the house using the substance.

On one unforgettable afternoon, after facing much stress from the day's job, I had a call from my children's daycare and was told to come "pick up my kids." It was strange, the daycare center had just recently closed for the day, and I had expected Rod to pick the kids up from school.

However, I was wrong. I picked up the kids and took them to McDonald's as they were hungry. Roderick would not stop crying because his dad did not pick him up from school. It was an experience I could not forget. I remember feeling a little of that vindictiveness and much anger. As I had arrived home, pulling into the garage, I remember hitting the remote control anxiously waiting just to figure out what happened to my husband. I watched the garage door lift (it seemed to take more time than usual). When the garage door got all the way up, all I saw was a man in a sleeveless wife-beater T-shirt, blue Levi jeans, and white tube socks. When I looked again, it felt surreal; I saw my husband bent over leaning on the washer and dryer snorting what I was sure to be crack cocaine. He did it quite uncaringly and had continued unperturbed, showing no signs of noticing my presence in the garage. It was more likely that he did not care. As you can image, I was in total shock. My heart nearly fell into my lap as I witnessed with my own eyes what was going on...Rod was getting high in our garage.

Things escalated and took a downward spiral from there. There were ups and downs and arguments and fights, and it got to a point where I began calling the police to come out for assistance. I remember the officer saying, "This is the last time we will come out and take a report since you aren't willing to move from this situation. If we get another domestic violence call, then we'll move forward with filing a civil claim against this individual, and he will have to deal with the State of California."

We continued living together. One thing about breaking through is that sometimes, even if the universe wants to help them, victims of abuse look for ways to cling to their past.

Are you sticking to your past? When will you let go?

It got to a point when we had another quarrel, and he socked me in the jaw. At that point, I called the police, and they said "This is it. We are filing a case against this individual." Make yourself open to receiving help and support from well-meaning individuals.

As you can image, the fights began to happen frequently even after the police intervention. The arguments got heated as well, and it got to a point where I asked my husband if he would move out. Asking him to remove himself from our home resulted in a heated fight in front of our young kids, and of course, they were crying and screaming wondering why daddy was hitting mommy. At the time the kids were two and four; too helpless and young to do anything but watch, yell, and scream.

One thing I know, I always felt in fear. Fear that he would hurt me more than he had already done. Fear that he would hurt my kids. Victims of domestic violence often are trapped in violent domestic situations through isolation, power, and control, cultural acceptance, lack of financial resources, fear and shame or to protect children. At this point, things only got worse.

I had to take care of our kids and at the same time, make sense of the dwindling situation. It was zapping all my energy; I often felt burnt out with the fights, arguments, and rancor that prevailed at every moment in time. I would call the police when I sensed an argument and during battles, so much so that it became recurring.

Unveiling My Mask

Unveiling your mask requires a turning point. An 'aha!' moment. One day, I got to the end of my rope and said: "enough is enough." I asked Rod to leave the house once and for all by placing a note on the bathroom mirror for Rod to see and read. I was finally ready to confront my demons and do something about it. I took the kids to the master bedroom and locked the door, so Rod could not enter the room. I realized later that night that locking the door was the wrong thing to do. That particular evening, Rod burst through the bedroom door and tore the hinges off the door and began to rant and rave and said he was not leaving. I was terrified because, at that point, it was in the middle of the night; probably 2:00 a.m. Rod woke up the kids and had us in the bedroom, while he blew a fuse, and sadly, it was witnessed by the kids who cried along with yells.

Subsequently, about three days later, Rod came to me and said that he was going to be moving out of the house. That was the best thing I had heard in a while. To say I was relieved was an understatement. I was finally going to be free. Unfortunately, my happiness was short-lived as Rod moved just around the corner from the kids and me. My joy immediately disappeared like evaporated smoke. I was not happy.

Shortly after moving out of the home, he began sending balloons, flowers, and gifts to my workplace in what I assumed was a ploy to win me back. It was both frustrating and disconcerting mostly because I did not know what was going to happen on any given day.

One day, he came to my home requesting that I see him outside. Fortunately, I noticed a weapon (gun) on the passenger seat of the car. When I saw that he had a gun in his car, I declined his request, calling the police almost immediately. He was arrested instantly. His parents wanted me to cover his bail, but I refused. I did not see any reason to bail someone out of jail who had caused me physical trauma and still impacting my life.

Shortly after that, I guess Rod got tired of his foolishness because he served me with divorce papers. The divorce, however, wasn't a friendly one. It was one that was a battle for custody over who was going to have full custody of the kids. He wanted to take care of the kids, and I did not want any of that because of the things I had endured with him. I did not want that kind of influence on my children. We battled over this, and I came out as the custodial parent.

The marriage was dissolved, and so was my only source of income. Because of going through my divorce and other life matters, things began to take a toll on work. I started slipping in my performance and ultimately made a mistake which resulted in "termination of employment." Wow…I was unemployed. No income and responsible for two kids. I quickly went from two incomes to one income, to nothing. I had zilch to my name. I was penniless, near homeless and a single mother on public assistance with food stamps and any other support I could get. The most important thing at that point was how to get back on my feet for my children.

I was so used to having two incomes in the household, and now I did not even have one. Dealing with the stress, taking care of the kids all alone, telling no one about the harrowing experience and the pain I suffered made it ten times worse. I had no shoulder to lean on.

In hindsight, I understand the situation would have been a lot easier if I had talked to someone about the issues and problems I was facing. I would have gotten some quality advice. I could not have persuaded Rod all on my own to go rehabilitation, but I might have if I had informed either of our parents about his problems.

> *Also, my relationship with God (or lack thereof) was another factor that stood against me. I was not deeply religious and was more of the lukewarm type if you know what I mean. Attending church came whenever the urge struck or when it was necessary for me.*

It took me about six months to recover from being off from a job, but during that time, I started picking up books and figuring how I could rebound and get back on my feet. Today, I say the same thing to you. It might take you some time, but you have to make continuous, logical steps towards change. It took me some time. However, I was able to salvage my home. Subsequently, I began to keep more of my earnings by putting money away in my employer 401K plan. I started to put money away into savings accounts for my kids so that they would have money to go off to college. I began to make automatic savings withdrawal so that I could buy Series EE savings bonds so that when the kids graduated and went to school, I would be in a position to cash the savings bonds and use as a deposit towards books and other expenses required for higher education.

Subsequently, I was able to bounce back, but it was not easy. It was a process that took years. Today as a single mom, I have positioned myself to leave a secure financial legacy for my family. We take our fiscal matters serious. I was very dedicated and diligent to reach my goal. There were days when I wanted to lose hope, but I kept going. Today, our financial portfolio looks excellent considering our start it was my commitment to change that made the difference.

I say all of this to encourage and inspire anyone that is in an abusive relationship surrounded by substance abuse. You too can get out of it. You do not have to stay in your situation. There is help, resources, and shelters that will take you in, help you and allow you to see the light at the end of the tunnel. That is the story of how I recovered. It can be yours too irrespective of your age, status or where ever you are in life. It is never too late.

Today, I am a successful businesswoman.
My kids are all grown up now,
Briana's 27 and Roderick's 25.

In retrospect, I often think how I could have handled the situation differently, but there's no point beating a dead horse. T.E Elliot said quite succinctly that "Only by acceptance of the past can you alter it."[5] Well, can you alter the past?

No, but can you alter the effects the past had on you? This book is for whosoever has experienced any abuse; you can get over the crippling effects. You do not have to stay in such relationships. Fear is the tool used in such instances to disarm you. You have got to find your anchor and use it to your benefit. You are beautiful; you are courageous, you have much good in you and don't let anybody tell you otherwise.

xxx

You do not have to be the confined captive in your own home. There are plenty of shelters and other resources that are ready to pull you up from that bottomless chaos and into the light. Have faith, believe in God, and fear nothing. Your past does not have to dictate your future, when there is a will, there'll always be a way.

How to Use This Material

This book is all about financial empowerment for women. It will challenge you to get your finances in order after any financial disaster. This book is useful to anyone seeking financial health. Grab your favorite journal, as I take you on a journey to getting your financial house in order. Putting pen to paper will enable you to retain the material and allow you to take notes that you can refer back to throughout the year, at your two-year mark, your five-year mark, and so on. Use the journal as a way to monitor your progress. As you read through the book, you will notice a few icons that you will want to take note of to use as a future reference too.

LOOK FOR THESE HELPFUL ICONS

MONEY QUOTES

PERSONAL FINANCE STATISTICS

COZETTE'S TIPS

Exercise Material

Cozette M. White

CHAPTER
1

FINANCIAL
HEALING

"Every morning when I open my curtains for that first look of the day, no matter what the day looks like — raining, foggy, overcast, and sunny — my heart swells with gratitude. I get another chance."

-Oprah Winfrey

Thee starting point for financial recovery is to stop wallowing in your misery and accept reality. Yes, it is a bummer. Yes, you're likely the victim of somebody else's wrongdoing. Yes, it is devastating. Most important– none of that matters now. What's done is done, and there is no turning back. Resisting what's already a fact is futile, so don't waste your energy. Accept reality.

Living in the past only makes forward progress more difficult. Instead, accept the setback, let go of it, and commit to forward movement. Not because it is the right thing to do, but because it's the best way to help yourself. As long as you waste your energy wallowing in your misery, you will have that much less energy to dedicate to solving the very real challenges you face to move forward in life. The best defense is a good offense, so get out of defensive mode and get started on the road to recovery with a clear offensive strategy.

Identify the Problems

The next step to overcoming financial disaster is to identify the problem that is causing difficulties. Financial problems are generally an indication of a larger issue and to come up with long term solutions, you have to identify the actual cause of your financial troubles. The idea behind the importance of uncovering the specific problem is to come up with a permanent solution. Just like a leaky tap in your house; placing a bucket below it is a temporary solution. Fix the tap, and the leak will stop permanently. Rather than dwelling on you stress, focus on resolving the problem that's causing your financial problems.

Stop Wasting Time

Many people respond to stress by using time- wasters to procrastinate. They will dump time and energy into activities that have nothing to do with their problem in order to distract themselves for a little while. The problem with that is that it usually makes the problem worse when they face it again.

Stop procrastinating. Focus on the problem at hand. If you're feeling overwhelmed with it at the moment, get real rest so you can attack it with mental focus tomorrow. So, how do you actually "focus on the problem at hand"? The next several strategies will help you do just that.

Let's first look at your money personality. This will assist you in telling you about your money habits.

Your Money Personality

Are you a big spender, saver, worrier or avoider? Are your decisions driven by more than one money personality perspective? Take a few moments to complete the below *Money Personality Quiz*. Besides being fun, this quiz with your results will help you better understand your instinctive responses to your financial habits.

Money Personality Quiz

1. You just arrived in Las Vegas, and you win $1,000 on your first bet. What do you do?

   a. Deposit your winnings into your savings account and stick to your prearranged spending plan for the rest of the trip.

   b. Bet it all in your next turn of the wheel or round of cards.

   c. Have no idea what to do because you never win anything.

   d. Spend it freely on shows, restaurants, and spa treatments.

2. You are shopping at your favorite store when you spot the perfect bathing suit. It fits perfectly! The only problem is that it is costly and way out of your budget. What do you do?

   a. Buy it anyway. Plastic is Power!

   b. Wait for the bathing suit to go on sale.

   c. Buy it, a g o n i z e all night long over the purchase and then return it the next day.

d. Think maybe you could buy it, but figure you better wait and decide later.

3. Good news! You have just inherited $50,000 from an Uncle that you have never met. You:

   a. Put the check in your drawer for right now.

      You do not want to act too quickly.

   b. Start booking your next vacation.

   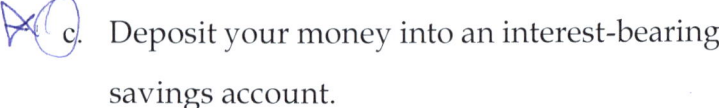 c. Deposit your money into an interest-bearing savings account.

   d. Deposit it into your checking account to pay bills.

4. When it comes to saving money, you:

   a. Can't do it.
   b. Know you should but aren't sure you know the best way.
   c. Have set up a system that works for you.

   d. Make and break a new savings plan every month.

5.   Honestly, how do you drive your car?

   a.   Reluctantly you wish you had a chauffeur.

   b.   Cautiously and safely-you are a defensive driver.

   c.   Quickly and aggressively-you do not let anyone get in your way!

   d.   Anxiously-there are a lot of crazy drivers out there.

6.   If you could choose any of the following occupations, regardless of income, it would be a:

   a.   Best-selling poet and novelist.

   b.   Stunt-woman.

   c.   Judge with the Supreme Court.

   d.   Elementary school teacher.

7.   Regarding money, your best wish for your children is that:

    a.   They do not take too many risks. Risks can get you into trouble.

    b.   They learn to control their spending.

       Someone has got to.

    c.   They have good luck. That is what it takes to make it in this world.

    d.   They have a good education. They will need to work hard to find a suitable occupation.

8.   Money-wise, what do you look for in a mate?

    a.   A stable income and very conservative with their money.

    b.   A hot car in his driveway and a lot of shiny plastic in his wallet.

    c.   Someone who will handle the family finances, so I do not have to.

    d.   A lack of concern for material things.

9. When you think about your retirement, you:

   a. Cross your fingers, close your eyes, and begin to pray.

   b. Remember you probably need to plan sometime soon.

   c. Hope your saving plan works well.

   d. Can't wait for the party to begin; I hear that the weather is beautiful in Florida!

10. Your worst money problem is your:

   a. Lack of financial education.

   b. Shopaholic tendencies.

   c. Procrastination.

   d. Concern it will dissipate.

11. Your worst fear of money is:

    a. The sound of creditors is knocking at your door.

    b. Losing over 50% of your assets in a stock market crash.

    c. Turning 55 and realizing that you have no assets other than your car.

    d. You will not get around to thinking about your finances in time.

12. If someone asked, "How much is your bank account right now?" you would say:

    a. "Enough, but I do not like to dwell on money."

    b. "Do you want me to include the outstanding checks not yet posted to the account?"

    c. "I am not sure."

    d. "I hope that I did not bounce any checks this week."

13. When you receive a savings and retirement account statement, you:

    a. Check it over very carefully.

    b. Give up trying to figure it out after a few minutes.

    c. Leave it with other unopened mail on the dining room table.

    d. Toss it in a drawer and assume the company must be right.

14. A quality that you admire about yourself is:

    a. Punctuality-you are always on time.

    b. Spirituality-you are not a money-grubber.

    c. Vivacity-you are always the life of the party.

    d. Caution-you do not tackle things of which you are unsure.

15. The reason you do not have as much money as you would like is:

    a. You are too cautious. You miss out on high investments because you do not want to take risks.

    b. You do not like thinking about money. It can be so complicated.

    c. You throw it away. You keep buying things you do not need.

    d. You are not sure why.

16. Guests are arriving for Thanksgiving dinner in one hour. In the kitchen, you are:

    a. Wishing you had not agreed to host.

    b. Frantic, messy, and creative; you're trying to perfect a new recipe you created just for this occasion.

    c. Disorganized, frustrated, and slow.

    d. Organized, fast, and clean; everything is in the oven already, and you are just setting up a few last-minute details.

17. When entertaining, you like:

    a. Spontaneous bashes with a few hundred of your closest friends.

    b. Well-planned parties for your monthly dinner group.

    c. Informal get-together with friends in the great outdoors.

    d. Someone else to suggest the plan to you and set things up.

Your Money Personality Quiz: Score your Results

	A	B	C	D
1	S	B	A	W
2	B	S	W	A
3	A	B	S	W
4	B	A	S	W
5	A	S	B	W
6	W	B	S	A
7	A	B	W	S
8	S	B	A	W
9	W	A	S	B
10	W	B	A	S
11	B	S	W	A
12	A	S	B	W
13	S	W	A	B
14	S	W	B	A
15	S	A	B	W
16	A	B	W	S
17	B	S	W	A

TOTALS

SAVER   _____   AVOIDER _____

WORRIER   _____   BIG SPENDER ___

RATINGS

From your scores above, see which style dominates your money personality. You may find that you possess some characteristics of each style, but one trait tends to dominate.

<u>THE SAVER</u>

Channel took the quiz, and she's the saver. The saver is deeply attached to her money. Her hobby is saving money, and she loves to see her bank account grow. She is also known to clip coupons, set budgets, and prioritize financial goals, although she may not be inclined to take on much risk. The saver enjoys keeping her money safe in the bank. She often worries that she may outlive her money and end up in poverty.

The saver also has difficulty spending money on herself and her loved ones, especially on things that are not a necessity. Many savers worry about money and feel that they will never have enough to be secure.

Others channel their thrifty tendencies into always

looking for the big sale. Getting a bargain makes her feel great but finding out there was a better deal somewhere else makes her feel terrible. The Saver attempts to assert financial control of her life by focusing on details, and she is usually very apprehensive about making mistakes.

THE AVOIDER

My girlfriend, Jennifer, fits the shoes here. She's our "avoider." The avoider would rather do almost anything than to think about her money. She typically handles financial matters at the very last minute, or even late-such as failing to pay bills on time and then owing a late charge premium. She does not like keeping financial records or a budget.

She tends to be quite fearful of making a mistake, so it is easier to do nothing.

Most avoiders feel some level of inadequacy when it comes to financial matters. They wish someone else would just take care of it. Money matters can be so complex and confusing, and there can be so many details and decisions to make. It is no wonder they may not prepare well for the future.

THE WORRIER

At one point, Tamara considered herself the saver but has become a worrier after she started caring for her mom. The worrier has a difficult time dealing with her finances, whether balancing her checkbook, budgeting, paying bills or investing. She is likely to engage in "robbing Peter to pay Paul" behaviors, all the while self- flagellating for doing so. The worrier continually thinks about money but rarely takes charge of her finances or strategizes for financial comfort.

The worrier may feel that money is evil and has the power to corrupt. She may believe that having too much money or making a profit on investments means she is being greedy or selling out on her values. Worriers are not inclined to keep tabs on their current spending or invest for the future, and they may alienate their loved ones with their self-righteous attitude toward affluence.

THE BIG SPENDER

I have friends, and I have good genuine friends. Well my colleague, Cheryl, has friended the credit cards as her besties. The big spender's credit cards are her best friends. She often spends money on things she really cannot afford. The b ig spender hates to limit herself; after all, she works hard for her money, and it makes her feel good to spend it!

At the same time, she may feel frustrated that she does not have more. Big spenders have a hard time budgeting and difficulty delaying gratification in the present to save for the future. The big spender is also prone to fantasies of the financial rescue, and fears of achieving success on her own. While she waits for the miracle person or event that will solve her financial woes, the Big spender may spend most of what she has at her disposal or rack up a hefty amount of debt.

72% of Americans report being financially stressed each month.[6]

CHAPTER 2

EMOTIONAL MONEY ELEMENTS

"Financial peace is not the acquisition of stuff. It is learning to live on less than you make, so you can give the money back and have money to invest. You cannot win until you do this."

-Dave Ramsey

GROWING YOURSELF BACK UP

Be aware that negative emotions are normal. Before addressing the financial elements ofa financial disaster, it is important to address the emotional elements. You have to recognize that emotional turmoil is a normal component of the process. Depending on the cause of your situation, you may experience stress, depression, or anxiety. This may be accompanied by a sense of guilt or failure. You may also feel as if you have no control over your situation.

These emotions are a normal component of going through a financial disaster. While it may be difficult at first, these emotions will likely pass over time as you adjust to your new circumstances and regain control of the situation by taking action.

Focus on accepting your financial situation. When faced with a difficult situation, people often try to deny or ignore the situation. While it may feel better to do this, it does not help in the long run. Accepting your situation can empower you to face your difficulties as they are and conquer them head-on. Accepting the situation is the first step to resolving it. Try to channel any negative energy about the situation into positive, solution-focused actions. For example, instead of dwelling or blaming yourself for a scenario, try taking that negative energy and using it to make a commitment to solve the situation once and for all.

Talk about your situation. I realize it's tough and uncomfortable for some, but it will help aid your problem. Confide in close friends or family members to talk out your worries and work out possible solutions aloud. Your confidants may be able to offer advice from their own experiences or those of their friends. Not only does this provide emotional support, but it exposes you to different and potentially more productive ways of approaching and dealing with the situation.

In extreme cases, you should consider seeking the help of a professional therapist. You should certainly seek professional help if your financial disaster is causing you to struggle with depression, have anxiety attacks, or consider harming yourself or others.

Be honest with your family. Let your loved ones know that you are going through a financial disaster. You may be surprised who might offer you a loan (although I'd shy away from borrowing and loaning to family), and even if your family is not in the position to provide you with financial assistance, letting them know what's going on could result in significant stress relief. In many cases, it can be beneficial to let children know that the family is experiencing tough times. This is because some extracurricular activities (music lessons, summer camp, etc.) might have to be sacrificed for the good of the family. Just be sure to reiterate the temporary nature of these sacrifices. You can also encourage older teenagers to get part-time jobs. If they are over age 18, consider having them pay rent.

Commit to staying positive. Before making a plan to remedy your situation, make a commitment to focus on the positive. Think about it this way: while the cause of your situation may not be in your control, how you choose to react to it is. Thinking positively can improve your mood, reduce your stress, and help you approach the situation in a way that is conducive to solving it. Remember that regardless of your situation, others have faced and solved it before.

Focus on being grateful for what you currently do have. For example, if you lost a job and have a large amount of debt, you could, perhaps, focus on support systems you have (like friends or family).

Let's take a moment to access how you feel about money and how you use the money.

Emotional Uses of Money

Answer the following questions about how you use your money. ***Be honest.***

True False

 I buy things I don't need because they are on sale.

T (F) I feel anxious and defensive when asked about my finances.

(T) F I can never have enough money saved to feel secure.

T (F) I buy things I don't need or want because they are "in."

T (F) I regularly overspend on "extras."

Cozette M. White

T (F) I often insist on paying more than my share at a restaurant or on a group gift.

T (F) I spend more freely, even foolishly, on others, but seldom for mys<u>elf</u>.

T (F) I feel "dumb" if I pay more for something that my neighbor did.

T F I don't trust others in my family to spend money wisely.

(T) F If I earn money, I think I should have the right to decide how it is spent.

T F If someone in my family acts selfishly in spending our money on himself/herself, I feel I have the right to do the same.

26

Scoring

A "true" answer to questions 1-3 might mean that you feel insecure about money.

If you answered "true" to either 4 or 5, you might use the money to gain status.

"True" answers to questions 6, 7, or 8 might mean that you use the money to compensate for your low self- esteem.

Did you answer "true" to questions 9 or 10? You may use the money to control others in the family.

A "true" answer to question 11 may indicate you use the money for retaliation.

Over the course of a family's life, 90% of married women will control the wealth.[7]

Exercise

My Money Story

We all have a personal **money story** which shapes our relationship, thoughts, and actions about our finances and how we live our lives. How our parents managed their relationship with money has a direct impact on our money habits.

In this section, take a moment to brainstorm and write down your thoughts that have had a direct impact on your emotions about money. Write down all ideas that come to mind on the Money Story Worksheet.

Exercise

Money Love Letter

Write a letter to yourself about what you would like to accomplish, what you would want to eliminate from your money story and more.

Exercise

Share "why" you are Financially Fabulous, Fierce and Fit.

This exercise is one you'll want to repeat continuously. As your mindset begins to shift, so will your behaviors surrounding money and values shift. After all, it's our subconscious negative talks with ourselves that have a direct impact

on our decision making. If you continuously affirm what you want your money to do for you, then you'll begin to see the shift in your money attitude.

Money Story Worksheet

MONEY LOVE LETTER

I am Financially Fabulous, Fierce and Fit because

_____

_____

_____

_____

_____

_____

_____

_____

_____

_____

_____

_____

_____

_____

_____

_____

_____

CHAPTER 3

GET YOUR ATTITUDE RIGHT

"Money can't buy happiness, but it will certainly get you a better class of memories."

-Ronald Reagan

CHANGE YOUR ATTITUDE;
CHANGE YOUR LIFE

P utting your financial disaster into proper perspective is the next step toward overcoming it. Brad Klontz, an associate research professor in personal financial planning at Kansas State University, says to frame it as an opportunity for growth. "We can learn much more from our failures than from our successes," Klontz says.[8] He urges victims of financial setbacks to examine their personal roles in helping create the outcome and says we should own our failures the way we do our successes. "If our focus is entirely outward, we doom ourselves to repeated failures," he says.[9]

Klontz recommends seeking professional help if money-related depression lingers. For those without the resources to pay for counseling, some charitable, religious and community-based organizations offer programs with reduced fees.

Cozette's Tip - When you hold onto an attitude long enough, it becomes your reality. To achieve a transformation, your thoughts and your attitudes about money must point to the results you want. Shifting to an attitude that points to the results you want is the first step you must take to transform your relationship with money.

"Half of the American households currently live paycheck to paycheck"[10]

Working on your money mind shift requires dedicated work. In the next exercise session, I provide money affirmations to assist you in your journey.

Exercise

Money Affirmation

Positive affirmations are extremely useful tools for programming your subconscious mind and changing your core beliefs. It is likely that you have some views that are holding you back from getting what you want in your life. We all do, but we all have the power to change that.

I have seen great success using positive affirmations and subliminal audio programs. I have compiled a list of affirmations for you. Just 5 minutes a day of reading the affirmations can change your life in ways you could not imagine. Take advantage of the incredible power of affirmations.

- Learning about money is fun!

- Budgeting is fun!

- Financial planning is fun!

- I love my money, and it loves me back!

- I release my need for debt.

- I am financially secure.

- I am open and willing to receive wealth into my life.

- I have more than I need in every area of my life.

- I focus on building my net worth.

- I manage my money with grace and ease.

- I permit myself to prosper.

- It is my choice to live in abundance, and I make that decision now.

- I quickly release all negative beliefs about money that no longer serve me.

- I trust that I will create abundance for myself.

- I promote my value to others with confidence.

- I am now earning a significant income doing what satisfies me.

- All my bills are paid in full, and I still have all this money.

- A lot more money is coming into my life.

- All my clients praise me and pay me!

- There's more where that came from.

- I love investing my money for the future.

Unveiling the Mask

- Money flows to me like water from a faucet.

- Money comes to me quickly and effortlessly, waking and sleeping.

- All my dues *debt* are paid in full.

Exercise

Affirm the Possibilities

- Write your own success story as if it were already true:

- List the reasons why it is possible for you to succeed: (Ex: others have done it, you have had smaller successes when you put your mind to it, you are more determined than ever before, etc.)

CHAPTER
4

SET GOALS
THAT SPEAK FREEDOM

"Wealth is the ability to experience life fully."

-Henry David Thoreau

FINANCIAL RECUPERATION

The next step in your financial recovery plan is to define your objective or goal. You must determine where you want to go financially.

This step is akin to locating your end destination on the map. Once you know where you are, and you know the end destination, it is simply a matter of plotting the course to get to your final goal. Setting your end destination is the same thing as setting a goal.

Goals

The "S.M.A.R.T." goal setting system provides helpful guidelines:

- *Specific*: There must be a clear and definable end result. For example, "I want to make more money" is too vague and general, but, "I want to have $1,000 per month residual income after taxes by December

31, 2019" is specific and points you in a clear direction.

- *Measurable:* You must have some way to measure your progress toward the goal. In the example above, the measurement is dollars of residual income per month. I also encourage you to add interim goals along the way to break big goals into more realistic chunks. For example, how much residual income should you have one year from now? Three years? Five years? And so on.

- *Attainable:* There's a fine balance between setting a goal that stretches your ability while still remaining within reach. If you set a goal that's too easy, then you are not challenging yourself, and if you make it too hard, then you're setting yourself up for failure. A properly designed goal achieves that razor-edge balance that stretches your comfort zone without being out of reach.

- *Realistic*: If you are deep in credit card debt and filing for bankruptcy, it probably isn't realistic to set a goal of becoming a millionaire in 12 months. Enough said?

- *Timely:* A goal without a deadline is just wishful thinking. You may want $1000 per month residual income, but unless you include a date for this to occur by, it doesn't qualify as a smart goal. It is just wishful thinking. Give yourself a deadline.

Having said all that, one must brace up to achieve great success in putting one's finances back together. Self-discipline and determination are essential keys in the process of bouncing back to proper financial status. In many cases, we need to consider the possibility that some individuals are in situations where their primary source of income is dependent upon the abuser, or they do not have sufficient resources to remove themselves from an abusive situation. Fortunately, this was not my case, but for many, this is a problem. I was not that individual that worried about staying put in my situation for fear of not having the resources of leaving. I was just stuck on an emotional rollercoaster. For some days, things were excellent, and other days, things were worse. When we marry, we are supposed to marry for better or worse. Unfortunately, this was not the case with my marriage.

For the person seeking to remove themselves from this abusive relationship, they will need to devise an exit plan and for **S.M.A.R.T.** goal for saving.

Achieving great success requires us to put in check anything that can cause financial chaos. This is where the old adage comes in, which categorically states that "One should cut his or her coat according to his or her cloth."

Size here remains ambiguous, which states that it can mean more than body size, the size of one's bank account should always be put into consideration. To remain financially independent, one must check a whole lot of things.

All in all, you must define the major goals you need to achieve in life so as not to miss out on having self-acclaimed progress in life. Attaining substantial goals makes one's story worth it!

Nearly half of Americans admit to having not saved anything at all for retirement.[11]

Exercise

Create an Effective Wealth Vision Board

Visualizing the process helps bring things into reality. What we think about we bring about. You can create your board on a large piece of cardboard, or you can use part of poster board. Make it as large or as small as you'd like. The board is there to serve your needs and your preferences matter. Outline the goals you want to accomplish over a set period.

Vision Board

CHAPTER 5

KNOW YOUR WORTH

"Before you speak, listen. Before you write, think. Before you spend, earn. Before you invest, investigate. Before you criticize, wait. Before you pray, forgive. Before you quit, try. Before you retire, save. Before you die, give."

-William A. Ward

ASSESS YOUR FINANCIAL SITUATION

Determine your assets: The first step to resolving a financial disaster is to get a clear picture of your entire financial situation. Begin by looking at your assets, which can simply be defined as what you own. Assets are a source of financial strength. They typically include any value you have in your home, cash in checking or savings accounts, any value you have in a car, and any money in retirement or investment accounts.

Assets can also include any other valuables that may be worth money like jewelry, collectibles. Consider taking your valuable assets to an appraiser or researching them online so you can know how much your assets are worth. Keep in mind, the value of any asset could appreciate or depreciate over time. However, knowing the current value can assist you in determining if you're getting a good deal. Create a column on a piece of paper that lists these assets and their values. At the bottom, sum up the values to determine what the total value of your assets is.

Asset Valuation		
Date Acquired	**Description**	**Asset Value**
1/1/19		
	Total Asset Value	

• Determine your liabilities: Liabilities refer to your debt, or more simply "what you owe." They are the opposite of assets. Liabilities include credit card debt, lines of credit, mortgages, unpaid bills, student loans, and your car loan.

Using, the same piece of paper you used for your list of assets, create a column that lists all your liabilities, and their values. At the bottom of the column, include the sum of your total liabilities.

• Calculate your net worth. Your net worth is simply your total assets minus your liabilities. This is the figure that represents how much is left if you were to sell all your assets to pay off your debt, and is a good figure to describe your current financial situation. For example, if you have $1. 3M in assets and $666K in various forms of debt. Your net worth would be $677K.

• Knowing your net worth helps you understand your options. For example, it may be necessary to sell assets in order to satisfy creditors if you are in debt, or to use any accumulated savings for the same purpose. Typically, any assets that are not absolutely essential could be sold to satisfy debt. For example, selling a car to pay off a credit card can improve your credit rating, reduce your debt payments every month, and get creditors off your back. Even during a bankruptcy proceeding, creditors and courts may demand that you sell off certain unnecessary assets before your liabilities can be settled. Therefore, its best to sell off the assets beforehand. See tables at the end of the chapter to determine your current Net Worth.

• Determine your income. Once you know your net worth, it is now necessary to look to your income and expenses. Knowing your income can help you determine whether or, not your net worth is shrinking or growing and affects your path to recovery. Income is fairly simple to calculate by adding all sources of revenue together. For most people, this will be their wages from work and any regular government payments (like social security or other forms of income such as child support, spousal support, Social Security or disability payments, pension income, investment income, etc.

Remember to include necessary automatic deductions so that your income figure represents how much cash you actually have available to use. Deductions include any taxes, insurance, or withheld amounts on your paycheck.

PROJECTED MONTHLY INCOME	Income 1	$2,500
	Extra income	$150
	Total monthly	**$2,650**
ACTUAL MONTHLY INCOME	Income 1	$2,525
	Extra income	$89
	Total monthly	**$2,614**
PROJECTED BALANCE (Projected income minus expenses)		**$2,650**
ACTUAL BALANCE (Actual income minus expenses)		**$2,614**
DIFFERENCE (Actual minus projected)		**($36)**

- Determine your expenses. In order to alleviate your financial disaster, you need to have a good idea about where and how you spend your money. The best way to determine how much money you are spending is to review your bank account statements from the last two months. Make a list of how much money you spend on utilities, food, housing, gas, clothing, and entertainment. Once you know where your money is going you can make adjustments geared towards decreasing the amount of money you spend so that you can get back on your feet.

Housing	Projected Cost	Actual Cost	Difference
Second mortgage or rent	$0	$0 ⬆	$0
Supplies	$0	$0 ⬆	$0
Other	$0	$0 ⬆	$0
Water and sewer	$8	$8 ⬆	$0
Waste removal	$10	$10 ⬆	$0
Maintenance or repairs	$23	$23 ⬆	$0
Gas	$22	$35 ⬇	-$13
Cable	$34	$34 ⬆	$0
Phone	$120	$120 ⬆	$0
Electricity	$44	$44 ⬆	$0
Mortgage or rent	$1,100	$1,100 ⬆	$0
Total	$1,361	$1,374	($13)

- Determine your monthly net income. If you subtract your expenses from your income, the resulting number is your net income. This represents how much you have left over at the end of the month. If this number is negative, it is a sign that reducing your expenditures will need to be a critical component of your overall plan to restore your financial well-being.

However, if your monthly net income is negative because you are receiving a very small amount of income each month, it becomes necessary to increase your income and cut your expenses.

- Assess the consequences of your situation. To motivate yourself to get out of this financial disaster, you'll have to remind yourself why you want to improve your situation. In other words, what will you be unable to do because of your current situation? Be realistic about your life goals and calculate the costs of achieving those goals. Think about how just sitting back and settling into your new financial situation will hurt you and those around you in the long run.

For example, if you have children and want to give them the opportunity to go to College one day, think about how you will be unable to do so unless you turn around your current situation.

58% of housing costs go to rent and mortgage payments,

with 21% spent on utilities, 10% on furnishings and 11% for other home costs, such as repairs and maintenance.[12]

Exercise

Financial Oath

I, _____acknowledge that this is the current state of my financial affairs. They may not be where I want them, but I am committed to improving my current financial situation.

I,_____ believe in the importance of my financial health.

I, _____ accept my new title as (CFO) Chief Financial Organizer by understanding and organizing of my personal finances.

I, _____ will welcome the strength financial clarity gives me to protect myself and my family.

_____

Signed & Dated

Exercise

Know Your Net Worth

1. Write down your assets on the attached Net Worth Worksheet.

2. Write down your liabilities on the attached Net Worth Worksheet.

3. Add up the Total Assets minus Total Liabilities to give you your Net Worth.

What are the results? _____

Are the results what you expected? _____

How do you feel about your results?

_____

_____

Where would you like to be in 12 months?

_____

_____

Where would you like to be in 3 years?

_____

_____

_____

Where would you like to be in 5 years?

_____

_____

_____

_____

Where would you like to be in 10 years?

_____

_____

_____

_____

_____

_____

_____

_____

Net Worth Calculator

Estimated Net Worth: $0

Assets

Personal Items	Estimated Value	
Primary Real Estate	$	-
Income Property	$	-
Vehicles		-
Jewelry		-
Artwork		-
Furniture		-
Electronics		-
Antiques		-
Other		-
Cash or Cash Equivalent		
Checking account	$	-
Savings account		-
Certificates of deposit		-
Money market account		-
Life insurance (cash value)		-
Other		-
Investments		
Retirement account	$	-
IRA	$	-
401K or 403B		-
Bonds		-
Mutual funds		-
Individual stock shares		-
Real estate other than home		-
Other		-
Assets Total	$	-

Liabilities

Loan Balances	Estimated Value	
Mortgage loan	$	-
Rental Property Loan		-
Home equity loan		-
Car loans		-
Real estate loans		-
Student loans		-
Other loans		-
Other Outstanding Debt		
Credit card debt	$	-
Charge Cards		-
Past-Due Taxes		-
401K Loans		-
Loan from family		-
Loan from friends		-
		-
		-
		-
		-
		-
		-
		-
		-
		-
Liabilities Total	$	-

Net Worth Calculator

Estimated Net Worth: $906,090

Assets

Personal Items	Estimated Value
Primary Real Estate	$ 620,000
Income Property	$ 900,000
Vehicles	30,000
Jewelry	6,000
Artwork	1,400
Furniture	6,500
Electronics	3,000
Antiques	100
Other	-

Cash or Cash Equivalent	
Checking account	$ 1,200
Savings account	24,890
Certificate of deposit	-
Money market account	-
Life insurance (cash value)	-
Other	-

Investments	
Retirement account	$ 21,000
IRA	$ 60,000
401K or 403B	480,000
Bonds	1,000
Mutual funds	5,000
Individual stock shares	10,000
Real estate other than home	-
Other	-

Assets Total: $ 1,572,090

Liabilities

Loan Balances	Estimated Value
Mortgage loan	$ 420,000
Rental Property Loan	200,000
Home equity loan	-
Car loans	17,000
Real estate loans	-
Student loans	20,000
Other loans	-

Other Outstanding Debt	
Credit card debt	$ 9,000
Charge Cards	-
Past-Due Taxes	-
401K Loans	-
Loan from family	-
Loan from friends	-

Liabilities Total: $ 666,000

CHAPTER
6

ESTABLISH A
SPENDING PLAN

*"Money never made a man happy yet, nor will it. There is
nothing in its nature to produce happiness.
The more a man has, the more he wants. Instead of filling a
vacuum, it makes one."*

-Benjamin Franklin

CREATE A SPENDING PLAN

One of the best weapons for combating financial problems is a budget. A budget is a monthly spending plan for your money. Creating a budget is like turning the lights on to find your way around a dark room. You no longer need to wonder in the dark; banging your shins, tripping over the furniture, and stepping on the dog. Instead, with the lights on, you can see what's going on and prevent problems before they happen. A budget works much the same way; it guides your spending decisions so that you're spending money on what's really important to you. In this case, you'll spend your money in a way that helps solve your financial problem.

I train clients to track their expenses for 14 to 30 days to gain a clearer picture of where their money is spent. Goodbudget app is a great personal finance tool for budget planning and money management. Tracking your expenses will enable you to build a budget that works. As you create your budget, it's important that your expenses aren't just guesses – they need to reflect reality. You may want to track your expenses for at least a couple of weeks (a month is best) to objectively see where you are spending your money and how much you're spending. Although you may think you know where your money is going, when most people tally up all their purchases for a month, they are usually quite surprised to notice that their spending doesn't always match up with what they thought their priorities were.

Once you're confident the numbers in your budget are realistic, you can look at your budget critically and search for areas where you can save money. You'll want to ask yourself things like:

- Do I need to eat out this frequently or not at all?

- Do I need to spend on entertainment or hobbies this month?

- Could I pack a lunch for work rather than buy one?

- Can I find FREE entertainment for a while?

- Can we use coupons?

- Can we buy generic vs. name brand?

Asking yourself these questions doesn't mean you're cheap or restricted by your budget. It means that you've got bigger things to accomplish or worry about, things that can be solved by making some small changes.

 *Cozette's Tip –*

When considering long-term goals,

think of anything over 12 months,

3 yrs, 5 yrs and beyond.

Short-term goals are typically soon

(< 12 months).

STEP 1 – *Determine Your Financial Goals.*

Make up a list of your long-range and immediate financial goals.

Long – Range Financial Goals

What do you see money offering you in the future? Your list might include:

- Retirement

- College education for children

- Ability to take family vacations

- Charitable donations, if possible.

Immediate Financial Goals

What do you want from your money today? Your list might include:

- Mortgage

- Private school tuition for children

- School supplies

- Food

- Clothing (business and casual)

- Household supplies

- Summer camp

- Vacations

- Car payments

- Utilities

- Dry cleaning

- Newspaper delivery, magazine subscriptions

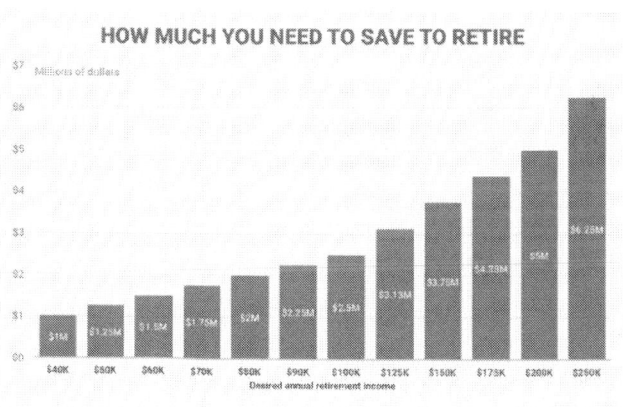

HOW MUCH YOU NEED TO SAVE TO RETIRE

Source: BusinessInsider – June 2017[13]

STEP 2 – *Add up all the individual figures.*

This is your monthly budget. You should sign and date the bottom of the budget. Don't duck out of this task because you think it is too time- consuming or figure out some other excuse for not gaining control of your spending and your marital finances. The goal here is to find a healthy way of dealing with money. Resist the urge just to smile and say, "All right, let's just do the best I can to spend a little less." You may as well say, "You know, my emotional issues are a little too intense for me on this money thing, so I'd rather pretend it away and risk continuing our dysfunctional way of dealing with it than actually taking responsibility for my actions."

S T E P 3 – *Write down your purchases.*

Commit to writing down every purchase for the next month. Each of you must write down in a little notebook every time money leaves your pocket, whether through check, cash or credit card. When you buy a magazine, shop for food, eat at a restaurant, go to the movies, buy a cup of coffee, or pay bills, have your book ready and simply jot down the date, the item purchased and the cost. You don't have to itemize the food shopping; just write the date and total cost. If you have a financial record program such as Quicken on your computer, you can just enter these daily totals into your computer records and truly simplify your budgeting. Other financial tools that I recommend for tracking your finances are:

- You Need A Budget
- MVelopes
- Money Dance (MAC users)
- Mint
- Personal Capital

STEP 4 – *Analyze your spending.*

After one month, sit down and begin to categorize your expenditures. How much are you spending a month on food, clothing, entertainment, utilities, dry cleaning and household help? I guarantee you'll have some unpleasant surprises. Fifty bucks just for lattés? Resign yourself to feeling sheepish or embarrassed, or perhaps a little out of control. Forgive yourself and congratulate yourself for taking a brave step. Now you will have a more precise sense of how much you spend and on what. You can decide on some areas in which you could spend less. If saving money is important to you, decide on an amount that seems reasonable – now's a great time to use the S.M.A.R.T goal plans as discussed in Chapter Five.

Read books like The Millionaire Next Door[14] and Your Money or Your Life[15] together; discuss the chapters with an accountability partner – a mentor or a coach; someone that will hold you accountable for your financial goals. Your accountability partner will help you begin to formulate a lifelong plan of how you want to use your money. Begin to be psychologically aware of your relationship with money and commit to creating a responsible financial lifestyle.

STEP 5 – *Revisit the budget you created.*

From your one-month tracking of expenses, you should be able to create a more detailed budget. Review what your estimates were before you started recording every purchase for the month and see how close you were to the real number.

First, add the entire month's expenses and see how this total compares with the amount you earn (after taxes). If you are spending more than you are earning, you must decide where you will spend less each month. Even if you're earning more than you are spending, consider whether you are comfortable with the amount of money you're spending in each category. You may realize that you're spending $250 each month on eating out and that you'd rather spend (or save) that $3,000 a year on something else.

Create a new realistic number for spending on each item that you can agree to. Commit to your new budget for a month. Agree to use cash as much as possible. For example, if your monthly food budget is $500, take it in cash at the start of the month and place it in an envelope designated solely for food purchases. This helps you regulate your spending. It also avoids impulse purchases of "unnecessary" items.

STEP 6 – *Keep it up!*

Continue reviewing the numbers with your accountability partner, if possible, and congratulate yourself on taking control of an intricate part of life. Revisit and update your budget every month. As you start to recognize how well you can approach complicated issues like spending, it will reinforce your confidence.

4 of 5 couples say they're on the same page as their partner about money. In truth, there seems to be a large financial perception gap.[16]

MONTHLY SPENDING BREAKDOWN

Personal Monthly Budget

PROJECTED MONTHLY INCOME	Income 1	$1,100
	Extra Income	$0
	Total monthly income	$1,100
ACTUAL MONTHLY INCOME	Income 1	$1,100
	Extra Income	$0
	Total monthly income	$10,000

PROJECTED BALANCE (Projected income minus expenses)		$8,914
ACTUAL BALANCE (Income minus expenses)	[Actual]	$9,373
DIFFERENCE (minus projected)	[Actual]	$559

HOUSING	Projected Cost	Actual Cost	Difference
Mortgage or rent	$2,900	$2,900	$0
Phone	$300	$300	$0
Electricity	$30	$30	$0
Gas	$35	$11	$24
Water and sewer	$175	$158	$17
Cable	$300	$334	($33)
Waste removal	$10	$10	$0
Maintenance or repairs	$0	$125	($125)
Supplies	$75	$100	($25)
Other	$0	$0	$0
Subtotals	**$3,395**	**$3,797**	**-$142**

TRANSPORTATION	Projected Cost	Actual Cost	Difference
Vehicle payment	$342	$342	$0
Bus/taxi fees			$0
Insurance	$87	$87	$0
Licensing			$0
Fuel	$60	$63	$22
Maintenance	$25	$25	$0
Other			$0
Subtotals	**$514**	**$492**	**$22**

INSURANCE	Projected Cost	Actual Cost	Difference
Home			$0
Health	$100		$100
Life	$132		$132
Other			$0
Subtotals	**$232**	**$0**	**$232**

FOOD	Projected Cost	Actual Cost	Difference
Groceries	$375	$278	$97
Dining out	$250	$50	$200
Other			$0
Subtotals	**$625**	**$328**	**$297**

PETS	Projected Cost	Actual Cost	Difference
Food			$0
Medical			$0
Grooming			$0
Toys			$0
Other			$0
Subtotals	**$0**	**$0**	**$0**

PERSONAL CARE	Projected Cost	Actual Cost	Difference
Medical			$0
Hair/nails	$135	$135	$0
Clothing	$100	$100	$0
Dry cleaning	$50	$0	$50
Health club	$25	$25	$0
Organization dues or fees	$0		$0
Other			$0
Subtotals	**$310**	**$260**	**$50**

ENTERTAINMENT	Projected Cost	Actual Cost	Difference
Video/DVD			$0
CDs			$0
Movies			$0
Concerts	$200	$0	$100
Sporting events			$0
Live theater			$0
Other			$0
Other			$0
Other			$0
Subtotals	**$100**	**$0**	**$100**

LOANS	Projected Cost	Actual Cost	Difference
Personal			$0
Student	$160	$160	$0
Credit card			$0
Credit card			$0
Credit card			$0
Other			$0
Subtotals	**$160**	**$160**	**$0**

TAXES	Projected Cost	Actual Cost	Difference
Federal			$0
State			$0
Local			$0
Other			$0
Subtotals	**$0**	**$0**	**$0**

SAVINGS OR INVESTMENTS	Projected Cost	Actual Cost	Difference
Retirement account	$500	$500	$0
Investment account	$250	$250	$0
Other			$0
Subtotals	**$650**	**$650**	**$0**

GIFTS AND DONATIONS	Projected Cost	Actual Cost	Difference
Charity 1			$0
Charity 2			$0
Charity 3			$0
Subtotals	**$0**	**$0**	**$0**

LEGAL	Projected Cost	Actual Cost	Difference
Attorney			$0
Alimony			$0
Payments on lien or judgment			$0
Other			$0
Subtotals	**$0**	**$0**	**$0**

TOTAL PROJECTED COST	$6,186
TOTAL ACTUAL COST	$5,627
TOTAL DIFFERENCE	$559

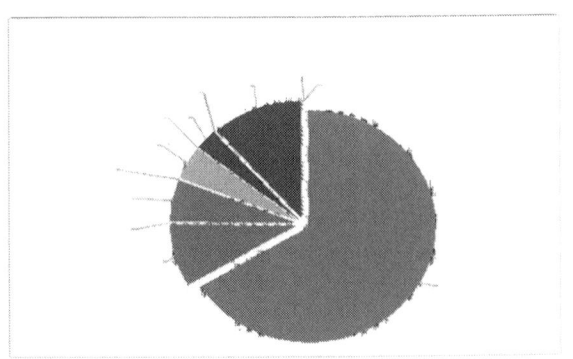

Personal Monthly Budget

PROJECTED MONTHLY INCOME	Income 1	$0
	Extra income	$0
	Total monthly income	$0

ACTUAL MONTHLY INCOME	Income 1	$0
	Extra income	$0
	Total monthly income	$0

PROJECTED BALANCE (Projected income minus expenses)	$0
ACTUAL BALANCE (Actual income minus expenses)	$0
DIFFERENCE (Actual minus projected)	$0

HOUSING	Projected Cost	Actual Cost	Difference
Mortgage or rent			$0
Phone			$0
Electricity			$0
Gas			$0
Water and sewer			$0
Cable			$0
Waste removal			$0
Maintenance or repairs			$0
Supplies			$0
Other			$0
Subtotals	$0	$0	$0

TRANSPORTATION	Projected Cost	Actual Cost	Difference
Vehicle payment			$0
Bus/taxi fare			$0
Insurance			$0
Licensing			$0
Fuel			$0
Maintenance			$0
Other			$0
Subtotals	$0	$0	$0

INSURANCE	Projected Cost	Actual Cost	Difference
Home			$0
Health			$0
Life			$0
Other			$0
Subtotals	$0	$0	$0

FOOD	Projected Cost	Actual Cost	Difference
Groceries			$0
Dining out			$0
Other			$0
Subtotals	$0	$0	$0

PETS	Projected Cost	Actual Cost	Difference
Food			$0
Medical			$0
Grooming			$0
Toys			$0
Other			$0
Subtotals	$0	$0	$0

PERSONAL CARE	Projected Cost	Actual Cost	Difference
Medical			$0
Hair/nails			$0
Clothing			$0
Dry cleaning			$0
Health club			$0
Organization dues or fees			$0
Other			$0
Subtotals	$0	$0	$0

ENTERTAINMENT	Projected Cost	Actual Cost	Difference
Video/DVD			$0
CDs			$0
Movies			$0
Concerts			$0
Sporting events			$0
Live theater			$0
Other			$0
Other			$0
Other			$0
Subtotals	$0	$0	$0

LOANS	Projected Cost	Actual Cost	Difference
Personal			$0
Student			$0
Credit card			$0
Credit card			$0
Credit card			$0
Other			$0
Subtotals	$0	$0	$0

TAXES	Projected Cost	Actual Cost	Difference
Federal			$0
State			$0
Local			$0
Other			$0
Subtotals	$0	$0	$0

SAVINGS OR INVESTMENTS	Projected Cost	Actual Cost	Difference
Retirement account			$0
Investment account			$0
Other			$0
Subtotals	$0	$0	$0

GIFTS AND DONATIONS	Projected Cost	Actual Cost	Difference
Charity 1			$0
Charity 2			$0
Charity 3			$0
Subtotals	$0	$0	$0

LEGAL	Projected Cost	Actual Cost	Difference
Attorney			$0
Alimony			$0
Payments on lien or judgment			$0
Other			$0
Subtotals	$0	$0	$0

TOTAL PROJECTED COST	$0
TOTAL ACTUAL COST	$0
TOTAL DIFFERENCE	$0

CHAPTER 7

GROUND LEVEL
FORWARD THINKING

"A wise person should have money in their head, but not in their heart."

-Jonathan Swift

ROAD TO RECOVERY

C reate a plan suited to your needs. The exact nature of your recovery plan will have to remedy the problem that got you into the financial disaster in the first place. Put simply, you will have to reduce debt if you have it and earn more income to replace your lost assets and financial security. This may mean getting a new job, getting another job, cutting your expenses, applying for government assistance, or seeking debt forgiveness. For example, if your financial disaster was caused by a divorce, you will have to find income to replace the joint income you had in marriage.

Determine your fixed and discretionary monthly expenses. Fixed expenses refer to expenses that do not vary between months. Discretionary expenses refer to expenses that are not essential and vary from month to month. Knowing the difference is important, since reducing discretionary expenses can be much simpler than reducing fixed ones. Your fixed monthly expenses are those bills and other costs that must be paid regularly so that your basic needs are met. Fixed monthly expenses include rent, mortgage payments, utilities, education, insurance, food, and transportation. Other fixed monthly expenses include any debt or other payment obligations. Variable or discretionary expenses include anything that you don't need to spend to survive, like eating out at restaurants, gym memberships, entertainment, and clothing.

Reduce your variable expenses. The first place to start with reducing expenses is with your variable expenses. These are your wants, as opposed to your needs, and cutting them can free up significant room in your budget for debt repayments. Ensure that you're not confusing your wants with your needs. For example, a cell phone may be a need, but a 64GB data plan with cell phone is almost certainly a want.

Decide now that you won't go out to eat at a restaurant until your situation changes (for example, when you get a new job). This can save you a large amount on food costs. Watch for small purchases that add up, like buying coffee every day. Eliminating these can save significant amounts of money each month.

Cancel unnecessary memberships to fitness centers, clubs, and other monthly recurring-cost entertainment. Check to make sure that you don't incur more charges if you must break a contract early. Consider canceling cable TV since with the internet and smartphones, cable is often redundant, and don't shop unless you need to. You can probably postpone buying clothes for many months. If you must purchase something, go to a second-hand store or a close-out store.

Reduce your fixed expenses. Expenses like housing, food, or transportation are traditionally considered fixed, but that does not mean, you can't significantly reduce your costs in these areas to free up space in your budget each month. If you are renting and your housing is too expensive, consider relocating to a more affordable apartment, or to a different area of town. Keep in mind what you want, versus what you need. For example, if you are single, a one-bedroom apartment may be ideal, but a studio is likely all you need, and downsizing can save you considerable amounts.

Consider getting a roommate if possible.

Rideshare with a co-worker, consider Uber or Lyft or take the bus to reduce transportation costs.

Pursue additional sources of income. In a perfect world, a 40 -hour a week full-time job would provide you with the funds you need to cover your costs and expenses. In reality, you may need to get creative in order to locate additional sources of income, especially if you've fallen on hard times. If you don't already have a full-time job, immediately start going out to businesses that may be hiring and submit your application. Apply to as many places as possible. Find a part-time job. Search on Craigslist, Monster and consult with friends in order to locate part-time job opportunities.

Focusing on jobs that provide seasonal employment may be a great option in that seasonal employers often hire people only looking for short-term employment i.e. working at the mall during the Christmas season, or as a lifeguard during the summer. Take on odd jobs like landscaping, babysitting, waiting tables, or bartending. Register with several, temporary, employment agencies. They might not have regular work or career-related work, but sometimes short assignments will help when you're in a pinch.

Producing multiple streams of income can have a big impact on your finances. An extra $500 per month could go a long way in paying down debt or raising your investment.

When I talk about multiple streams of income, I am not insisting that you get a second job to supplement your current income. A second job does not provide you with the flexibility and freedom to increase your income. In fact, it can hurt you when you think about it. You are trading time for money, and in the long run, you lose! I want you to create something that will allow you to give yourself a pay raise when you need and want it.

When evaluating and researching ways to produce income, consider the following:

- **Investment** – should require minimal investment.

- **Sustainable** – ultimately, something that generates income without you.

- **Scalable** – produces substantial amounts of income.

- **Flexibility** – you call the shots.

Here's what an extra $500 per month could look like:

Savings account: If you deposited $500 each month for one year with an interest rate of 4.00%, compounded annually, and an initial starting balance of $500, your yield will be $6,629.22.

Investment account: Now transfer the amount above from your savings into a 5- year CD with an interest rate of 2%, compounded annually, for five years, your yield will be $7,319.99.

Financial Freedom

Extra income of $500 per month could cover car payments, auto insurance, help pay down credit card debt, or cover some or even all of a mortgage payment. Small incremental savings can ultimately go a long way.

Think about some of the things you are great at and create your additional source of revenue.

Below are steadfast ideas guaranteed to help you generate multiple streams of income this year.

1. Sell an e-book

If publishing a book, the traditional ways is a long shot, and then consider an e-book. An e-book is simple; many people publish them for free, but many sell them as well on Amazon. Of course, there are other expenses to consider such as an editor, covers, advertising, etc. but this is an opportunity to generate additional income.

2. Affiliate marketing

If you have a blog or other type of site, you can build affiliate links to different services on the website.

3. Write a book

A well-written book will undoubtedly rake in some profits for you. Although the process of getting it published is sometimes tedious, it is not entirely impossible. Contrary to what many believe, self-publishing can be easy, fun, invigorating, and life changing!

4. Start a small business

Many of the above examples are also small businesses. However, you can start a more traditional kind of business - one that sells a service or product. Consider the one thing you're good at or the one thing you are constantly complimented on. Before starting, make sure you have all the legal documents in alignment.

5. Teach a class

If you have excellent skills or knowledge, then consider teaching at a university; make a series of seminars or create your e-courses.

6. Offer consulting or coaching

Instead of teaching a full class, you can coach clients one-on-one.

7. Start a blog

It may take a while for a blog to earn any money, as with any business, but with consistency and commitment, it will eventually pay off.

8. Develop a product

A typical way of making money is to transform service into a product. For example, as a freelancer, you offer a service once and earn money once. However, if you can change your service into a product, you can put it up for sale once and get paid lots of times.

9. Have multiple clients

If you depend on one main client for your main source of revenue, consider branching out to newly organic customers. Build your client list through list building

10. Launch a magazine

You can select a topic, develop content, transform it into a perfect magazine and sell it for a profit.

11. Expert advice on clarity

The technique here charges for calls from people who want guidance in the topic/field you are knowledgeable in.

12. Make a membership website and get money

If you can make valuable content, there will almost forever be people willing to pay a monthly fee for membership.

13. **Investments**

Stocks, bonds, 401K's, annuities, etc., are great ways to earn passive income. Place proceeds in high-interest savings account or a high-interest checking account to establish your emergency fund account.

14. Real estate

Real estate is an excellent way to earn extra income. Real estate investing includes fixing and flipping houses, which requires capital in the form of cash and credit. Speak with seasoned investors and realtors to find out if this passive income strategy is right for you.

Producing additional income is the foundation for building wealth. While earning extra income does take work, the return on your investment ROI can be enormous and pay off for years to come. Now's the time to create your plan and build your financial legacy for you and your family.

Never think small –
DREAM BIG!

Other options include - consider selling assets and using the proceeds to pay off debt. Any assets you don't absolutely need can and should be sold to pay off your debt. This is because the value of your assets is likely decreasing and the value of your debt is always increasing. The simplest thing you can do to improve your net worth is pay off as much of your debt as possible as quickly as possible. If you are in a very dire debt situation, it can be a good idea to use retirement savings to pay off debt, or sell assets like a car. You can replace the car with a cheaper one or use public transportation instead if possible.

If using savings to pay off debt, it is important to consider a few things. Firstly, only use savings to pay off very high-interest debt (like credit card debt). Not only is paying off this debt with savings financially reasonable (due to the fact the debt is extremely costly and it is unlikely an equivalent amount of interest is being earned on savings), it can improve your credit rating, get creditors off your back, and reduce your monthly expenses.

While planning your recovery, make a schedule of how much you can pay off each debt each month. This should also include when you estimate to be able to pay off each debt completely.

Consider filing for bankruptcy. If you lack sufficient assets and income to pay for basic necessities and pay off your debt at the same time, filing for bankruptcy can be your only option. Bankruptcy can erase your debts and give you a clean financial slate, but is not without its downsides. The process also destroys your credit score and can force you to sell off certain assets deemed unnecessary, even if you don't want.

Most people will file for what is known Chapter 7 Bankruptcy. This allows the court to settle your debts by selling off some of your assets. Protected assets are those that cannot be sold during bankruptcy proceedings. These typically include your primary residence, primary transportation, and personal items like wedding rings. Specific protected asset always vary by state.

If all else fails and you still require assistance, consider visiting a food bank or soup kitchen, and using food stamps. If qualified, temporarily using these resources can significantly reduce your costs until you are in a better place financially. The Supplemental Nutrition Assistance Program (SNAP), once known as the food stamps program, provides low-income Americans with supplemental funds to purchase food. Eligibility for SNAP is based on household monthly income, as well as other factors such as the number of children in a household. Contact your state's government assistance program to learn about applying for SNAP.

Apply for government assistance programs. The U.S. federal government provides a wide range of services; however, accessing government assistance programs requires patience because of varying application processes, and bureaucratic delays. As a result, government assistance programs can provide additional funds when you are going through a long-term financial crises, but you shouldn't expect to receive quick financial-aid from government assistance program.

Unveiling the Mask

Unemployment insurance is a great option for those workers who are in a financial crisis because they have lost their job, or are otherwise unable to work. An unemployment insurance claim can be filed if you fulfill specific requirements, which vary by state.

Check with your local state department of social services to determine which other governmental assistance programs that you may be eligible to access. If you live outside of the United States, contact your local government to inquire about government assistance. Most developed countries offer unemployment assistance and subsidized necessities to those in need.

Only about 1/3 of Americans (32%) maintain a household budget[17] and 65% of Americans literally live paycheck to paycheck.[18]

CHAPTER
8

INSPECT WHAT
YOU EXPECT

"If we command our wealth, we shall be rich and free. If our wealth commands us, we are poor indeed."

-Edmund Burke

TRACK YOUR PROGRESS

The last step takes place once you are a few months into working on your plan. Every week, take a few minutes to track your progress. Is your plan working? Are you making progress toward your goals? If not, you'll need to take a closer look to figure out why not and adjust your plan. Your plan needs to be realistic, or its not going to work. It should also contain some things you weren't doing before you put the plan in place.

If you keep doing what you were doing before, then you'll continue to get the same result as before – problems. You've got to do something different to get a different outcome. As you follow your plan and see improvements in your situation, be open to the possibility of fine-tuning the plan. Once you start making some progress, you may realize that you're doing better than you thought, or you may come up with some new insights. Improving your plan so that you accomplish your goals more quickly is good as long as your budget can afford the changes and everyone who relies on your budget is okay with the more aggressive approach.

Being in control in the area of your finances is both empowering and necessary. When you can keep this part of your life well-managed, you prevent unnecessary stress and worries. I've outlined practical strategies to assist in tracking your finances.

1.   Be motivated. Before tracking your finances, you must know why you want to do it. Perhaps you are finding it difficult to pay the bills, or maybe you don't have enough money for groceries each month. Knowing the "why" helps you stay on track when you are losing focus.

2.   Be disciplined. When tracking your finances, you must be willing to sacrifice temporary pleasures to prepare for the future. Choose willpower over instant gratification, as this is necessary, yet the most significant hurdle to cross.

3.   Learn what you are spending right now. Find out what your habits are. Keep track of where

your money goes, and every place it goes to. Anytime you leave your home, take your notebook with you. Keep it on the computer when you are indoors in case you should need to record an online purchase or to remind you not to make that purchase at all.

4.   Keep track of everything. Record both big and small spendings. You may not think that your coffee and breakfast muffin was a big deal, but over a period, this kind of indiscriminate spending can cause significant problems.

5.   Don't forget to track cash. It is somewhat easier to keep track of what is being spent on credit and debit cards since there is a record of it. But don't forget cash, as this can drain your pockets when not carefully watched.

6.   Sort your spending into categories. Tracking is made easier when there is a logical system to follow. Divide your spending into classifications such as "entertainment," "living expenses," "savings," and any other areas your spending may fall into.

7. Use a spreadsheet. This can help you with quick data entry of your numbers, and with being able to retrieve your info quickly. By using one of a variety of programs, you will save time with your tracking.

8. Use an App. By searching terms such as "finance tracker," there are several Apps available to help make this part of your life easier. Many are free, so there is no reason not to try it. Use a few before deciding which one suits you and works best for your situation.

9. Revise your spending plan and budget repeatedly. You may begin to see patterns and be able to make choices about what needs to be changed. It is always beneficial to regularly review your goals and budget to keep it updated continuously and suitable for your present lifestyle.

10. Persevere no matter how tiresome it gets. Tracking your finances is no easy chore, but it gets more manageable with practice. Keep on going, even when you wish you didn't have to think about it anymore.

Tracking finances is a life skill that takes practice. It may feel unnatural and restrictive at first, but with a little bit of effort, you will be able to pinpoint your financial issues and create a plan to make your spending habits more effective and appropriate. Take control of your finances today and see what a difference it can make for you.

A Career Builder survey found 2/3 of the minimum workers they surveyed struggled to make ends meet and 50% said they must work more than one job to break even.[19]

CHAPTER 9

BOOST YOUR

CREDIT WORTHINESS

"A simple fact that is hard to learn is that the time to save money is when you have some."

-Joe Moore

SURVEY THE DAMAGES

Speaking of credit scores, the next thing to do is to checKyour credit reports and scores to see what damage your debt may have caused them. If you only want to survey the damage and make the necessary changes to raise your score, you can apply for your free credit reports. The free credit reports are online at www.annualcreditreport.com. Every consumer is entitled to one report every twelve months, but this report doesn't include credit scores. If you would rather keep track of the improvements you are making to your scores, you can sign up for a credit report monitoring service which will keep track of all three of your scores.

If you need to rebuild your credit score, there are a few things you can do. First, if your score is really bad and all of your credit cards have been closed, try signing up for a secured credit card in order to build your credit back up. Secured credit cards are specifically for people looking to build their credit, and most of them report to all three credit bureaus monthly. Another last-ditch step would be to sign up for a credit repair service. The best of these services will work with the credit card lenders to raise your credit score through goodwill outreach or loopholes in credit law. Just be careful, although many of these services offer a guarantee, they only guarantee to raise your score, they never say by how much and there could be a fee associated with the card. My best advice is for you to work on repairing your credit first personally, and if you do not see any improvement, then seek outside services.

Unveiling the Mask

How Does Credit Work?

Consumer credit comes into play whenever you borrow money as an individual. If you are brand new to the idea of credit, let's start with the very basics. The person borrowing is responsible for making payment and the information about amounts borrowed and timing of repayment is recorded on that person's individual credit file. Debts like car loans, mortgages, and credit cards are the most positive types of credit accounts, and creditors in these categories report both positive and negative payment histories to credit bureaus. But those aren't the only forms of credit that exist. If you rent an apartment, have a cell phone, or use utilities for your home, those are all considered credit accounts as well, the company or creditor in question offers you a service and expects you to remit payment after the fact. However, these creditors differ in that they don't typically report positive payment information. They will only be relevant to your credit history down the line if you are significantly delinquent in payment.

Cozette M. White

What Are Credit Bureaus?

The credit bureau is an agency that researches and collects individual credit information and sells it for a fee to creditors so they can make a decision on granting loans. Unfortunately for borrowers, your credit score isn't a memoir. Instead, each borrower's financial story is controlled by credit bureaus; the agencies that collect information about individual credit reports and synthesize it on behalf of lenders. Think of credit bureaus as journalist collecting the facts and telling your story. They are well- meaning, and most of the time they get the story quite right…but every now and then mistakes are made, or they might show an angle of your financial story that doesn't provide full context. The main three credit reporting agencies are Experian,[20] Equifax,[21] and TransUnion.[22] Each agency has their own proprietary method of collecting information about borrowers, meaning they can gather slightly different information at different times. And because different creditors report their payment information to different agencies, you can't be sure that these journalists are all using the same (or the most

108

accurate) sources. We will talk more in a bit about taking control of your narrative to make sure that your credit history is accurately reported. First, though, it's comforting to know that there is one place where these different journalists reporting styles, all come together through the use of the FICO credit score. A FICO score is a type of credit score created by the Fair Isaac Corporation.

Disputing Your Credit

Nothing gets your heart rate going quite like discovering an error on your credit report. Whether it's a line of credit you never opened, a closed account that is registering as unpaid or a bankruptcy that isn't yours, an error can spoil your credit history and damage your credit score. There are six steps to contest items on your credit report.

- **Identify the error**: The best way to sniff out errors on your credit report is to check it regularly. AnnualCreditReport.com allows you to obtain an annual copy of your credit report from each of the three credit-reporting bureaus: Equifax, Experian and TransUnion.

- **Make sure that it's an error**: Before you start spinning your wheels through the dispute process, make sure you're actually reporting an error. You may think you see an incorrect item when, in fact, it's just a debt you don't recognize. For example, you may not recognize the name of a debt collector reporting late payments on your account (but you may still owe that debt). An unfamiliar debt issuer may be the third-party company that manages a store credit card you applied for a few months ago. There's no point in contesting correct information with the credit bureaus. Up-to-date and accurate information will stay on your report, even if you dispute it.

•**Consider your method**: When reporting an error to the credit-reporting bureaus, you may choose to pursue the process online, over the phone or through the postal service. You'll need to provide identifying information, pinpoint which data points are incorrect and possibly provide supporting documentation.

•**Be specific**: Be as detailed as possible when disputing information on your credit report, experts say. That may include providing supporting paperwork and clearly identifying each item on the report you want to contest. If you've been dealing with financial fraud, for example, a police report may be useful. If you're sending a dispute via snail mail, make sure to send photocopies of your background information, not the originals.

•**Know your rights**: The credit-reporting bureaus and information provider (the credit issuer, debt collector or bank, for example) are responsible for correcting errors on your report under the Fair Credit Reporting Act. Credit-reporting companies must consider your dispute, typically within 30 days, unless it's deemed frivolous, according to the FTC. The bureaus should work together with the information provider to clear up any inaccuracies. You can also write a letter directly to the information provider – the FTC provides a sample letter – instructing the company to investigate the error. When everything's squared away, you should receive the results and a free copy of your report if there's a change, according to the FTC.

•**File a complaint**: If you feel like the credit bureaus or information provider are not doing their due diligence when it comes to your credit-reporting dispute say, you're experiencing long delays or the company is not appropriately considering your dispute you can file a complaint with the Consumer Financial Protection Bureau. "The complaint program is almost like an appeals court in terms of these disputes," says Jonah Kaplan, markets analyst for consumer reporting at the CFPB.[23] The credit bureaus will be alerted once your complaint is filed and potentially be motivated to address your concerns. You may also reach out to your state's attorney general, department of consumer affairs or consumer advocate law office to file a complaint, investigate next steps or, when all else fails, even file a lawsuit.

Dispute Sample Letter 1

[Your Name]
[Street Address]
[City, ST ZIP Code]
[Date]

[Recipient Name]
[Title]
[Company Name]
[Street Address]
[City, ST ZIP Code]

RE: [Account Number]

Dear [Recipient Name]:

I am disputing a credit charge from [Merchant Name] in the amount of $[amount], which is included on my statement dated [click to select a date].

On [click to select a date], I ordered [product] from the web site, [website URL]. I received an email the same day that confirmed my order in the amount above. I was also told that I would receive the merchandise within two to four weeks. However, I never received the merchandise. On [click to select a date], I contacted [Merchant Name] via email and phone, and was told that my merchandise was on backorder and expected to arrive on [click to select a date]. Again, I did not receive the merchandise.

On [click to select a date], I contacted [Merchant Name] via email and phone to request that my order be cancelled and my money refunded. [Merchant Name] would not agree to refund my money, insisting that the merchandise was on the way. On [click to select a date], I again requested that my order be cancelled and my money refunded, but I did not receive a response from the company. I have not yet received my order.

I have enclosed a copy of the bill with the disputed charge highlighted, and copies of my email correspondence with [Merchant Name]. Please investigate this dispute and provide me with a written statement of the outcome.

Thank you for your time and attention to this matter.

Dispute Sample Letter 2

No Response Regarding Disputed Information After 30 Days-- Equifax

[Date]

Equifax
Disclosure Department
PO Box 740241
Atlanta. GA 30374

RE: [Your name]

        [Your current address]

        Previous address:

        Social Security number:

        Date of Birth:

To Whom It May Concern:

Over thirty days ago, I wrote to your company indicating my dispute of information in my credit report. A copy of my original letter accompanies this correspondence. As of today's date, Equifax has not responded to my dispute and therefore must remove from my credit file all information disputed in my correspondence.

Under the Fair Credit Reporting Act, your bureau was to have completed its reinvestigation of disputed information within 30 days. This 30-day mark has come and gone without any response from your office.

I am requesting your assistance in the verification of the removal of the disputed data from my credit report. Please send to my address provided above an updated credit report at no cost to me as proof that these items have been removed.

Thank you for your attention to this matter. I await your response.

Sincerely,

   (Signature)
Enclosure

Credit Score

A credit score is a numerical expression based on a level analysis of a person's credit files, to represent the credit worthiness of an individual. A credit score is primarily based on a credit report information typically sourced from credit bureaus.

Lenders, such as banks and credit card companies, use credit scores to evaluate the potential risk posed by lending money to consumers and mitigate losses due to bad debt. Lenders use credit scores to determine who qualifies for a loan, at what interest rate, and what credit limits. Lenders also use credit scores to determine which customers are likely to bring in the most revenue.

The use of credit or identity scoring prior to authorizing access or granting credit is an implementation of a trusted system. Credit scoring is not limited to banks. Other organizations, such as mobile phone companies, insurance companies, landlords, and government departments employ the same techniques. Digital finance companies such as online lenders also use alternative data sources to calculate the creditworthiness of borrowers. Credit scoring also has much overlap with data mining, which uses many similar techniques. These techniques combine thousands of factors but are similar or identical.

Cozette M. White

How Much Debt Should
Go Toward Our Paycheck?

No one likes to be in debt, but the truth is, almost everyone is. Your goal should be to have as little debt as possible so that you can keep as much of your hard-earned paycheck... The trick is how to get there. You need to have realistic expectations and, with a little discipline, you can have peace of mind that you are in good financial shape. The following steps will help out.

Step 1: Debt-to-income Ratio: If you went to a bank and asked for a loan, one of the first things they would want to know is what is your debt-to-income ratio. Banks believe that the amount you pay for your monthly debt should be no higher than 36 percent of your gross monthly income.[24] Ideally, it should be around 10 percent, but if it's less than 20 percent, you're still considered to be in pretty good shape. This means that the money you pay out every month for your mortgage, including taxes and insurance, credit card payments, car and other loans should not be more than the 36 percent figure. Before you panic, remember that the calculation is on your gross income, not your take-home pay. What's left over has to pay for everything else: living expenses, utilities, clothes, food, entertainment and those lattes purchases that some get every morning on the way to work. Sure, you put some of those things on a credit card, but that increases your debt, which increases your monthly payment and besides, the whole point is to get out right?

Step 2: Mortgage Debt: Your monthly mortgage, plus taxes and insurance, should not be any more than 28 percent of your gross monthly income.[25] So, if you make $6,000 per month, your monthly mortgage debt should not be any more than $1,680.

Step 3: Credit Card Debt: Credit cards, unless you pay them off every month, are a cancer on your finances. Bite the bullet. Pay them off as soon as you can; then only charge what you can pay for in full when the statement comes. Here's why, interest on credit cards is ridiculously high and all that money you are paying in interest can be put to much better use. What's more, 30 percent of your credit score is based on your "credit utilization rate," or how much you have used up of the credit that has been extended to you.[26] Add up all the amounts of your credit limits on your cards then divide it by the sum of all your outstanding balances; that's your credit utilization rate. So, if the sum of credit limit is $10,000, and you owe $5,000, then your credit utilization rate is 50 percent. As a rule of thumb, anything more than 30 percent could negatively affect your credit score.

Step 4: You Owe It to Yourself: Give yourself some credit and be a creditor to yourself. Pay yourself a monthly payment for savings and investment. Treat it as you would any other debt you have to pay every month. This is the one monthly debt payment that should be as high as possible.

Unveiling the Mask

How Credit History Works

Credit history is a record of a borrower's responsible repayment of debts. A credit report is a record of the borrower's credit history from many sources, including banks, credit card companies, collection agencies, and governments. A borrower's credit score is the result of a mathematical algorithm applied to a credit report and other sources of information to predict future delinquency. When a customer fills out an application for credit from a bank, credit card Company, or a store, their information is forwarded to a credit bureau.

The credit bureau matches the name, address and other identifying information on the credit applicant with information retained by the bureau in its files.

Cozette's Tip – CREDIT = MONEY One way to rebuild your credit is through a secured card. This is a card that is fully funded by you. You will be required to leave a deposit. After making regular payments over a period, ask the financial institution to drop the deposit and convert the card to an unsecured card.

The gathered records are then used by lenders to determine an individual's credit worthiness; that is, determining an individual's ability and track record of repaying a debt. The willingness to repay a debt is indicated by how timely past payments have been made to other lenders. Lenders like to see consumer debt obligations paid regularly and on time, and therefore focus particularly on missed payments and may not, for example, consider an overpayment as an offset for a missed payment.

Cozette M. White

Length of Credit History

The longer you have been using credit, the better your chances of a high FICO score in the credit scoring world. What is the 'FICO Score'? A FICO score is a type of credit score created by the Fair Isaac Corporation.[27] Lenders use borrowers' FICO scores along with other details on borrowers' credit reports to assess credit risk and determine whether to extend credit. FICO scores take into account various factors in five areas to determine credit worthiness: payment history, current level of indebtedness, types of credit used, length of credit history and new credit accounts. To earn a FICO credit score, borrowers need to have at least some credit history. Although it's not the most heavily weighted factor used to calculate a borrower's FICO score, the length of a borrower's credit history does matter. And within that component, age and experience typically prove beneficial. Generally, the older your length of credit history, the better it is for your FICO score. Lenders use Credit scores – including credit card issuers and mortgage lenders – to predict the risk of a borrower not repaying their loans. There

124

are many credit scores available, but its the FICO score that gets the most frequent use. As a result, to improve their ability to qualify for low interest credit, borrowers will want to work on building up their FICO scores.

To calculate its score, FICO looks at five differently weighted factors:[28]

How you have handled credit (otherwise known as your payment history).

- How much debt you have available compared to how much you use, known as credit utilization.
- How long you have had credit.
- How much new credit you have.
- The mix of credit you have.

Accounting for 15 percent of a FICO score, "length of credit history falls in the middle of those five factors in terms of its importance. There's a saying in the credit industry, "The best credit is old credit." According to to Experian's State of Credit 2017 report, members of the Silent Generation (born before 1946) have the highest average credit score (729) of any age group.[29] That's nearly 30 points higher than baby boomers. But you don't necessarily have to be a "grizzled veteran" of credit to have an excellent credit score. It's quite possible for a person with a relatively short credit history to have a score equal to a score for a person with 30 years of credit history. It's really about how you manage the credit you have available. Of course, you do need to have some length of history in order for scores to be calculated. Even if your history isn't perfect, it's still important to have one. That's because, without a credit history, banks don't know what kind of borrower you will be in the future. And when banks are uncertain, that usually means higher interest rates for borrowers – if they can get a loan at all. When considering 'length of credit history,' the FICO scoring formula evaluates the ages of your oldest and newest accounts, along with the average age of all your other cards.

 *Cozette's Tip –*

What factors determine your credit score?

Payment History-35%;

Total Amount Owed- 30%;

Length of Credit, History- 15%;

New Credit- 10%;

Types of Credit Used- 10%.[30]

The minimum amount of credit history needed to generate a FICO score is six months or more on at least one credit account.[31] That means a consumer who opened her first credit card three months ago – and had no other loans – would not yet have a FICO score, regardless of how responsible she has been with that card. Although accounts don't need to be open, they do need to still appear on your credit report to be counted by FICO. So even if an account was closed five years ago, for example, its continued appearance on a credit report would help extend a borrower's length of credit. Those closed accounts won't appear indefinitely, however. Closed accounts that were always paid on time remain on credit reports for 10 years from the date of closure or last account update, while accounts with late payments remain for seven years from the date of the first delinquency.[32]

Types of Credit to Have

Credit refers to the concept of a lender providing a loan for a borrower. There are various different types of credit – such as credit cards, overdraft facilities, higher purchase agreements and personal loans depending on how the borrower intends on repaying the finance.

Credit cards: Credit cards are a type of credit that allow users to borrow money from a bank or credit card issuing company to purchase goods and services or to withdraw cash. There are countless credit card types, and various forms of charge cards, store cards, rewards cards and balance transfer cards available.

Bank loans: Bank loans which can be paid off in monthly installments over a particular period. Mortgages are a type of credit often used to purchase property. They are secured against a property and are usually paid off in monthly payments over an extended period of time.

Cozette M. White

Overdrafts: Overdraft facilities are another type of credit that, because of a pre-arranged agreement authorized by your bank, allows you to withdraw money after the bank account balance reaches zero. An overdraft has a limit depending on your account history and needs. They are helpful in providing a safety net to cover short-term arrears and to compensate for a temporary lack of cashflow. Be aware that overdrafts incur interest and, depending on your agreement, may include an administration fee or monthly payment charges.

Higher Purchase and Personal Loans: Higher purchase agreement is a mechanism for borrowing money in order to purchase goods. Once the purchase is paid off you then own it, but if you don't make regular payments, creditors can ask you to return the goods. Personal loans allow you to borrow an agreed amount and pay it back with interest over a fixed period of time.

The average FICO credit score broke records in 2017 – the average American has a 700 FICO score.[33]

3 Credit Bureaus

The three major credit bureaus in the United States are Equifax, Experian, and the TransUnion.

EQUIFAX

Equifax Credit Information Services, LLC

P.O. Box 740241, Atlanta, GA 30374

866-349-5186: Dispute Credit Report Items

800-685-1111: Request Free Credit Report

EXPERIAN

Experian National Consumer Assistance Center
P.O. Box 4500, Allen, TX 75013

800-509-8495: Dispute Credit Report Items

888-397-3742: Report Requests & Fraud Help

TRANSUNION

TransUnion Consumer Relations
P.O. Box 2000, Chester, PA 19016-2000
800-916-8800: Disputes Items & Status Checks
877-322-8228: Free Annual Credit Report

CHAPTER 10

ROADMAP TO FINANCIAL FREEDOM

"It is better to have a permanent income than to be fascinating."

-Oscar Wilde

FOLLOW YOUR PLAN
AND MANAGE YOUR DEBT

Implement your recovery plan. After you've decided on a recovery plan, whether that is getting a new job, reducing debts, bankruptcy, or some combination of those, get started as quickly as possible. The longer you delay, the more your debt will pile up.

Most of these will be abrupt changes that will negatively impact your quality of life. As stated previously, the most important thing is to remain positive throughout this situation change, and try to see the light at the end of the tunnel.

Prioritize your debt repayment. Understand that in a financial disaster situation, not all debt is valued equally. If after reducing expenses, you have a fairly small amount to pay off debt, it is important to use that amount to pay off debts in the following order of importance.

Pay off any secured loans first. These include mortgages or car payments. Not paying these loans can ultimately result in foreclosure or repossession. Focus next on unsecured loans, specifically on high-interest accounts like credit cards.

Unveiling the Mask

Finally, focus on unsecured loans with low debt. For any debts you cannot afford to pay, ensure that you contact the creditor and explain your situation. You may be able to renegotiate repayment in these cases.

Understand the importance of staying in touch with your creditors. While it may be tempting to ignore your creditors, this will only worsen your situation. Often, creditors will begin garnishing wages simply because they have not been able to make contact with borrowers. Be aware that creditors will not stop attempting to contact you, nor will they forget about you. Therefore, being proactive and working with, rather than against creditors is critical.

Contact your creditors and explain your situation in open and honest terms. Phone your creditors, and make sure you have with you all your financial information, as they will likely ask. Honestly explain to your creditors that you are unable to make payments, and that you would like to work with them to come upon a solution.

Ask for a rate reduction, deferred payments for several months, or a reduced payment plan. Creditors are very eager to work with borrowers, since it is more costly for a creditor to utilize debt collection services and risk losing principle than to work constructively with a borrower. Suggest that you are willing to pay the ongoing interest during any period of debt relief, this signals to creditors that you are serious about your obligation. Inform your creditors that you are planning on staying in touch every month. By contacting them and staying readily available, they will be more likely to extend favorable terms and be more flexible in their needs.

Consider debt consolidation loans and/or balance transfer cards to reduce payment amounts. Both of these solutions involve transferring debt balances to new loans with more favorable terms. A debt consolidation loan involves taking out a new loan with lower interest, like a line of credit, and transferring your higher interest debts to that loan. For example, you would transfer all your credit card debts to a line of credit, which rolls all of your payments into one payment that will often cost less than the previous payments combined due to lower interest rates. Be aware that although interest rates are lower, the loan terms are often longer, which means you may actually spend more in interest over time.

A balance transfer card is another solution for credit card debts. A balance transfer card is credit card which offers very low to no interest rates for the first 12-24 months for individuals who transfer their balances from another credit card. Doing this can give you a much needed break on payments until your financial situation is in order.

Consider debt counseling. If you feel overwhelmed, then consider consulting not-for-profit debt counseling services. These services can help you make, plan and work with creditors to restructure your debt in a way that fits within your current means to pay.

The most commonly reported sources of stress include money (64 percent report that this is a very or somewhat significant source of stress), work (60 percent), the economy (49 percent), family responsibilities (47 percent) and personal health concerns (46 percent).34

CHAPTER
11

DISCIPLINE NOT
DEPRIVATION

"I will tell you the secret to getting rich on Wall Street. You try to be greedy when others are fearful. And you try to be fearful when others are greedy."

-Warren Buffett

RECOVER FROM Y O U R
FINANCIAL INSTABILITY

Maintain your recovery habits. As you begin to pay off debt and increase your income, you will begin to feel more financially secure again. However, this feeling can be quickly reversed if you get ahead of yourself and spend your newfound excess as quickly as you earn it. Make sure that even when you feel your financial health returning, you keep your spending low and don't incur any new debt until all of your old debts are repaid.

Consider allowing yourself one luxury each time you pay off a debt. For example, you might have cancelled your Netflix subscription to save money. You can set an allowance where you can renew your subscription once your credit card debt has been paid off. Allowing one luxury like this can help keep you on track.

Rebuild your credit. If you ever had significant debt and were late on payments or went through bankruptcy proceedings, there is a good chance that your credit limits and credit score are low. In order to secure your financial future, you will have to rebuild a good credit score. This will allow you to take on lower cost loans in the future.

Even though unpaid debts or a bankruptcy can remain on your credit report for years, it is possible to begin building a good credit score once you get back on your feet.

Build credit by paying off credit card in full and on time. This should be simpler now that you've reduced your discretionary spending. You can also build credit by paying back other loans on time and in the full amount. These include mortgage and car payments. Again, be sure to avoid taking out any new loans like these until you've paid off your old ones.

Apply the lessons you've learned. Examine the practices and situations that got you into the financial disaster that you've just struggled to climb out of. Were you living above your means? Were you often using expensive forms of debt to finance purchases? Perhaps you realize now that you can get by with spending much less than you did before, especially on discretionary expenses. Apply these experiences to your new financial situation to become even more financially sound than you were before.

Save or prepare to prevent another crisis. If your financial disaster was due to an unavoidable cause, like a lost job or a medical emergency, you should take steps to be ready if it happens again. Once you're back on your feet with debts paid, be sure to save the money you have been using to pay off debts. Part of this saved money can be your "emergency fund." An ideal amount to save is enough to cover your fixed expenses for around six months. Having this money set aside will give you a financial buffer if you ever find yourself in a similar crisis.

39% of consumers say they spend three hours a week, at work thinking about their personal finances.[35]

CHAPTER 12

PROPTECT YOUR
FINANCIAL HEALTH

"Many folks think they aren't good at earning money when what they don't know is how to use it."

-Frank A. Clark

MANAGE AND PROTECT
YOUR FAMILY

The question that often comes up to every individual occasionally, is, do you have a saving plan to cover financial emergencies? If your family was to suddenly lose an income, would they be able to maintain their lifestyles and so on.

Life insurance is an important component of a sound financial plan. The proceeds from a life insurance policy can help your loved ones continue to manage financially after your death. Life insurance can protect your survivors financially by replacing your lost income due to death.

Life is uncertain, and we need to be prepared for the unexpected. In fact, the only things certain in life are taxes and death. One or both of these things are bound to happen at some point in a person's life. While taxes will always be present in every society, and death can come like a thief in the night. Sickness and death are particularly frightening as it is. Death is certain part of life and its certain that one day we will go back to our creator. What's really frightening though is if we are not prepared when this happens.

This is the reason why every person should have a life insurance policy. A life insurance policy can go a long way toward helping dependents who have experienced the death of a loved one. If the breadwinner of the family dies, then the dependents can be left with nowhere to turn. If primary wage earner has a life insurance policy, however, then their dependents will have a safety net until they can fend for themselves.

Policies can do more than serve as a lifeline for dependents after the insured dies. However, they can also help defray death-related expenses, including funeral costs and the cost of probate for the insured's will. Some people are not as lucky as others and they will not be able to leave mansions and lands to their dependents. With this insurance, a parent can be sure to leave an inheritance especially for those who have young children the benefits will help cover their expenses until they are able to work and fend for themselves.

Why Life Insurance?

Life insurance is a form of insurance in which a person makes regular payments to an insurance company, in return for a lump sum of money to be paid to them after a period of time, or to their family if they die. A life insurance policy is a contract with an insurance company. In exchange for premium payments, the insurance company provides a lump-sum payment, known as a death benefit, to beneficiaries upon the insured's death. A accidental death benefit is a provision that may be added to a life insurance policy which provides payment of an additional benefit in the case of death resulting from an accident. Typically, life insurance is chosen based on the needs and goals of the owner. Term life insurance generally provides protection for a set period of time, while permanent insurance, such as whole and universal life, provides lifetime coverage. It's important to note that death benefits from all types of life insurance are generally income tax-free.

Uses and Purpose of Insurance

If you fill out a life insurance application, it will ask that very question: "What is the purpose for your life insurance policy?" That is because the purpose varies from person to person. Some purposes for which people buy life insurance are:

- To replace their income that would be lost upon their death.
- To hire others to replace their contributions to the family that would be lost upon their death (daycare, transportation, cleaning services, lawn services, etc.)
- To give a business time and resources to replace an employee when a key employee dies.
- To pass their estate to their heirs in a tax-friendly fashion.
- To pay taxes, administrative fees, and debts upon their death.
- To pay for chronic, critical or terminal illness expenses (when the policy has living benefits).

• To pay off mortgage, school loans, business loans, and other debts.

• To pay for all final expenses, including funeral, memorial service, burial, transportation, etc.

• To leave a gift to charity.

• To provide cash value for retirement.

How Much Can You Afford
in Life Insurance

No matter how it may sometimes seem, life insurance premiums aren't arbitrary. Insurance companies use various criteria to determine what your premiums will be, or if they will even approve you for a policy. There are several factors used to determine your life insurance premiums, including the following:

Age – Age is probably the single primary factor that determines your life insurance premiums. Since the policies will pay out upon your death, the insurance company wants to make sure that it won't happen too soon. True enough, everyone will die sooner or later, but the company needs a sufficient number of years to pass and the accumulation of the premiums you will pay in the meantime that the policy will be adequately funded to pay the claim. The older you are when you buy your policy, the higher the premium will be. That will be the case whether the policy you buy is term or whole life. By age 65 the premiums might be prohibitive if the company will even be willing to accept the policy at all.

Gender - Statistically, women live longer than men so they will generally pay less in life insurance premiums for a policy with the same face value and at the same age as a man. Though the average life expectancy in the US is78.8, the gap between men and women is substantial.[36] The average life expectancy for men is 76.4 and for women it's 81.2, a difference of slightly more than five years.

However, life expectancies have shifted allowing for longer lifespans.

Physical Condition - Life insurance premiums are also based on your weight, or at least the proportion of your weight to your height. There are ranges and a theoretical norm at the center that indicate a "normal" proportion. To the degree your own height-to-weight ratio varies from the ideal range, you will pay more in premiums.

Smoking - Smoking is a heavyweight negative when it comes to life insurance premiums. Smoking is closely linked to cardio vascular disease and to numerous forms of cancer. Premiums can increase by 15-20% as a result of cigarette smoking. And it's not just smoking that raises premiums. Various health issues have been linked to chewing tobacco. So expect to see a higher rate if you participate in this activity. It does help if you quit. Insurance companies will often lower your premium if you have quit for at least two years. Some even offer smoking cessation programs to help you along.

Your Medical History - Your medical history – (including any current health conditions) will have an effect on your premiums. That isn't to say that any healthconditions will result in higher premiums, but only those that have the potential to reduce your lifespan. The insurance company will rely heavily on your answers provided on the medical questionnaire, so it's important to be as truthful and accurate as possible. Companies will also often require a physical and will likely request a report from the Medical

Information Bureau, or MIB. This report will provide a history of surgeries, hospital stays and known health conditions. Between your information given on the questionnaire, the results of your physical and the MIB report, they'll have a pretty thorough assessment of your medical history. It is important to mention that there are options for no exam life insurance in the market as well.

Your Family Medical History - Since so many health conditions that affect longevity are genetic, the insurance company will be interested in your family's medical history, in addition to yours. There is at least some predictive potential in studying family medical history, otherwise, healthy individual might develop certain medical conditions that are prevalent in the family tree. The insurance company will be most interested in linear family – your parents, grandparents and siblings more than any others. Aunts, uncles and cousins aren't considered as relevant if their histories will even be considered at all.

Occupation - Some occupations carry greater risk than others, and that will be a factor in determining premiums. An engineer might be considered a "safer" occupation than a police officer, a pilot or fire fighter, where the risk of being killed on the job is higher. It is even possible that a career that is considered too dangerous will result in a declined insurance application. The insurance companies are, after all, looking to build a client list comprised of the lowest risk customers possible.

Types of Insurance

There are two major types of life insurance term and whole life. Whole life is sometimes called permanent life insurance, and it encompasses several subcategories, including traditional whole life, universal life, variable life and variable universal life. In 2003, about 6.4 million individual life insurance policies bought were term and about 7.1 million were whole life.[37] Life insurance products for groups are different from life insurance sold to individuals. The information below focuses on life insurance sold to individuals.

Term Insurance is the simplest form of life insurance. It pays only if death occurs during the term of the policy, which is usually from one to 30 years. Most term policies have no other benefit provisions.

There are two basic types of term life insurance policies: level term and decreasing term.

- Level term means that the death benefit stays the same throughout the duration of the policy.
- Decreasing term means that the death benefit drops, usually in one-year increments, over the course of the policy's term.

Whole Life/Permanent - insurance pays a death benefit whenever you die even if you live to 100! There are three major types of whole life or permanent life insurance, traditional whole life, universal life, and variable universal life, and there are variations within each type.

Traditional Whole Life Insurance - in the case of traditional whole life, both the death benefit and the premium is designed to stay the same (level) throughout the life of the policy. The cost per $1,000 of benefit increases as the insured person ages, and it obviously gets very high when the insured lives to 80 and beyond. The insurance company could charge a premium that increases each year, but that would make it very hard for most people to afford life insurance at advanced ages. So, the company, keeps the premium level by charging a premium that, in the early years, is higher than what's needed to pay claims, investing that money, and then using it to supplement the level premium to help pay the cost of life insurance for older people. By law, when these "overpayments" reach a certain amount, they must be available to the policyholder as a cash value if he or she decides not to continue with the original plan. The cash value is an alternative, and not an additional benefit under the policy.

Universal Life Insurance – this type of life insurance offers very high death coverages. It combines this with a savings component; the premium that the policyholder pays is for the most part invested by the life insurance company to provide a cash value build-up (every policy will have a so-called Cash Value). And this can be viewed by the policyholder as an alternative asset class akin to a savings account or investment product.

Universal life insurance policies are mostly used:

- As a liquidity planning tool in case of demise (estate planning).
- To compensate for inheritance tax charges, for example on foreign property (tax planning); e.g., UK inheritance tax (40%) will be applicable to the value of London real estate on the demise of the owner.[38]
- To plan for complex estates with numerous family members (succession planning); i.e. to create liquidity in the context of family business succession to benefit non-active family members or to settle existing debts without liquidating businesses or investments.
  - To provide family security – protect the family's lifestyle in the event of a tragic loss (wealth planning);
  - To avoid probate;

  - or As an attractive alternative investment (diversification).

Variable life insurance – This is a type of permanent life insurance where the cash value is invested in a number of sub-accounts that are similar to mutual funds. These sub-accounts can be thought of as similar to mutual funds, except you can only invest them through.

Unveiling the Mask

How Does the Insurance
Part Work?

Like all life insurance policies, variable life insurance policies have three important parts - the death benefit is a tax-free chunk of cash paid out by the life insurance company in the event that you die. In permanent life insurance policies, the death benefit is made up of two components -a regular term life insurance policy and the cash value.

A beneficiary is a person or organization that is set to receive the death benefit. Besides the obvious choices (your spouse, your children), almost anyone, any organization, or any kind of legal relationship (such as a trust) can be a beneficiary. There can be more than one beneficiary.

Your premiums are how you pay for your life insurance policy. You can usually pay either monthly or annually. Variable life insurance lasts for your entire lifetime, assuming you continue to pay the premiums.

How Does the Cash Value
Part Work?

Every time you pay your premium, a certain percentage of it will go into the cash value of your policy. This cash value will then be invested some of the sub-accounts that you choose.

The easiest way to think about this sub-accounts is to imagine them as mutual funds. These sub-accounts are only available through the life insurance policy; you could not invest in them outside of the variable life insurance policy.

Like all investments, the cash value will fluctuate depending on how well each investment is doing. The stock market is in free fall? Your cash value probably is, too. Typically, however, your cash value will grow incrementally over the course of decades. Your investments are tax-deferred as well, which is why some refer to variable life insurance as a "super-IRA."

Remember when we talked about how cash value i t is one component of your death benefit? In all permanent life insurance policies, your death benefit is made up of a regular term life insurance policy and your cash value. Over time, as your cash value grows, your term life insurance policy will get smaller.

Eventually, your cash value will cover the entirety of your death benefit, and your variable life insurance policy will no longer have a term component.

This can be confusing to people who think that, by buying a variable life insurance policy, they will receive both the accrued cash value and the term component's death benefit when they die. Instead, the cash value slowly replaces the term policy until it represents the entirety of your death benefit.

There are various strategies you can use to withdraw the cash value from your variable life insurance policy before you die, though they are typically less flexible than whole life insurance policies.

You can also surrender your policy to get the cash value. You can surrender at any time, however, most of the growth won't happen for two or three decades. If you surrender your policy within the first twenty years, you'll end up paying more in surrender fees than you will have made in profit.

Conclusion

Life insurance is a form of insurance in which a person makes regular payments to an insurance company, in return for a lump sum of money to be paid to them after a period of time, or to their family if they die. I encourage every family to obtain a life insurance policy once they've positioned their finances to afford a life insurance policy into their monthly household expenses as a life insurance policy for death and accident.

28% of parents agree with the statement "I am not good with money, so I should not be the one to teach my Kids about money."[39]

CHAPTER 13

THE DEVIL LURKS
IN THE DETAILS

"The real measure of your wealth is how much you'd be worth if you lost all your money."

-Unknown

GETTING IT ALL TOGETHER

Believe it or not, you have an estate. In fact, nearly everyone does. Your estate is comprised of everything you own - our car, home, other real estate, checking and savings accounts, investments, life insurance, furniture, personal possessions.

No matter how large or how modest, everyone has an estate and something in common, you can't take it with you when you die. When that happens and it is a "when" and not an "if" you probably want to control how those things are given to the people or organizations you care most about.

To ensure your wishes are carried out, you need to provide instructions stating whom you want to receive your items, what you want them to receive, and when they are to receive it. You will, of course, want this to happen with the least amount paid in taxes, legal fees, and court costs. This is what we call estate planning -

making a plan in advance and naming whom you want to receive the things you own after you die.

However, good estate planning is much more than that. It should also include instructions for passing your values (religion, education, hard work, etc). In addition, to your valuables, include instructions for your care if you become disabled before you die.

Name a guardian and an inheritance manager for minor children. Provide for family members with special needs without disrupting government benefits. Provide for loved ones who might be irresponsible with money or who may need future protection from creditors or divorce.

Include life insurance to provide for your family at your death, disability income insurance to replace your income if you cannot work due to illness or injury, and long-term care insurance to help pay for your care in case of an extended illness or injury.

Provide for the transfer of your business at your retirement, disability, or death. Minimize taxes, court costs, and unnecessary legal fees, and make it an ongoing process, and not a one-time event. Your plan should be reviewed and updated as your family and financial situations (and laws) change over your lifetime.

Estate Planning

It is not just for "retired" people, although people do tend to think about it more as they get older. Unfortunately, we can't successfully predict how long we will live, and illness and accidents happen to people of all ages.

Estate planning is not just for "the wealthy," either, although people who have built some wealth do often think more about how to preserve it. Good estate planning often means more to families with modest assets, because they can afford to lose the least.

Too many people don't plan. Individuals put off estate planning because they think they don't own enough, they're not old enough, they're busy, think they have plenty of time, they're confused and don't know who can help them, or they just don't want to think estate planning. Then, when something happens to them, their families have to pick up the pieces. If you don't have a plan, your state has one for you, but you probably won't like it.

At disability, if your name is on the title of your assets and you can't conduct business due to mental or physical incapacity, only a court appointee can sign for you. The court, not your family, will control how your assets are used to care for you through a conservatorship or guardianship (depending on the term used in your state). When the court intervenes and has control over how the assets used, it become expensive and time consuming; it is open to the public, and it can be difficult to end even if you recover.

At your death, if you die without an intentional estate plan, your assets will be distributed according to the probate laws in your state. In many states, if you have remarried and have children, your spouse and children will each receive a share. That means your spouse could receive only a fraction of your estate, which may not be enough to live on. If you have minor children, the court will control their inheritance.

If both parents die (i.e., in a car accident), the court will appoint a guardian without knowing whom you would have chosen. Given the choice and you do have the choice wouldn't you prefer these matters be handled privately by your family, not by the courts? Wouldn't you prefer to keep control of who receives what and when? And, if you have young children, wouldn't you prefer to have a say in who will raise them if you can't?

Wills

A will provides your instructions, but it does not avoid probate. Any assets titled in your name or directed by your will must go through your state's probate process before they can be distributed to your heirs. (If you own property in other states, your family would probably face multiple probates, each one according to to the laws in that state.) The process varies greatly from state to state, but it can become expensive with legal fees, executor fees, and court costs. It can also take anywhere from nine months to two years or longer. With the rare exception, probate files are open to the public and excluded heirs are encouraged to come forward and seek a share of your estate.

In short, the court system, not your family, controls the process. Not everything you own will go through probate. Jointly-owned property and assets that let you name a beneficiary (for example, life insurance, annuities, etc.) are not controlled by your will and usually will transfer to the new owner or beneficiary without probate.

But there are many problems with joint ownership, and avoidance of probate is not guaranteed. For example, if a valid beneficiary is not named, the assets will have to go through probate and will be distributed along with the rest of your estate. If you name a minor as a beneficiary, the court would probably insist on a guardianship until the child legally becomes an adult. For these reasons, a revocable living trust is preferred by many families' and professionals. It can avoid probate at death (including multiple probates if you own property in other states), prevent court control of assets at incapacity, bring all of your assets (even those with beneficiary designations) together into one plan, provide maximum privacy, is valid in every state, and can be changed by you at any time. It can also reflect your love and values to your family and future generations.

Chances You Need an Estate Plan

Chances are you already have a last will and testament. (If not, that should be your priority for the sake and sanity of your loved ones.) But you could also make life much easier for your loved ones (and yourself) if you prepare a comprehensive estate plan. A well-conceived estate plan can accomplish two important goals. It can protect your assets during your life and streamline the dispersal of your assets to your beneficiaries after you're gone, while minimizing their tax burden. A trust also allows you to set the terms and conditions upon which those dispersals are granted. In essence, a trust is an assortment of legal documents that lay out the terms of the administration and disposition of an individual's assets— which, as you might note, sounds almost identical to the objective of a will. So why go to the extra time, effort and expense of preparing an estate plan? The fact is, a will is one component of an estate plan, but there are other elements that give an estate plan far more than power and flexibility:

• An estate plan offers you immediate financial benefits. A trust within an estate plan can protect your assets and minimize the taxes on some of your investment gains while you are still alive.

• It streamlines the disbursement process by bypassing probate court. Otherwise, your beneficiaries might be forced to settle your estate in court in a divisive legal battle that could drag on for many years at a cost of thousands of dollars.

• It gives you the opportunity to set more explicit terms on the dispersal of the assets. For instance, money can be doled out in delayed installments or when certain goals are obtained, such as graduation from college. A trust gives you a great deal of flexibility to rule over the disposition of your estate for many years after you're gone.

• It minimizes inheritance taxes. An estate plan can be structured in a way that minimizes the taxes that your beneficiaries' pay on their inheritance, giving you the benefit of passing more of your money to your loved ones and less to Uncle Sam.

• Provides for care and oversight. It gives you the chance to choose the type of care you'll receive and to designate specific individuals to manage your money and your health care decisions when you are no longer capable of making those decisions on your own.

• It can avoid investment gains taxes for your charitable endowments. Certain trusts can be structured in a way that transfers your invested assets, such as stocks, directly to a charitable organization without paying taxes on the gains. Setting up an estate plan requires the services of an experienced estate attorney. It is also helpful to involve your investment advisor, your tax accountant and any other key advisors in your estate planning decisions. While it entails a fair amount of time and effort on your part, setting up an estate plan will ultimately make your life easier while sparing your loved ones from a significant tax burden, as well as many difficult months or years of costly litigation.

Conclusion

Many lawyers now provide flat-fee estate planning services, creating a will for a fixed sum of a few hundred dollars. And if you want to save a few bucks by doing some of the work yourself, there are plenty of self-directed resources online — including websites like Rocket Lawyer[40] and LegalZoom[41] — that help guide you. There are even do-it-yourself products like Quicken's Will Maker, which works similarly to its taxpreparation software.

Whatever method you choose, the important thing is to engage seriously on your estate plan and not leave things up to chance.

Only 4 in 10 American adults have a will or living trust.[42]

Team of Professionals Checklist

Name	Phone/Email

Financial Planner

_____

Accountant/CPA

_____

Bookkeeper

_____

Estate Planning Attorney

_____

HR Director at work

_____

Business Lawyer

_____

Insurance Agent

_____

Mortgage Broker

_____

CHAPTER 14

CONQUER YOUR PAST FOR
A POWERFUL FURTURE

"Health is the money. We never have a true idea of its true value until we lose it."

-Dr. Cozette M. White

CONQUERING ABUSE

Abuse occurs or happens when an individual either physically or emotionally treats another violently. Abuse occurs in continuous process typically, in something like a cycle. It continues until the individual who is being abused gets assistance. Some of the time, another person, a companion or, relative perceives the abuse and hops in to aid.

Ordinarily, abuse can be difficult to perceive because the abuser most of the time may not appear to be damaging. An abuser, most of the time, may seem like a decent and everyday kind of person, and they may state that they give it a second thought or are infatuated.

Types of Abuse

There are different kinds of abuse in the world, but it can be generalized to these two categories.

- Physical abuse: this type of abuse involves physically injuring or causing trauma to a person.

- Emotional abuse: it can also be referred to as Psychological or mental abuse, and it is characterized by an individual subjecting another person to a behavior that may result in psychological trauma such as anxiety or chronic depression.

Why Do People Abuse?

There are different reasons why people abuse. Some abusers learned how to abuse at a very young age by watching either of their parents abuse the other (most of the time it is a man abusing the woman). Because these individuals were exposed to this behavior at a young age abuse becomes a typical state of life for them. Such individuals disguised a specific relationship dynamic, specifically the correlative parts of "abuser" and "casualty." They know about and completely comprehend what it is like to be the powerless casualty from their experience.

Abusive behavior can also come about from emotional well-being issues or distress. For instance, somebody with anger, drinking, or medication issues may effortlessly gain out of power amid contentions (e.g., because there is some problem with their capacity to hinder themselves at the mind level) and verbally or physically strike out at their partners, friends, or children.

Cozette's Tip –

If you have been isolated from most family and friends, confide in someone you can trust from whom you do have contact with. Telling someone is a way of breaking out of suffering in silence. And in emergency cases, it could mean contact with someone who could one day save your life.

Warning Signs of Abuse

Before any relationship becomes an abusive relationship, there would be signs that would indicate that the relationship may develop into an abusive one. Those signs are:

1. Blames you for tricking or backstabbing him or her: If there's a cycle of doubt and false allegations, and your partner continually blames you for trying to cheat or backstab him or her, then you should beware.

2. Makes you feel useless: If your partner regularly makes you feel broken, then you should beware as he or she ought to be your greatest encourager; not your greatest commentator. This is a type of psychological abuse.

3. Continually restricts your movement: If your partner always tries to limit where you go and is always obsessed with having you in his or her sight, then you

should keep a keen eye on them in case of any change in behavior.

4.   Tries to control your cash: Money related abuse is one of the most widely recognized types of abuse in a relationship. When your partner demands that he or she controls the majority of the cash and also restricts your access to the family, then there are signs that you might be abused.

5.   Tries to control what you do and who you see; this can be possible in various ways, and this is very different from essentially having sentiments about what you ought to or shouldn't do. If it gets to a point when your partner starts giving you guidelines like a parent would implement with a child, at this point, the marriage is not an organization anymore but rather tyranny.

STATISTICS OF ABUSE

Abuse does not segregate. It does not look at gender, race, or color. Be that as it may, there is a considerable probability that somebody will be abused from a sentimental point of view, for example, sex, race, training, and wage, but there are other influences, some of which are sexual abuse, substance abuse, family history, and criminal history. You will be amazed at some of the statistics that are associated with abuse in America. They are listed below:

- Averagely 20 people per minute are physically abused by an intimate partner in the United States.[43]

- Each day, there are more than 20,000 phone calls placed to domestic violence hotlines in America.[44]

- The presence of a gun increases the risk of homicide in domestic violence for women by 500%.[45]

- Intimate partners cause 15% of all violent crime.[46]

- 19% of all domestic violence involves aweapon.[47]

- in 5 women and 1 in 71 men in the United States have been raped in their lifetime.[48]

- Almost half of the female (46.7%) and male (44.9%) victims of rape in the United States were raped by an acquaintance. Of these, 45.4% of female rape victims and 29% of male rape victims were raped by an intimate partner.[49]

- 72% of all murder-suicides involve an intimate partner; 94% of the victims of these murder-suicides are female.[50]

- in 15 children are exposed to intimate partner violence each year, and 90% of these children are eyewitnesses to this violence.[51]

HOTLINES AND NUMBERS
TO CALL FOR ASSISSTANCE

If you are a victim of abuse in any form, you do not need to fret or be in the dark. Many communities and societies are ready to help in any way possible even legally. Below are some of the communities with their websites and numbers that you can call for help.

The National Domestic Violence Hotline
1-800-799-7233 (SAFE)
www.ndvh.org

National Dating Abuse Helpline
1-866-331-9474
www.loveisrespect.org

Americans Overseas Domestic Violence Crisis Center
International Toll-Free (24/7)
1-866-USWOMEN (879-6636)
www.866uswomen.org

National Child Abuse Hotline/Childhelp
1-800-4-ACHILD (1-800-422-4453)

www.childhelp.org

National Sexual Assault Hotline

1-800-656-4673 (HOPE)

www.rainn.org

National Resource Center on Domestic Violence

1-800-537-2238

www.nrcdv.org and www.vawnet.org

Childhelp USA/National Child Abuse Hotline

1-800-422-4453

www.childhelpusa.org

Domestic Violence Initiative
1-303-839-5510/ 1-877-839-5510
www.dviforwomen.org

Deaf Abused Women's Network (DAWN)

Email: Hotline@deafdawn.org

1-202-559-5366

www.deafdawn.org

National Latin Network for Healthy
Families and Communities
1-651-646-5553
www.nationallatinonetwork.org

The National Immigrant Women's Advocacy Project

1-202-274-4457

http://www.niwap.org/

Committee against Anti-Asian Violence (CAAAV)

1-212- 473-6485

www.caaav.org

Institute on Domestic Violence in the African
American

Community

1-877-643-8222
 www.dvinstitute.org

National Gay and Lesbian Task Force
1-202-393-5177
www.ngltf.org

National Center for Elder Abuse
1-855-500-3537

www.aginginplace.org

Men Stopping Violence
1-866-717-9317

www.menstoppingviolence.org

American Bar Association Commission on Domestic Violence

1-202-662-1000
www.abanet.org/domviol

Battered Women's Justice Project

1-800-903-0111

www.bwjp.org

National Clearinghouse for the Defense of Battered Women

1-800-903-0111 x 3
www.ncdbw.org

FINAL WORDS -
WINNER IN YOU

Unexpected financial challenges are bound to arise in life - in fact, research shows that 6 in 10 people will experience major life events that will challenge their prior financial plans.[52] The key to tackling these challenges is to be flexible. Review your budget occasionally and make necessary changes. Build up savings so that you can handle unanticipated expenses without going into debt and putting yourself in a difficult situation.

Dealing with a financial disaster can be incredibly challenging for anyone, but if you don't have some smart strategies in mind, the challenge becomes even more overbearing. No matter what financial issues you're dealing with, these strategies will help you cut through the stress and tackle the problem with a clear mind and a strong spirit. *There's a winner in you!*

Cozette M. White

Dr. Cozette M. White is an acclaimed bestselling author, nationally recognized finance and tax strategist, international speaker and philanthropist. She inspires individuals to live in purpose, embrace passion, and achieve personal greatness through a balance in work and life. White has been coined the "Financial Physician" because of her unparalleled ability to empower her clients to ditch debt and develop a plan to create the kind of wealth that leaves a secure financial legacy. She's able to diagnose negative money stories and provide a cure to transform limited beliefs to the sky's the limit! White prescribes the right Financial Rx to boost your financial health.

Dr. White has more than 20 years of experience in corporate America. In her roles, she was responsible for the financial affairs of the organization and focused on a broad range of financial, operational, strategic and executive leadership issues impacting the organization. During her tenure, Dr. White was instrumental in developing processes to ensure that SarbanesOxley (SOX) protocols were in compliance with company standards and were maintained within the business.

Dr. White is the Founder and CEO of My Financial Home Enterprises a global financial consultancy firm providing comprehensive accounting, tax and financial management services for businesses and individuals. White received her Master of Business Administration degree from the University of La Verne and her Bachelor of Science degree in Accounting from California State University, Dominguez Hills. Later Dr. White was awarded an Honorary Doctorate Degree of Philosophy Letters. She is involved in her community and is a member of Alpha Kappa Alpha Sorority, Inc., and she is a member of the National Association of Black Accountants. Additionally, Dr. White is the Founder and Executive Director of Achieving My Dreams Foundation, Inc., a non-profit organization that provides scholarships to graduating high school seniors.

Dr. White's advice has been called upon by ABC and FOX television stations. She has been featured on the numerous radio shows, a recurring voice to millions making regular appearances in various national media outlets, including Black Enterprise, Forbes, Women of Wealth, Upscale, The Huffington Post, and countless newspapers across the country. Women of Wealth dubbed White, "Wealth Builders Extraordinaire." Dr. White was awarded the President's Lifetime Achievement Award by President Barack Obama. Huffington Post name her as "Top Female to Watch in 2018."

Dr. White resides in Southern California and enjoys, traveling, reading, and outdoor activities. When not working, you will likely find Cozette at home enjoying time with her loving kids – Briana M. and Roderick J. and other loved ones.

Customer Support or General Inquires
Attn: Client Relations Manager
info@cozettemwhite.com
(805) 983-1151

Speaking Requests, Media & Press Inquiries
Attn: Admin Assistant
info@cozettemwhite.com
(805) 983-1151

*Serious Speaking Inquiries, review:
www.cozettemwhite.com

Interested in hiring me as your business coach?
Visit www.cozettemwhite.com for details.

Yes, I am A Social Girl!
Want to follow me behind the scenes?

STAY CONNECTED

@cozettemwhite

Grab a copy at www.attractingthebest.com

Grab your FREE downloadable copy.
Grab a copy at www.myfinancialhome.com/financialproducts

INDEX

D

E

F

1   S.G. Smith et al., *The National Intimate Parter and Sexual Violence Survey (NISVS): 2010-2012* (Atlanta, GA: National Center for Injury Prevention and Control, Centers for Disease Control and Prevention, April 2017): 118, 122.

2   Dr. Patricia A. Barrier, "Domestic Violence," *Mayo Clinic Proceedings* 73 (1998): 271.

3   Office of Violence Against Women, "What Is Domestic Violence?," *The United States Department of Justice*, June 16 2017, https://www.justice.gov /ovw/domestic-violence.

4   Dr. Nicole P. Yost, et al., "A Prospective Observational Study of Domestic Violence During Pregnancy," *Obstetrics & Gynecology* 106, no. 1 (July 2005):
61.

5   T.S. Elliot, *The Cocktail Party* (Orlando, FL: Harcourt Brace & Company, 1950).

6   "American Psychological Association Survey Shows Money Stress Weighing on Americans' Health Nationwide," *American Psychological Association*, February 4, 2015, http://www.apa.org/news/press/releases/2015/ 02/money-stress.aspx.

7   Jill Krasny, "Infographic: Women Control The Money In America," *Business Insider*, February 17, 2012, http://www.businessinsider.com/ infographicwomen-control-the-money-in-america-2012-2.

8   Dr. Brad Klontz and Dr. Ted Klontz, *Mind Over Money* (New York: NY: Broadway Books, 2009).

9   Ibid.

10 Quentin Fottrell, "Half of American Families are Living Paycheck to Paycheck," *Market Watch*, April 30, 2017, https://www.marketwatch.com/ story/half-of-americans-are-desperately-living-paycheck-to-paycheck-201704-04.

11 Monique Morrissey, *The State of American Retirement: How 401(k)s Have Failed Most American Workers* (Washington D.C.: Economic Policy Institute, March 3, 2016): 5, 11.

12 "Compare Your Finances to Financial Statistics For the Average American Household to See How You Stack Up," *Debt.com*, December 21, 2017, https://www.debt.com/edu/personal-finance-statistics/.

13 Lauren L. Cole and Andy Kiersz, "There's a Simple Calculation to Determine How Much You Need to Have Saved Before You Can Retire," *Business Insider*, July 6, 2017, http://www.businessinsider.com/how-to-retire-by-income2017-6.

14 Dr. Thomas J. Stanley and Dr. William D. Danko, *The Millionaire Next Door: The Surprising Secrets of America's Wealthy* (Lanham, MD: Taylor Trade Publishing, 2010).

15 Vicki Robin and Joe Dominguez, *Your Money or Your Life* (New York, NY: Penguin Books, 2008).

16 Ameriprise Financial, *An Ameriprise Study on Couples and Money: How Couples Manage Their Finances and Develop Successful Financial Relationships* (Minneapolis, MN: Ameriprise Financial Services, September 2016): 3. Finding that while 77% of couples claim they are aligned when it comes to managing their household finances, a deeper look at the data shows all is not what it seems. Ibid., 4.

17 Dennis Jacobe, "One in Three Americans Prepare a Detailed Household Budget," *GALLUP News*, June 3, 2013, http://news.gallup.com/poll/162872/one-three-americans-prepare-detailedhousehold-budget.aspx.

18 Vivian Manning-Schaffel, "Most of Us Live Paycheck-to-Paycheck: This is What it Does to Your Health," *NBC News*, November 2, 2017,

https://www.nbcnews.com/better/health/most-us-live-paycheck-paycheckwhat-it-does-your-health-ncna816411.

[19] "Two Thirds of Minimum Wage Workers Can't Make Ends Meet, CareerBuilder Survey Finds," press release, *CareerBuilder*, August 11, 2016, http://www.careerbuilder.com/share/aboutus/pressreleasesdetail.aspx?ed=12%2F31%2F2016&id=pr963&sd=8%2F11%2F2016.

[20] https://www.experian.com/.

[21] https://www.equifax.com/personal/.

[22] https://www.transunion.com/.

[23] Susannah Snider, "6 Steps to Contest an Error on Your Credit Report," *U.S. News*, February 28, 2017, https://money.usnews.com/money/personalfinance/banking-credit/articles/2017-02-28/6-steps-to-contest-an-error-onyour-credit-report.

[24] For example, Wells Fargo – a major banking institution – views a debt-toincome ratio of 35% or lower as good. "What is a Good Debt-to-Income Ratio?," *Wells Fargo*, accessed March 1, 2018, https://www.wellsfargo.com/ goals-credit/smarter-credit/credit-101/debt-to-income-ratio/understandingdti/.

[25] "How Much of My Monthly Income Should I Spend on a Mortgage?," *Forbes*, March 1, 2017, https://www.forbes.com/sites/trulia/2017/03/01/how-much-of-my-monthly-income-should-i-spend-on-amortgage/#478ddd477a90.

[26] "What is a Credit Utilization Rate?," *Experian*, accessed March 1, 2018, https://www.experian.com/blogs/ask-experian/credit-education/scorebasics/credit-utilization-rate/.

[27] "What is a Credit Score?," *myFICO*, accessed March 1, 2018, https://www.myfico.com/credit-education/credit-scores/.

28 "How to Repair My Credit and Improve My FICO Scores," *myFICO,* accessed March 1, 2018, https://www.myfico.com/credit-education/improve-yourcredit-score/.

29 Bob Sullivan, "State of Credit: 2017," *Experian*, January 11, 2018, https://www.experian.com/blogs/ask-experian/state-of-credit/.

30 "Keeping Score on Your Credit Score," *Equifax*, accessed March 1, 2018, https://www.equifax.com/cs/Satellite?c=DS_General_Cont_C&childpage na me=DecisionSimple%2FDS_General_Cont_C%2FDSGeneralContentTempl ate &cid=1189578994233&pagename=DecisionSimple%2FPage%2FDSLayout Te mplate&ParentLinkID=1162919656130.

31 "What Are the Minimum Requirements for a FICO Score?," *myFICO*, accessed March 1, 2018, https://www.myfico.com/CreditEducation/ questions/requirement-for-fico-score.aspx.

32 "Closed Accounts Will Remain in Credit History for up to 10 Years," *Experian*, January 15, 2014, https://www.experian.com/blogs/askexperian/closed-accounts-will-remain-in-credit-history-for-10-years/.

33 Jessica Dickler, "Average FICO Score Hits an All-Time High," *CNBC*, July 10, 2017, https://www.cnbc.com/2017/07/10/average-fico-score-hits-an-alltime-high.html.

34 American Psychological Association, *Stress in America: Paying With Our Health* (Washington D.C.: American Psychological Association, February 2015): 9.

35 Consumer Financial Protection Bureau, *Financial Wellness at Work: A Review of Promising Practices and Policies* (Washington D.C.: Consumer Financial Protection Bureau, August 2014): 8.

36 Kenneth D. Kochanek, et al., "Deaths: Final Data for 2014," *National Vital Statistics Report* 65, no. 4 (June 30, 2016): 7.

37 "What Are The Principal Types of Life Insurance?," *Insurance Information Institute*, accessed 1 March 2018, https://www.iii.org/article/what-areprincipal-types-life-insurance.

38 "Inheritance Tax," *Gov.uk*, accessed 1 March 2018, https://www.gov.uk/inheritance-tax.

39 "Parents Bribe Kids For Good Behavior While Behaving Badly Themselves on Money Matters," press release, *T. Rowe Price*, March 25, 2014, https://www3.troweprice.com/usis/corporate/en/press/t--rowe-price-parents-bribe-kids-for-good-behavior-while-behavi.html?id=64214.

40 https://www.rocketlawyer.com/.

41 https://www.legalzoom.com/.

42 Jeffrey M. Jones, "Majority in U.S. Do Not Have a Will," *GALLUP News*, May 18, 2016, http://news.gallup.com/poll/191651/majority-not.aspx.

43 M.C. Black, et al., *The National Intimate Partner and Sexual Violence Survey (NISVS): 2010 Summary Report* (Atlanta, GA: National Center for Injury Prevention and Control, Centers for Disease Control and Prevention, November 2011): 38. This statistic was derived by summing the total estimated number of victims of intimate partner violence (both men and women) in 12 months from Tables 4.1 and 4.2.

44 "Statistics," *The National Coalition Against Domestic Violence (NCADV)*, accessed 1 March 2018, https://ncadv.org/statistics.

45 Dr. Jacquelyn C. Campbell, et al., "Risk Factors for Femicide in Abusive Relationships: Results From a Multisite Case Control Study," *American Journal of Public Health* 93, no. 7 (July, 2003): 1090-92.

46 Dr. Jennifer L. Truman and Dr. Rachel E. Morgan, "Nonfatal Domestic Violence, 2003-2013," special report, *Bureau of Justice Statistics, U.S. Department of Justice*, April, 2014: 1.

47 Ibid.

[48] Black, *Intimate Partner and Sexual Violence Survey*, 18.

[49] Dr. Matthew J. Breiding, et al., "Prevalence and Characteristics of Sexual Violence, Stalking, and Intimate Partner Violence Victimization – National Intimate Partner and Sexual Violence Survey, United States, 2011," *MMWR* 63, no. 8 (September 5, 2014): 6-7.

[50] Violence Policy Center, *American Roulette: Murder-Suicide in the United States* (Washington D.C.: Violence Policy Center, October 2015): 5.

[51] Sherry Hamby, et al., "Children's Exposure to Intimate Partner Violence and Other Family Violence," *Juvenile Justice Bulletin* (Washington D.C.: U.S. Department of Justice, October 2011): 1.

[52] "The Role of Emergency Savings in Family Financial Security: How Do Families Cope With Financial Shocks?," brief, *Pew Charitable Trusts*, October 2015: 2.

Cozette M. White

good budget apt

1 2853013

FB
Felicia Cox
Thon Driver
469-394-3259
Instasr ceo
Irondivas38@yahoo

ANIMALES FANTÁSTICOS

LOS SECRETOS DE DUMBLEDORE

GUIÓN ORIGINAL DE LA PELÍCULA

WIZARDING
WORLD

ANIMALES FANTÁSTICOS

LOS SECRETOS DE DUMBLEDORE

GUIÓN ORIGINAL DE LA PELÍCULA

Guión de

J.K. ROWLING & STEVE KLOVES

Basado en un guión de

J.K. ROWLING

Prólogo de

DAVID YATES

Con contenido adicional y comentarios de

DAVID HEYMAN, JUDE LAW, EDDIE REDMAYNE Y COLLEEN ATWOOD, ENTRE OTROS

salamandra

Papel certificado por el Forest Stewardship Council®

Título original: *The Secrets of Dumbledore. The Complete Screenplay*
Publicado por primera vez en Gran Bretaña en 2022 por Scholastic Inc.
Primera edición: julio de 2022

Printed in Spain – Impreso en España

ISBN: 978-84-18797-77-4
Depósito legal: B-9.645-2022

Impreso en RODESA
Villatuerta (Navarra)

SI97774

＊ ✻ ＊

PRÓLOGO

ZAMBULLIRSE de nuevo en el mundo mágico de J. K. Rowling con *Los secretos de Dumbledore* fue emocionante y, a la vez, todo un reto logístico, dado que la producción comenzó al mismo tiempo que la pandemia, y contábamos con trabajar, en gran parte, fuera de los Leavesden Studios de Hertfordshire, Inglaterra. Fue ahí donde Stuart Craig y su fabuloso equipo de dirección artística, frustrados por las diversas restricciones de viaje a causa de la CO-VID-19, crearon las versiones mágicas de Berlín, Bután y China. También reconstruimos algunos de los escenarios más memorables de otras historias y películas del mundo mágico, como la taberna Cabeza de Puerco, la Sala de los Menesteres o el propio Hogwarts.

El guión de Jo y Steve se mueve con habilidad entre lo antiguo y lo nuevo, y además equilibra una oportuna trama política con encanto y emoción. En el centro de la historia, uno de los personajes más perdurables y queridos de Jo, Albus Dumbledore, se enfrenta a los peligros del presente y a los remordimientos del pasado, mientras Newt Scamander lidera una misión para impedir que Grindelwald acceda al poder.

Durante muchos meses, mientras el mundo se sumía en una extraña hibernación, nosotros trabajamos para traducir a imágenes las palabras de Jo y Steve y llevarlas a la pantalla.

En *Los secretos de Dumbledore*, los tiempos peligrosos quizá favorezcan a los hombres peligrosos, pero la tenacidad y el coraje de Dumbledore y Newt, y del resto del grupo que componen para pararle los pies al mago más letal que ha existido desde hace más de un siglo, ofrecen la promesa de que, al final, la luz y el amor pueden imponerse, por muy escasas que sean las probabilidades.

DAVID YATES
21 de marzo de 2022

Warner Bros. Pictures Presenta
Una producción de Heyday Films
Una película de David Yates Film

ANIMALES FANTÁSTICOS:
LOS SECRETOS DE DUMBLEDORE

Dirigida por .... David Yates

Escrita por .... J.K. Rowling y Steve Kloves

Basada en un guión de .... J.K. Rowling

Producida por .... David Heyman, p.g.a., J.K. Rowling, Steve Kloves, p.g.a., Lionel Wigram, p.g.a., Tim Lewis, p.g.a.

Productores ejecutivos .... Neil Blair, Danny Cohen, Josh Berger, Courtenay Valenti, Michael Sharp

Director de fotografía .... George Richmond, BSC

Diseñadores de producción .... Stuart Craig, Neil Lamont

Edición .... Mark Day

Vestuario .... Colleen Atwood

Música .... James Newton Howard

PROTAGONISTAS

Newt Scamander .... Eddie Redmayne

Albus Dumbledore .... Jude Law

Credence Barebone .... Ezra Miller

Jacob Kowalski .... Dan Fogler

Queenie Goldstein .... Alison Sudol

Theseus Scamander .... Callum Turner

Eulalie «Lally» Hicks .... Jessica Williams

Tina Goldstein .... Katherine Waterston

y

Gellert Grindelwald .... Mads Mikkelsen

1   INT. VAGÓN DE TREN – DÍA

HOMBRES y MUJERES sentados en silencio bajo una luz parpadeante. LA CÁMARA SE DESLIZA poco a poco y vemos a un HOMBRE que va de pie sujeto a un asidero y que oscila suavemente con el movimiento del tren. No distinguimos su cara, pero su SOMBRERO, que lleva un poco ladeado, resulta familiar.

2   EXT. ESTACIÓN – MOMENTOS MÁS TARDE – DÍA

El tren se detiene. Las puertas se abren. Los hombres y mujeres se apean, incluido el hombre del sombrero.

3   EXT. PICCADILLY CIRCUS – MOMENTOS MÁS TARDE – DÍA

El hombre del sombrero sale a la luz del día y se separa de los otros pasajeros. Mira brevemente alrededor y continúa.

4   INT. CAFETERÍA – DÍA

Concurrida. Ruidosa. Una CAMARERA con el PELO CASTAÑO cortado a lo GARÇON entra en el plano y la seguimos. Se desliza con elegancia entre la clientela, hasta una mesa que hay situada al fondo, donde deja una taza de algo caliente delante del hombre del sombrero: DUMBLEDORE.

(arriba) BOCETO DEL VESTUARIO DE ALBUS DUMBLEDORE

(pág. siguiente) DISEÑO PRELIMINAR DEL EXPEDIENTE JUDICIAL DE
ALBUS DUMBLEDORE CON ESPACIO EN BLANCO PARA LA FOTOGRAFÍA MÓVIL

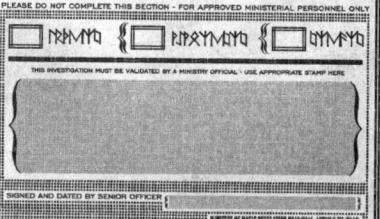

4546231₺

MINISTRY OF MAGIC
DEPARTMENT OF MAGICAL LAW ENFORCEMENT

FORM NO. 298/7122DY

- AUROR OFFICE - IMPROPER USE OF MAGIC - HIT WIZARDS -
- WIZENGAMOT ADMINISTRATION SERVICES -

PLEASE DO NOT COMPLETE THIS SECTION - FOR APPROVED MINISTERIAL PERSONNEL ONLY

☐ ᛗᚱᛗᚤᛗ   ☐ ᚠᛗᚱᚤᛗᚤᛗ   ☐ ᛟᛗᛗᚤᛗ

THIS INVESTIGATION MUST BE VALIDATED BY A MINISTRY OFFICIAL - USE APPROPRIATE STAMP HERE

SIGNED AND DATED BY SENIOR OFFICER

MINISTRY OF MAGIC REGULATION BM4048041 ARTICLE 74/45AF

DEPT. OF MAGICAL LAW ENFORCEMENT - CASE FILE

ALL WITCHES AND WIZARDS BEING INVESTIGATED BY THE DEPARTMENT OF MAGICAL LAW ENFORCEMENT UNDER THE JURISDICTION OF THE MINISTRY OF MAGIC ARE SUBJECT TO THE STRICTEST CONFIDENTIALITY, UNTIL OTHERWISE DEEMED NECESSARY BY THE MINISTER FOR MAGIC. THIS FILE IS CONFIDENTIAL AND INFORMATION APPERTAINING TO THIS CASE FILE MUST BE REPORTED BACK TO THE SUPERIOR MINISTERIAL EMPLOYEE OVER SEEING SAID INVESTIGATION.

⚡ CASE FILE NUMBER:

ALL INFORMATION REGARDING CASE FILES AND INVESTIGATIVE WORK UNDERTAKEN FOR THE DEPARTMENT OF MAGICAL LAW ENFORCEMENT IS STRICTLY CONFIDENTIAL.

0	0	0	8	1	9	1	7	7	X

1 - SECTION 19087/A

NAME OF WITCH OR WIZARD: ALBUS PERCIVAL WULFRIC BRIAN DUMBLEDORE

NATIONALITY: BRITISH

PRESENT ADDRESS: HOGWARTS SCHOOL OF WITCHCRAFT AND WIZARDRY

DATE OF BIRTH: ✳6/✳/⊕₮

PROFESSION OR OCCUPATION: PROFESSOR OF DEFENCE AGAINST THE DARK ARTS

INVESTIGATIVE NUMBER:
INVESTIGATIVE NUMBER MUST BE CONFIRMED BY SUPERIOR - AS MENTIONED IN ARTICLE 35

2	X	₮	0	0	1	8	ᚱ	ᚷ	ᚦ

PHOTO MUST BE RECENT

2 - SECTION 19087/B

1 - R. THUMB	2 - R. MERCURY	3 - R. APOLLO	4 - R. SATURN	5 - R. JUPITER

APPLICANT'S RIGHT HAND FINGER PRINTS - ONLY USE ROYAL PURPLE INK

THE PERSONS MENTIONED BELOW ARE THE KNOWN MEMBERS OF SUBJECTS FAMILY:

SPOUSE: N/A, ... BORN AT ......

FATHER: PERCIVAL DUMBLEDORE, BORN AT XX PLACE ... XX ... XX

MOTHER: KENDRA DUMBLEDORE, BORN AT XX PLACE ... XX ... XX

HEIGHT: 5' 11"
WEIGHT: 175 LBS
COLOUR OF HAIR: FAIR
COLOUR OF EYES: BLUE
COMPLEXION: FAIR

SPECIAL PARTICULARS: DESCRIBE ANY MARKS OR SCARS
XXX

3 - SECTION 19087/C

KNOWN HISTORY OF SUBJECT (INCLUDING FAMILY HISTORY & EDUCATION)

KNOWN TO HAVE ATTENDED HOGWARTS SCHOOL OF WITCHCRAFT AND WIZARDRY - SORTED INTO GRYFFINDOR. FATHER PERCIVAL DUMBLEDORE SENTENCED TO LIFE IN AZKABAN FOR CRIMES AGAINST MUGGLES. MOTHER AND SISTER, KENDRA AND ARIANA DECEASED IN UNKNOWN CIRCUMSTANCES. DURING ALBUS DUMBLEDORES TEENAGE YEARS, HE IS KNOWN TO HAVE MET AND BEFRIENDED THE DARK WIZARD GELLERT GRINDELWALD.

REASON FOR INVESTIGATION: TICK ALL APPROPRIATE OPTIONS

( ) KNOWN ILLEGAL ACTIVITIES   ( ) INFORMANT
(X) SUSPECTED ILLEGAL ACTIVITIES
(X) OTHER KNOWN AFFILIATION WITH DARK WIZARD

SECURITY STATUS

CURRENTLY UNDER INVESTIGATION.

4 - SECTION 19087/D

in dolemrei, at commodo mauris. Sed viverra tempus laoreet. Nam tempor pretium metus id tempus. Proin eleifend felis lorem, eget posuere diam. Praesent onena vulput ate. Praesent sit amet neque leo, ac bibendum ligula. Pellentesque vitae eros tellus. Ut et libero nisl. Integer iaculis euismod sem, et adipi molestie ut. Nunc ultricies sem eu massa rhoncus accumsan. Curabitur sed scelerisque juste. Sed nulla ligula, pretium vitae tincidunt a, comm modo quis sem habitant morbi tristique senectus et netus et malesuada fames ac turpis egestas. Proin ullamcorper rhoncus nisl vitae dictum. Aenean et pellen tesque s id posuere turpis. Curabitur sed velit neo sapien malesuada eleifend. Phasellus sollicitudin magna quis quam mattis vel porttitor mi adipiscing. Nulla fa sto tellus, ultrices eu dictum neo, rutrum nec lacus. Aenean viverra fermentum mi, non bibendum libero laoreet vel. Mauris nulla lectus, porta vitae ornar e placerat odio. Vivamus quis tellus arcu, at malesuada risus. Nulla mauris leo, pulvinar sed auctor id, tempor nec turpis. Phasellus fringilla tinci duntia

MINISTRY AUTHORIZATION CODE

∝ ÷ ⅔ ÷ ⅓ ÷ ½ ÷ ⅐ ÷ ⅖ ÷ ∝

* ALL INFORMATION IN THIS CASE FILE IS STRICTLY CONFIDENTIAL, AND MUST NOT BE DISCUSSED OUTSIDE OF INVESTIGATIONAL TEAM.

SIGNATURE OF SUPERIOR OFFICER   DATE

4546231₺

PRINTED IN ENGLAND BY THE MINISTRY OF MAGIC PRESS

DUMBLEDORE

Gracias.

CAMARERA

¿Desea algo más?

DUMBLEDORE

No, no, de momento no. Eh... Eh...
(frunce el ceño)
Espero a alguien.

La camarera asiente y se da la vuelta. Dumbledore la ve marchar; entonces mete un terrón de azúcar en su té y lo remueve, echa la cabeza hacia atrás y cierra los ojos. LA CÁMARA SE MANTIENE en Dumbledore, en su cara en reposo, largo rato, hasta que una LUZ le ilumina la cara.

Dumbledore abre los ojos y mira al hombre que está de pie junto a su mesa: GRINDELWALD.

GRINDELWALD

¿Éste es uno de los sitios que
frecuentas?

DUMBLEDORE

Yo no frecuento ningún sitio.

Grindelwald se queda observándolo un momento y luego se sienta frente a él.

LOS SECRETOS DE DUMBLEDORE

GRINDELWALD

Déjame verlo.

Dumbledore lo mira fijamente; luego, despacio, enseña una mano y le muestra el PACTO DE SANGRE. Mientras lo sostiene, la cadena se desliza poco a poco entre los dedos de Dumbledore, como si tuviese vida propia.

GRINDELWALD (CONT'D)

A veces imagino que aún lo llevo alrededor del cuello. Fueron tantos años... ¿Te gusta llevarlo?

DUMBLEDORE

Podemos liberarnos de él.

Grindelwald ignora el comentario y mira alrededor.

GRINDELWALD

Les encanta charlar, ¿verdad?, a nuestros queridos muggles. Pero hay que reconocer que hacen bien el té.

DUMBLEDORE

Lo que pretendes hacer... es una locura.

GRINDELWALD

Es lo que dijimos que haríamos.

DUMBLEDORE

Era joven. Me había...

GRINDELWALD

Comprometido. Conmigo. Con nosotros.

DUMBLEDORE

No, accedí porque...

GRINDELWALD

¿Porque...?

DUMBLEDORE

Porque estaba enamorado de ti.

Se miran a los ojos, y entonces Dumbledore vuelve a apartar la vista.

GRINDELWALD

Sí. Pero no accediste por eso. Fuiste
tú quien dijo que podíamos cambiar
el mundo. Que era nuestro derecho
natural.

Grindelwald se recuesta, entorna los ojos. INHALA.

GRINDELWALD (CONT'D)
¿Lo hueles? ¿Ese hedor? ¿De verdad
pretendes dar la espalda a los tuyos por
estos animales?

La mirada de Dumbledore vuelve a fijarse en los fríos ojos de Grindelwald.

GRINDELWALD (CONT'D)
Contigo o sin ti, arrasaré su mundo...
Albus. No puedes hacer nada para
detenerme. Que disfrutes del té.

Cuando Grindelwald se marcha, empieza a oírse un RUIDO SORDO. Dumbledore baja la vista hacia su taza de té y la ve TEMBLAR débilmente sobre el tablero de la mesa. El líquido que contiene la taza se ESTREMECE, y Dumbledore parece absorto en él.

Las llamas lo envuelven todo, y permanecemos así unos momentos, hasta que estamos en...

5 INT. HABITACIÓN DE DUMBLEDORE – HOGWARTS – MAÑANA

Vemos a Dumbledore de pie junto a su ventana, con los ojos cerrados. A medida que la cámara lo enfoca, poco a poco, él abre los ojos y volvemos al presente.

Tiene el pacto de sangre en la mano y la cadena enroscada alrededor de la muñeca.

CUANDO eran jóvenes, Dumbledore y Grindelwald idearon un plan para controlar el mundo de los magos, un plan que ahora Grindelwald intenta llevar a cabo. Pero Dumbledore ha cambiado. Se da cuenta de los errores que ha cometido y hace todo lo posible para enmendarlos. Creo que ésa es una idea muy poderosa: todos hemos cometido errores en la vida y, seamos quienes seamos, tenemos que aprender de ellos, admitirlos y seguir adelante.

—DAVID HEYMAN

(Productor)

6   EXT. LAGO – MONTAÑA TIANZI – AL MISMO TIEMPO – NOCHE

Un paisaje extenso y hermoso. Bajo la luz de la luna, que apenas se eleva sobre el horizonte, surgen del agua, majestuosas, unas columnas de piedra caliza a la sombra de una MONTAÑA: el Ojo del Ángel.

NEWT rema por el lago.

7   EXT. MONTAÑA TIANZI – MOMENTOS MÁS TARDE – NOCHE

Unos pies pisan delicadamente la orilla dejando atrás la balsa, que se zarandea, y vemos a NEWT SCAMANDER.

Más allá de los lagos y afluentes, inicia el ascenso por el bosque de bambú.

El grito lejano de un animal resuena de manera evocadora por el paisaje. Newt se detiene un momento a escuchar. PICKETT, que va en el hombro de Newt, también escucha.

> NEWT
> *(susurra)*
Está preparada.

BOCETO DEL VESTUARIO DE NEWT SCAMANDER

POR fin vemos a Newt feliz y haciendo lo que más le gusta: rastrear animales en la naturaleza. Y en este caso se trata de una criatura hermosa y extraordinaria llamada qilin, que en el mundo de los magos se considera mítica. Una de las cosas que siempre me han encantado de Newt es que hay una especie de desajuste entre sus características físicas y su ligera torpeza social y la destreza y la facilidad con que se desenvuelve en la naturaleza. Por eso me emocioné cuando vi el guión por primera vez y encontré ese momento tan «Indiana Jones» al principio de la película, porque ahí es donde Newt se siente más cómodo.

—EDDIE REDMAYNE
(*Newt Scamander*)

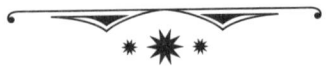
8   EXT. HONDONADA – MONTAÑA TIANZI – MOMENTOS MÁS
TARDE – NOCHE

Newt avanza con rapidez pero con cuidado hacia la entrada de una gran cueva que recuerda a una catedral. Cuando se acerca, algo se mueve en el interior, semioculto en la oscuridad.

9   EXT. HONDONADA – MONTAÑA TIANZI – MOMENTOS MÁS
TARDE – NOCHE

Con ternura, Newt extiende un brazo para acariciar el lomo del animal mientras éste gira suavemente sobre sí mismo, y vemos que es una hembra de QILIN: mitad dragón, mitad yegua, poderosa pero mansa. Respira agitadamente; tiene la piel moteada y estremecida, sucia de polvo y con hojas e insectos enganchados.

Vuelve a gritar.

Una LUZ DORADA empieza a extenderse por el suelo donde está tendido el animal. Newt sonríe fascinado. Poco a poco, de debajo de la madre sale una CRÍA DE QILIN, hermosa y frágil, que parpadea, ciega todavía. OLFATEA con curiosidad y emite un débil BALIDO; dentro de su diminuto cuerpo hay una pulsante LUZ DORADA que ilumina brevemente las caras de Newt y de Pickett, que la miran con atención.

Newt se aparta y observa cómo la madre qilin lame a la cría para limpiarla; la cría tiembla y se tambalea.

ANIMALES FANTÁSTICOS

NEWT

(fuera de cuadro mientras vemos a PICKETT)
Muy bonito.

(pausa)
Muy bien. Ahora viene lo complicado.

Newt extiende un brazo y, con cuidado, abre su maleta. Vemos una fotografía de TINA pegada en el interior de la tapa.

A través de la densa maleza se acercan unas figuras que enarbolan sus varitas.

Son los ACÓLITOS ROSIER y CARROW, que avanzan con ansia, mirando fijamente a la cría de qilin.

Rosier y Carrow levantan la varita y, con un FUERTE ZUMBIDO, lanzan HECHIZOS con los que hieren a la madre qilin. Ésta se tambalea y BRAMA en la oscuridad, hasta que las patas ya no la sostienen y se derrumba.

DURANTE EL ATAQUE:

Newt lanza un hechizo defensivo que se convierte en un escudo, pero es demasiado tarde.

Vuelve la cabeza y ve a una FIGURA OSCURA entre los otros acólitos: es CREDENCE, que parece mayor y más seguro de sí mismo. Credence rompe el escudo de Newt con su varita.

COMPARADO con Harry Potter y otros héroes del mundo de los magos, Newt no se nos representa como un mago poderosísimo, pero sí tiene una habilidad mágica peculiar. Cuando pelea contra Credence, en lugar de emplear los clásicos hechizos para batirse en duelo, Newt recurre a cosas más orgánicas y forma torbellinos o escudos de hojas, por ejemplo. Quizá su magia no sea la más impresionante, pero encaja perfectamente con su personalidad.

—EDDIE REDMAYNE

(Newt Scamander)

Newt apunta con su varita a su maleta.

NEWT (CONT'D)

¡Accio!

La maleta vuela hasta su mano.

Credence atraviesa el escudo; Newt se lanza desde el borde de la hondonada y se precipita por una peligrosa cuesta, rodando, saltando y tropezando con la maleza.

Detrás de él se oye el fuerte CHASQUIDO de un hechizo que rompe los tallos de BAMBÚ a su alrededor y hace que se le CAIGA la maleta de las manos.

Un poco más allá, en el sotobosque, vemos a la cría de qilin, que se ha levantado, asustada y frágil.

Newt se apresura, BUSCA CON LA MIRADA y ve...

... unas patas que salen de la MALETA mientras ésta rueda cuesta abajo, y la dirigen de nuevo hacia su dueño.

Carrow va volando hacia Newt con los brazos extendidos para arrebatarle la cría de qilin. Newt contraataca y la hace salir despedida hacia atrás.

¡ZAS! Otro HECHIZO pasa zumbando por encima de la cabeza de Newt, que se agacha justo a tiempo y recoge a la cría

de qilin del suelo. Un instante después recibe el IMPACTO de otro hechizo que lo hace SALTAR POR LOS AIRES y VOLVER A CAER.

DESDE ABAJO, vemos caer a Newt en una masa de agua turbulenta.

En la espuma de la superficie aparece la cabeza de Pickett, que nada hasta la orilla y mira PREOCUPADO hacia la orilla opuesta, adonde la corriente ha arrastrado el cuerpo de Newt.

PLANO GENERAL...

... para revelar que nos hallamos al pie de una serie de hermosas cascadas que descienden desde el Ojo del Ángel.

Por un instante, Newt yace semiinconsciente boca arriba, y entonces parpadea. Finalmente levanta la cabeza.

PLANO SUBJETIVO (NEWT)...

... de ZABINI sujetando un saco y Rosier cogiendo a la cría de qilin y metiéndola dentro de cualquier manera. ¡FIU! Un instante después, han desaparecido.

Newt se levanta con dificultad.

CORTE A:

Newt tambaleándose hacia la hondonada, con la maleta bajo el brazo. Llega a la parte más alta de la hondonada. La madre qilin yace en la oscuridad, inmóvil. Newt, que respira con dificultad, se deja caer sobre el cuerpo inerte de la madre qilin.

NEWT (CONT'D)
Lo siento mucho.

Newt mira hacia arriba y escudriña el cielo vacío. Le pesan los párpados... está a punto de dejarse vencer por el sueño... su respiración se vuelve más acompasada... Y entonces...

Su cara se ILUMINA DÉBILMENTE.

Parpadea y abre los ojos. A su alrededor, el suelo está FLO-RECIENDO.

Se incorpora y observa a la madre qilin; ve cómo le TIEMBLA la piel alrededor de los ojos y...

... un DÉBIL BALIDO rompe el silencio. La LUZ que brilla detrás se INTENSIFICA; Newt se incorpora un poco más y ve que se asoma...

... otra CRÍA DE QILIN. La cría se libera, mira a su alrededor con incertidumbre y entonces mira a Newt. Newt sonríe, se vuelve hacia la madre y... se detiene.

NEWT (CONT'D)

Gemelos. Has tenido gemelos.

Mientras Newt la observa, una LÁGRIMA se desliza de uno de los ojos de la madre y su PUPILA se DILATA. El rostro de Newt se ensombrece. Se apoya en el cuerpo sin vida de la madre.

Poco a poco, Pickett saca la cabeza del bolsillo de Newt y contempla maravillado a la cría de qilin.

Newt señala la maleta y Pickett se sube a ella de un salto; se detiene sobre uno de los cierres y mira a Newt, esperando instrucciones.

Sin soltar al qilin, Newt abre un cierre mientras Pickett abre el otro.

TEDDY saca la cabeza, ve a Newt y mira a la cría de qilin.

De las profundidades de la maleta asoma un GUIVERNO de largas patas. Lo vemos ascender y dejar atrás a Teddy y la fotografía de TINA GOLDSTEIN pegada en el interior de la tapa, hasta que SALE POR COMPLETO de la maleta y se eleva hacia el Ojo del Ángel.

El cuerpo del guiverno empieza a expandirse de forma mágica y hermosa ante nosotros. Con las pocas fuerzas que le quedan,

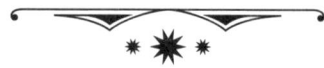

NEWT abraza a la cría de qilin y se la mete entre los pliegues del abrigo. La cría, temblorosa, bala débilmente en sus brazos.

La cola del guiverno se enrosca alrededor de Newt y los hace ascender a él y a la cría de qilin.

El guiverno se eleva por el cielo, extiende con elegancia sus magníficas alas y transporta a Newt y a la cría de qilin por encima de las extensas cascadas hacia el horizonte, donde empieza a brillar la primera luz del amanecer.

APARECE EL TÍTULO:

LOS SECRETOS DE DUMBLEDORE

10 EXT. PATIO DEL CASTILLO – NURMENGARD – MAÑANA

LA CÁMARA PLANEA y vemos salir a Grindelwald del castillo; al mismo tiempo, los acólitos se aparecen al fondo del patio.

Credence se separa de los otros.

Grindelwald clava la mirada en el saco que Credence lleva en la mano. Rosier se queda cerca, silenciosa y atenta. Grindelwald da unos pasos hacia delante.

GRINDELWALD

Dejadnos.

RENDER DEL CASTILLO DE
NURMENGARD

Los acólitos se retiran sin decir nada. Uno o dos vuelven la cabeza, conscientes de que ahora Credence es el favorito. Cuando se queda a solas con Credence, Grindelwald señala el saco con la barbilla.

> GRINDELWALD (CONT'D)
> Enséñamelo.

Grindelwald coge el qilin y escudriña sus apagados ojos. Del tembloroso hocico del animal caen gotas de FLEMA.

> CREDENCE
> Los otros han dicho que es especial.

> GRINDELWALD
> Oh, es mucho más que especial. ¿Ves...
> los ojos? Estos ojos lo ven todo. Con el
> nacimiento de un qilin, un líder justo
> surge para cambiar nuestro mundo para
> siempre. Su nacimiento trae consigo
> cambios, Credence. Drásticos.

Credence observa al qilin con curiosidad.

> GRINDELWALD (CONT'D)
> Buen trabajo.

Grindelwald le pone una mano en la mejilla a Credence, y Credence apoya la suya en la mano de Grindelwald sin saber

muy bien qué hacer, como si no estuviese acostumbrado a un contacto tan íntimo.

GRINDELWALD (CONT'D)
Vete. Descansa.

11 INT. SALÓN – AL MISMO TIEMPO – MAÑANA

QUEENIE ve marcharse a Credence y luego vuelve a fijarse en Grindelwald, que deja al qilin con cuidado sobre las losas del suelo mientras lo observa claramente fascinado.

Grindelwald levanta al qilin del suelo con suavidad y lo ayuda a sostenerse, se incorpora y se coloca delante del animal. Durante unos instantes no pasa nada. Entonces, despacio, el qilin alza la cabeza y su mirada cansada se cruza con la expectante de Grindelwald. Se quedan los dos así largo rato. Y finalmente...

... el qilin se aparta. El semblante de Grindelwald se endurece. Coge al qilin en brazos, se mete una mano dentro de la chaqueta, y algo DESTELLA brevemente cuando vuelve a sacarla. Grindelwald levanta el brazo y...

... la sangre rocía las losas y la navaja reluciente que Grindelwald tiene en la mano se tiñe de rojo. Queenie da un grito ahogado, apenas audible.

La sangre forma un charco en el suelo, y en él aparecen DOS FIGURAS vistas desde arriba CAMINANDO por la nieve.

RENDER DE HOGSMEADE

CORTE A:

12 EXT. HOGSMEADE – DÍA

Newt y THESEUS avanzan trabajosamente por la nieve y dejan atrás unos AJADOS CARTELES de Grindelwald: «¿HAS VISTO A ESTE MAGO?»

> THESEUS
> Supongo que no vas a decirme de qué
> va todo esto, ¿verdad?

> NEWT
> Me ha pedido que nos viéramos y que
> me asegurara de que vinieras.

> THESEUS
> Fantástico.

Theseus observa a NEWT mientras se internan en HOGSMEADE.

13 INT. CABEZA DE PUERCO – MOMENTOS MÁS TARDE – DÍA

El barbudo dueño del local (ABERFORTH DUMBLEDORE) pasa un trapo sucio por el ESPEJO de detrás de la barra y desvía la mirada, receloso, cuando entran Newt y Theseus, a los que ve REFLEJADOS. Los recién llegados echan un vistazo al sórdido local, y él sigue limpiando.

ABERFORTH

Vienen a ver a mi hermano, entiendo.

Newt se adelanta.

NEWT

Ah, no, señor, venimos a ver a Albus
Dumbledore.

Aberforth vuelve a mirarlos por el espejo y se da la vuelta.

ABERFORTH

Ése es mi hermano.

NEWT

Oh, disculpe, eh... Fenomenal. Soy
Newt Scamander y él es Theseus.

Newt le tiende la mano vendada a Aberforth, que se aparta.

ABERFORTH

Suban las escaleras. Primera puerta a la
izquierda.

*Newt se queda un momento con la mano tendida; entonces
asiente y se da la vuelta hacia Theseus, que arquea las cejas.*

RENDER DE CABEZA DE PUERCO

14 INT. HABITACIÓN DEL PISO DE ARRIBA – CABEZA DE PUERCO
– CONTINUO – DÍA

> DUMBLEDORE
> ¿Te ha dicho Newt para qué has venido?

> THESEUS
> ¿Debería?

Dumbledore lo mira y toma nota de su tono algo desafiante.

> DUMBLEDORE
> No, la verdad es que no.

Theseus mira a Newt, que se esfuerza por sostenerle la mirada.

> NEWT
> Hay algo de lo que queremos... de lo
> que Dumbledore quiere hablarte. Se
> trata de... una proposición.

Theseus mira a su hermano y luego a Dumbledore.

> THESEUS
> De acuerdo.

Dumbledore, que ha cruzado la habitación, coge el PACTO DE SANGRE de una mesa y lo hace oscilar, dejando que lo ilumine la luz del fuego de la chimenea.

DUMBLEDORE siempre ha sido un enigma. Tiene chispa, es juguetón, y al mismo tiempo corre riesgos altísimos. Pero entre Newt y él también hay una relación que recuerda a la de padre e hijo o maestro y aprendiz. En las películas anteriores, Dumbledore enviaba a Newt a hacer el trabajo sucio. En ésta empieza a compartir sus secretos con él.

—EDDIE REDMAYNE
(Newt Scamander)

DUMBLEDORE

Supongo que sabes lo que es esto.

THESEUS

Se lo vi a Newt en París. No es que
sepa... mucho de esas cosas, pero diría
que es un pacto de sangre.

DUMBLEDORE

Así es, correcto.

THESEUS

¿Y de quién es la sangre que contiene?

DUMBLEDORE

Mía.

(pausa)

Y de Grindelwald.

THESEUS

Supongo que por eso no puede
enfrentarse a él.

DUMBLEDORE

Exacto. Ni él a mí.

*Theseus asiente. Observa el frasco y ve cómo las gotas de
sangre giran una alrededor de otra, como las pesas de un reloj.*

THESEUS

¿Puedo preguntar qué le llevó a hacer
tal cosa?

DUMBLEDORE

El amor... la arrogancia... la
ingenuidad... Tienes donde elegir.
Éramos jóvenes, íbamos a cambiar el
mundo. Así nos asegurábamos de que
lo haríamos, aunque uno de los dos
cambiara de parecer.

THESEUS

¿Y qué pasaría si se enfrentara a él?

Newt mira a Dumbledore expectante, pero él permanece callado mientras observa el pacto de sangre.

DUMBLEDORE

Es una... preciosidad, las cosas como
son. Sólo con que se me pasara por la
cabeza quebrantarlo...

El frasco lanza un destello rojo, se suelta y rebota contra el suelo y la pared. Cuando Dumbledore saca la varita y apunta, la cadena del pacto de sangre, unida todavía a su brazo, se contrae y se le hunde profundamente en la piel.

ES un momento interesante de la vida de Dumbledore: el hombre al que todos amábamos en las películas de Harry Potter todavía no está completamente formado, así que vemos a Albus en situaciones muy emotivas y tomando decisiones que cambiarán su vida, y todo eso es lo que lo lleva a convertirse en el admirado y sabio director Albus Dumbledore años más tarde. Así que lo vemos enfrentarse con su pasado, con viejos amigos y viejos enemigos, y también enfrentándose consigo mismo.

—JUDE LAW
(Albus Dumbledore)

Newt y Theseus observan a Dumbledore cuando empieza a acercarse al frasco, que araña la pared. Dumbledore compone una sonrisa extraña, como si se sintiera cautivado por él.

DUMBLEDORE (CONT'D)
Lo sabe, ¿ves?

Dumbledore lo contempla embelesado. La cadena hace que las venas de la mano se le hinchen de forma monstruosa. Dumbledore hace una mueca de dolor, y la varita se le cae de la mano.

DUMBLEDORE (CONT'D)
Siente la traición en mi corazón.

Newt mira las GOTAS DE SANGRE, que ahora giran frenéticamente una alrededor de otra dentro del frasco.

Dumbledore sigue mirando fijamente el pacto de sangre, que tiembla con más violencia contra la pared. La cadena se desliza despacio hasta su cuello y lo rodea...

NEWT
Albus...

... se enrosca en él y lo aprieta...

NEWT (CONT'D)
Albus...

... Dumbledore pone los ojos en blanco...

NEWT (CONT'D)

¡Albus!

El pacto de sangre cae al suelo y de ahí salta a la mano de Dumbledore; la cadena desciende de su cuello y vuelve a unirse al frasco, su anfitrión. Poco a poco la cadena se afloja y Dumbledore respira hondo, como si acabase de recordar que necesita respirar. Abre la mano. En la palma, el frasco tiembla brevemente y luego se queda quieto.

DUMBLEDORE

Y eso no sería lo peor. Una magia
joven, pero, como veis, poderosa. No se
puede deshacer.

THESEUS

Supongo que... el qilin tiene algo que
ver con la proposición.

Dumbledore desvía la mirada hacia Newt.

NEWT

Promete no decírselo a nadie.

Dumbledore se vuelve hacia Theseus y responde a su pregunta.

DUMBLEDORE

Si queremos derrotarlo, el qilin es
sólo parte del plan. El mundo que
conocemos se desmorona. Gellert
lo está destruyendo a base de odio y
fanatismo. Las cosas que hoy parecen
inimaginables mañana parecerán...
inevitables si no lo detenemos. Si
aceptas hacer lo que te pido, tendrás
que confiar en mí. Aunque tu instinto
te aconseje lo contrario.

Theseus mira a Newt. Finalmente vuelve a mirar a Dumbledore.

THESEUS

Le escucho.

15 INT. HABITACIÓN DE CREDENCE – NURMENGARD – DÍA

*La cara de Credence entra en el plano. Se mira en el espejo y
levanta una mano, y vemos que tiene las venas oscuras. Una
mosca camina por su antebrazo. Él la observa atentamente, y
entonces desvía la mirada.*

Queenie está en el umbral.

CREDENCE

¿Te manda... a espiarme?

BOCETO DEL VESTUARIO DE QUEENIE GOLDSTEIN

QUEENIE

No. Pero quiere... saber qué piensas y
qué sientes.

CREDENCE

¿Y de los otros? ¿También quiere saber
qué piensan y qué sienten?

QUEENIE

Sí. Pero especialmente de ti.

CREDENCE

¿Y se lo cuentas?

Ella va a responder, pero titubea. Las venas de la mano de
Credence se aclaran y recuperan su aspecto normal. Credence
se da la vuelta y mira directamente a Queenie por primera vez.

CREDENCE (CONT'D)

¿Se lo cuentas?

Credence sonríe, pero de forma un tanto inquietante.

CREDENCE (CONT'D)

¿Ahora quién le lee la mente a quién?
(la sonrisa empieza a borrarse)
Dime lo que ves.

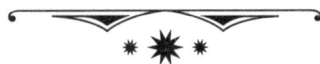

Ella lo mira y entonces:

QUEENIE

Eres un Dumbledore. Es una familia
importante. Lo sabes porque él te lo
ha dicho. También te ha dicho que te
abandonaron. Que se avergonzaban de
ti. Dice que... Dumbledore también lo
ha abandonado a él y que sabe cómo
te sientes, y que por esa razón te ha
pedido que lo mates.

La sonrisa se borra por completo de los labios de Credence.

CREDENCE

Quiero que te vayas, Queenie.

*Ella asiente y hace ademán de marcharse, pero en el último
momento se detiene.*

QUEENIE

No le cuento... siempre... todo.

*Queenie se retira y cierra suavemente la puerta. Credence se
queda un momento quieto, y entonces se fija en el espejo. Poco
a poco, como si las trazara una mano invisible, empiezan a
APARECER unas LETRAS en la SUPERFICIE de cristal.*

... PERDÓNAME...

Credence no se muestra sorprendido. Se acerca, levanta la mano... y limpia el espejo.

16 EXT. PASTELERÍA KOWALSKI – LOWER EAST SIDE – ANTES DEL AMANECER

Una maltrecha persiana metálica se levanta con ESTRUEN-DO y revela la triste y solitaria figura de JACOB KOWALSKI plantado en la calle. Se queda mirando el interior de la tienda con melancolía.

17 INT. PASTELERÍA KOWALSKI – CONTINUO – ANTES DEL AMA-NECER

Se abre la puerta del horno y desde el interior vemos a Jacob, que comprueba si todavía está encendido.

Coge una ESCOBA, se acerca al escaparate y empieza a barrer las migas del día anterior, ahuyentando a alguna que otra CU-CARACHA.

18 INT. TRASTIENDA – PASTELERÍA KOWALSKI – MOMENTOS MÁS TARDE – ANTES DEL AMANECER

PRIMER PLANO — PASTEL DE BODA

Un manto de glaseado blanco. Un ALTAR de hilo de azúcar. Y dos FIGURILLAS: una NOVIA ante el altar y un NOVIO caído boca abajo en el glaseado.

Jacob coge al novio con cuidado y, de pronto, ¡TILÍN!, suena la CAMPANILLA de la puerta. Vuelve a dejar la figurilla tumbada sobre el glaseado.

19 INT. PASTELERÍA KOWALSKI – MOMENTOS MÁS TARDE – ANTES DEL AMANECER

Sale Jacob con el delantal echado sobre el hombro y se para en seco.

> JACOB
> Perdone, está ce...

Una MUJER está mirando el expositor de pasteles de la entrada.

> JACOB (CONT'D)
> Queenie.

La mujer se da la vuelta y sonríe abiertamente. Es Queenie.

> QUEENIE
> Hola, tesoro.

Jacob se acerca a ella.

> QUEENIE (CONT'D)
> Cielo, mira la pastelería. Está
> abandonada.

BOCETO DEL VESTUARIO DE JACOB KOWALSKI

KOWALSKI K BAKERY

WE MAKE

BREAD, PASTRIES, CAKES

AND

FANCY CONFECTIONS.

PIERNIK ~ PACZKIS

FAWORKI AKA ~ CHRUST

FROM 2¢ EACH, OR 4 FOR 6¢.

BABKA ~ MAKOWIEC

SERNIK ~ BY THE SLICE.

BREADS FROM 5¢ A LOAF.

INCLUDING

OBWARZANEK KRAKOWSK

CHALLAH ~ ANGIELKA

AND

SLĄSK BREADS.

KOWALSKI BAKERY

443 RIVINGTON STREET. N.Y.

BREAD, PASTRIES, CAKES
AND FANCY CONFECTIONS.

WE DELIVER ～ ASK IN STORE.

M _____

DATE _____ 192___

SALESMAN _____

SIGNED _____

THANK YOU FOR YOUR CUSTOM.

(arriba) BLOC DE RECIBOS DE LA PASTELERÍA KOWALSKI
(pág. anterior) LISTA DE PRECIOS DE LA PASTELERÍA KOWALSKI

JACOB

Sí, es que te he echado de menos.

A Jacob se le llenan los ojos de lágrimas.

QUEENIE

Oh, mi vida. Ven aquí... Ven aquí...

Ella lo abraza. Él cierra los ojos.

QUEENIE (CONT'D)

Todo va a salir bien. Todo va a salir
fenomenal.

NUEVA TOMA — JACOB SE ABRAZA A SÍ MISMO EN LA TIENDA VACÍA

Abre los ojos. Se mira los brazos vacíos. Suspira. A través del sucio cristal del escaparate ve a una joven de aspecto tímido (LALLY HICKS) sentada en el banco de la parada de autobús de la acera de enfrente.

20 EXT. PARADA DE AUTOBÚS – LOWER EAST SIDE – CONTINUO – ANTES DEL AMANECER

Lally empieza a leer. No muy lejos vemos acercarse a TRES OBREROS.

Uno de los obreros se separa de los otros.

OBRERO 1

Hola, encanto, ¿qué te trae por aquí?

Lally sigue leyendo su libro.

LALLY

¿Se te ha ocurrido a ti solo esa frasecita?

El obrero da un paso más hacia Lally, que sigue enfrascada en el libro que tiene en el regazo.

OBRERO 1

Ah, quieres que te asuste, ¿es eso lo que quieres?

El obrero espera mientras Lally lo observa con solemnidad. Entonces:

LALLY

¿Sabes lo que pasa? No eres lo bastante peligroso.

OBRERO 1

Yo creo que soy bastante peligroso... Soy... ¿No soy peligroso?

Se vuelve hacia sus compañeros, que parecen indecisos.

LALLY

A lo mejor, si agitaras los brazos... Ya sabes, como un loco. Parecerías más peligroso.

El obrero sigue gesticulando exageradamente y Lally se inclina un poco hacia la izquierda y mira hacia la acera de enfrente.

LALLY (CONT'D)

Bien. Un poco más.

21 INT. PASTELERÍA KOWALSKI – CONTINUO – ANTES DEL AMA-NECER

Jacob, con los ojos entornados, observa al obrero que se cierne sobre Lally y agita los brazos.

22 EXT. PARADA DE AUTOBÚS – LOWER EAST SIDE – CONTINUO – ANTES DEL AMANECER

LALLY

Sigue. Perfecto. Tres, dos, uno...

JACOB (FUERA DE CUADRO)

¡Eh!

Jacob sale precipitadamente de la pastelería en medio de una nube de harina Colonial Girl, GOLPEANDO una SARTÉN

con una CUCHARA DE METAL. Cruza la calle a grandes zancadas. Los tres obreros se apartan de Lally y van hacia Jacob.

JACOB (CONT'D)

¡Eh! ¡Ya basta! ¡Largo de aquí!

OBRERO 1

¿Adónde vas, pastelero?

JACOB

Por Dios. Vergüenza debería daros.

Lally observa atentamente a los tres obreros, que rodean a Jacob.

JACOB (CONT'D)

Es una dama. ¡Será posible...! ¿Sabes
qué? Te dejo que me pegues tú primero.
Adelante.

OBRERO 1

¿Estás seguro?

¡PUM!

El obrero 1 se cae al suelo. Jacob se queda de piedra. Al cabo de unos segundos, se le cae la SARTÉN, provocando un gran estrépito.

El obrero 1 se sienta en el suelo y se frota la nuca.

OBRERO 1

Es la última vez que ayudo a esa mujer.
¡Lally!

Lally se toca la sosa melena corta con la varita y, todo en rápida sucesión, se le suelta una lustrosa cabellera, le desaparecen las gafas, y el vestido sin gracia y la camisa de cuello almidonado se transforman en unos pantalones de confección elegante y una blusa suelta y suave.

LALLY

Perdona, Frank, a veces se me olvida
la fuerza que tengo. Ya me ocupo yo.
¡Gracias!

OBRERO 3

De nada.

OBRERO 2

Hasta luego, Lally.

LALLY

Adiós, Stanley. Volveré uno de estos
días para jugar a Dudley el tonto.

OBRERO 2

Vale.

LALLY

Es mi primo Stanley. Es mago.

Jacob recoge la sartén al instante y empieza a retroceder mientras sacude la cabeza.

JACOB

¡No!

LALLY

¡Por favor! No me haga trabajar tan
temprano.

JACOB

Dije que no quería saber nada más.
Y no quiero.

LALLY

¡Vamos, señor Kowalski!

Jacob entra en la pastelería.

JACOB

Mi psicólogo me decía que los magos
no existían. ¡Vaya forma de tirar el
dinero!

Lally se aparece mágicamente delante de él dentro de la pastelería, comiéndose un rollo de canela.

LALLY

Sabe que soy una bruja, ¿no?

JACOB

Sí. Mire, usted parece una bruja muy
agradable, pero no se imagina lo que
me han hecho pasar. Así que ¿podría,
por favor, desaparecer de mi vida?

Jacob abre la puerta y le hace un gesto a Lally para que salga.
Como ella sigue hablando, Jacob sale de la tienda (todavía
lleva la sartén en la mano). Lally lo sigue.

LALLY

(de un tirón)

Hace poco más de un año, con la
esperanza de obtener un préstamo
para un pequeño negocio, cruzó las
puertas del Steen National Bank,
ubicado a unas seis manzanas de
aquí. Allí conoció a Newt Scamander,
el magizoólogo más importante del
mundo y, por otro lado, el único.
Entonces descubrió un mundo del que
era totalmente desconocedor. Conoció
y se enamoró de una bruja llamada
Queenie Goldstein, le borraron la
memoria con la desmemorización, sólo
que no funcionó. Y, por consiguiente,

se reencontró con la señorita Goldstein,
quien, tras su negativa a casarse con ella,
decidió unirse a Gellert Grindelwald
y a su oscuro ejército de seguidores,
quienes han supuesto la mayor amenaza
que se haya cernido sobre su mundo y
el nuestro en los últimos cuatro siglos.
¿Qué tal lo he hecho?

Jacob se sienta y se queda mirándola.

JACOB

Bastante bien. Salvo lo de que Quennie
se pasó al lado oscuro. A ver, sí, está
chiflada. Pero tiene un corazón más
grande que esta disparatada isla, y es tan
inteligente... Puede leer la mente
legítimamente. Es una... ¿cómo se llama?

LALLY

Una legeremante.

JACOB

Eso.

*Jacob suspira, se levanta y echa a andar hacia la pastelería. Al
cabo de un momento se da la vuelta y mira a Lally.*

JACOB (CONT'D)

Mire. ¿Ve esto? ¿Ve esta sartén?

(levanta la sartén)

Soy yo. Soy como esta sartén. Llena de abolladuras, por todas partes. Soy un cabeza hueca. No sé qué ideas absurdas tiene en la cabeza, señorita, pero estoy seguro de que podría buscarse a alguien mejor que yo. Adiós.

Jacob se da la vuelta y camina renqueante hacia la débil luz de la pastelería.

LALLY

No creo que podamos, señor Kowalski.

Él se detiene, pero no se da la vuelta.

LALLY (CONT'D)

Podría haberse escondido bajo el mostrador y no lo ha hecho. Podría haber mirado hacia otro lado y no lo ha hecho. Es más, no le ha importado arriesgar su vida para salvar a una completa desconocida. A mí me parece que usted es la clase de ciudadano que el mundo necesita ahora mismo. Sólo que aún no lo sabe. Por eso tenía que demostrárselo.

(pausa)
Lo necesitamos, señor Kowalski.

Jacob mira el pastel de boda de la pastelería y toma una decisión. Se da la vuelta y mira a Lally.

JACOB
Está bien. Llámeme Jacob.

LALLY
Llámeme Lally.

JACOB
Lally. Tengo que cerrar.

Lally agita la varita. La puerta se cierra, se apagan las luces y caen las persianas de la pastelería. La ropa de Jacob se transforma.

JACOB (CONT'D)
Gracias.

LALLY
Mucho mejor, Jacob.

Lally suelta el libro que tiene en la mano, y el libro, abierto, flota en el aire y las páginas empiezan a pasar suavemente.

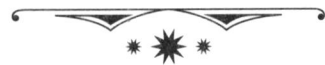
Lally extiende la mano y las páginas pasan cada vez más deprisa, hasta que se sueltan de la encuadernación y se esparcen por el aire como un caleidoscopio de mariposas.

LALLY (CONT'D)
Creo que ya sabes cómo funciona, Jacob.

Cuando sus manos se tocan, el torbellino de páginas desciende y los envuelve hasta que... ¡FIU!, DESAPARECEN. Pasados unos segundos, las hojas vuelven a su encuadernación.

Unos segundos más tarde... lo único que queda del libro son unas pocas páginas que descienden flotando hasta el suelo.

23   EXT. PAISAJE RURAL ALEMÁN – DÍA

El TREN avanza por un paisaje rural de Brandenburgo. Mientras lo observamos, un VAGÓN se materializa en la cola del tren.

24   INT. VAGÓN DE TREN MÁGICO – DÍA

YUSUF KAMA, de pie junto a la ventanilla, ve pasar el paisaje nevado al otro lado del cristal. Newt y Theseus están junto a una CHIMENEA ENCENDIDA. Theseus sostiene un ejemplar de El Profeta, *en el que leemos:*

ESPECIAL ELECCIONES

¿Quién ganará? ¿LIU o SANTOS?

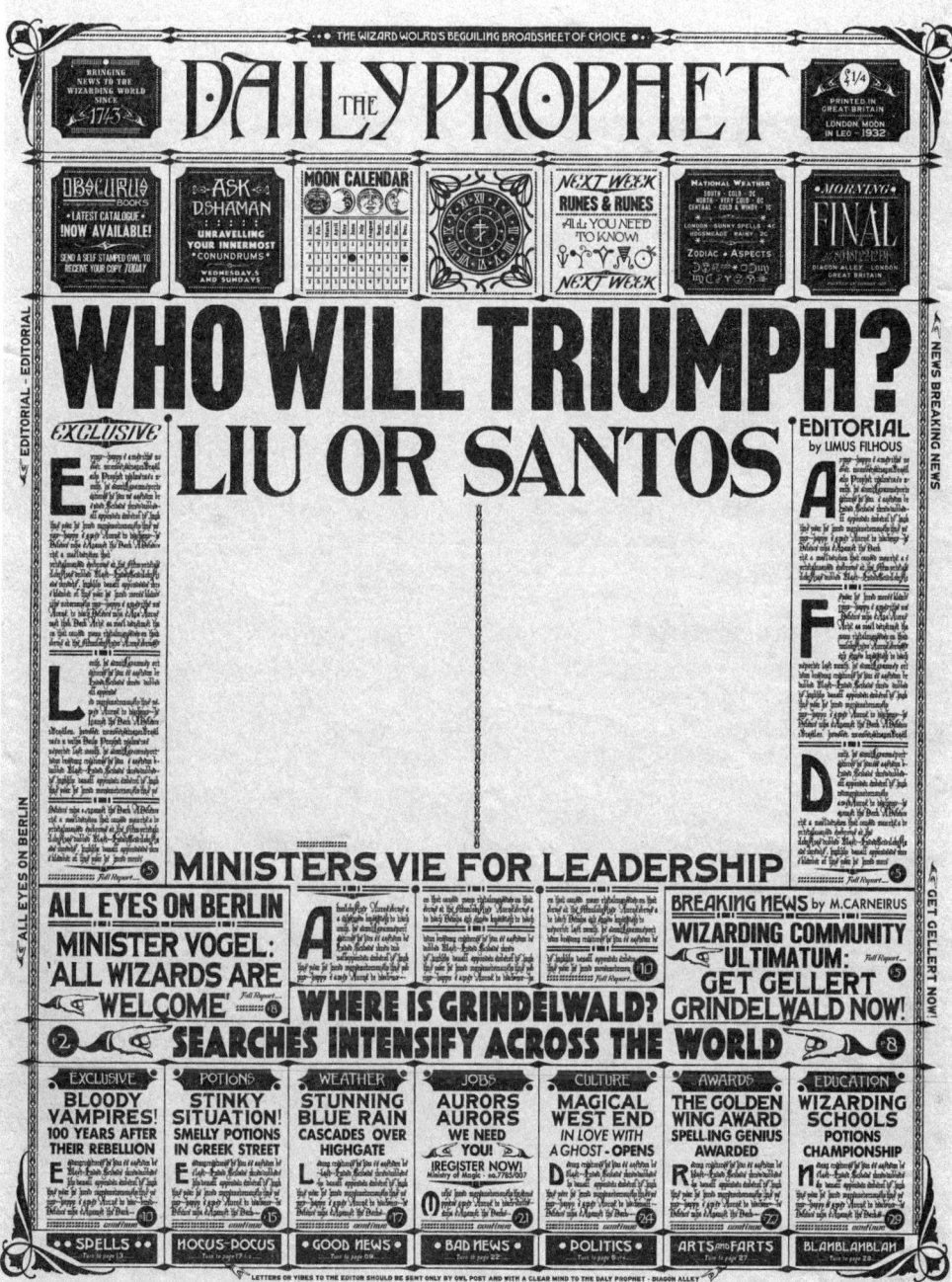

DISEÑO PRELIMINAR DE *EL PROFETA*, CON ESPACIOS
EN BLANCO PARA LAS FOTOGRAFÍAS MÓVILES DE LIU Y SANTOS

RENDER DEL INTERIOR DEL TREN

ES evidente que en las películas de Harry Potter hemos visto mucho el expreso de Hogwarts, al que siempre hemos tratado como un tren real que los muggles no pueden ver. Aquí la diferencia consiste en que van en un vagón unido a un tren muggle, de modo que teníamos que prescindir del concepto de un tren que es invisible desde fuera. Cuando vemos entrar el tren en la estación de Berlín y la cámara pasa del exterior al interior, se revela un precioso vagón dentro del destartalado furgón de equipaje de la cola del tren. Así que está escondido mediante magia en lugar de ser invisible, lo que nos pareció más interesante para el contexto de esta película.

—CHRISTIAN MANZ

(Efectos especiales)

Justo debajo hay un par de FOTOGRAFÍAS de los CANDIDA-TOS: LIU TAO y VICÊNCIA SANTOS.

En la contraportada, el cartel de «SE BUSCA» de Grindelwald.

NEWT
¿Qué se dice en el ministerio? ¿Liu o Santos?

THESEUS
Bueno, oficialmente el ministerio no se posiciona. Extraoficialmente, se apuesta por Santos. Aunque cualquiera sería mejor que Vogel.

KAMA
¿Cualquiera?

Kama mira con atención la fotografía de Grindelwald. Theseus se da cuenta.

THESEUS
No creo que sea un candidato, Kama. Aparte de que es un fugitivo.

KAMA
¿Y qué diferencia hay?

EL tren mágico que transporta a nuestros héroes de Londres a Berlín era una excelente oportunidad para desarrollar el estilo *art déco*. Los paneles esculpidos de las chimeneas están inspirados en ornamentos de pared de ese estilo. Luego cogimos algunos elementos de esos paneles y creamos el logo de la empresa del ferrocarril mágico. Una vez que tuvimos eso como insignia —y lo mismo ocurre con todas las insignias del mundo de los magos: las de los Ministerios de Magia, *El Profeta*, etcétera—, pudimos aplicarla a diversos medios. Por ejemplo, creamos una revista de a bordo y los billetes de tren, que quizá no salgan en primer plano, pero ayudan a llenar ese mundo con las piezas relevantes.

—MIRAPHORA MINA

(Diseñadora gráfica)

(arriba) LOGO DE LA COMPAÑÍA DE FERROCARRIL

(pág. siguiente) DISEÑO DE PANEL EN BAJORRELIEVE DEL INTERIOR DEL TREN

Justo entonces el FUEGO CHISPORROTEA, se vuelve ligeramente VERDE y Jacob sale bruscamente de la chimenea. Todavía lleva la sartén en la mano.

> JACOB
> ¡Más vueltas! Y dale con las vueltecitas.

> NEWT
> Jacob, bienvenido. ¡Qué alegría! Lo
> siento. Estaba totalmente seguro de que
> la profesora Hicks te convencería.

> JACOB
> Sí. Cómo me conoces, amigo. No puedo
> decir que no a un buen traslador.

Justo entonces, las llamas vuelven a chisporrotear y, al cabo de unos segundos, Lally sale tan campante de la chimenea, con el libro sujeto contra el pecho.

> LALLY
> Señor Scamander.

> NEWT
> Profesora Hicks.

> LALLY/NEWT
> Por fin.

NEWT

(a los otros)

La profesora Hicks...

(un poco turbado)

y yo hemos mantenido
correspondencia durante muchos años,
pero no nos conocíamos. Su libro
sobre hechizos de nivel avanzado es de
obligada lectura.

LALLY

Newt exagera. Hago leer *Animales
fantásticos* a todos mis alumnos de
quinto.

NEWT

Bien, déjeme que le presente a... Ella
es... Bunty Broadacre, mi indispensable
ayudante estos últimos siete años.

BUNTY

Ocho...

Dos escarbatos adolescentes se sientan en los hombros de Bunty.

BUNTY (CONT'D)

... años y ciento sesenta y cuatro días.

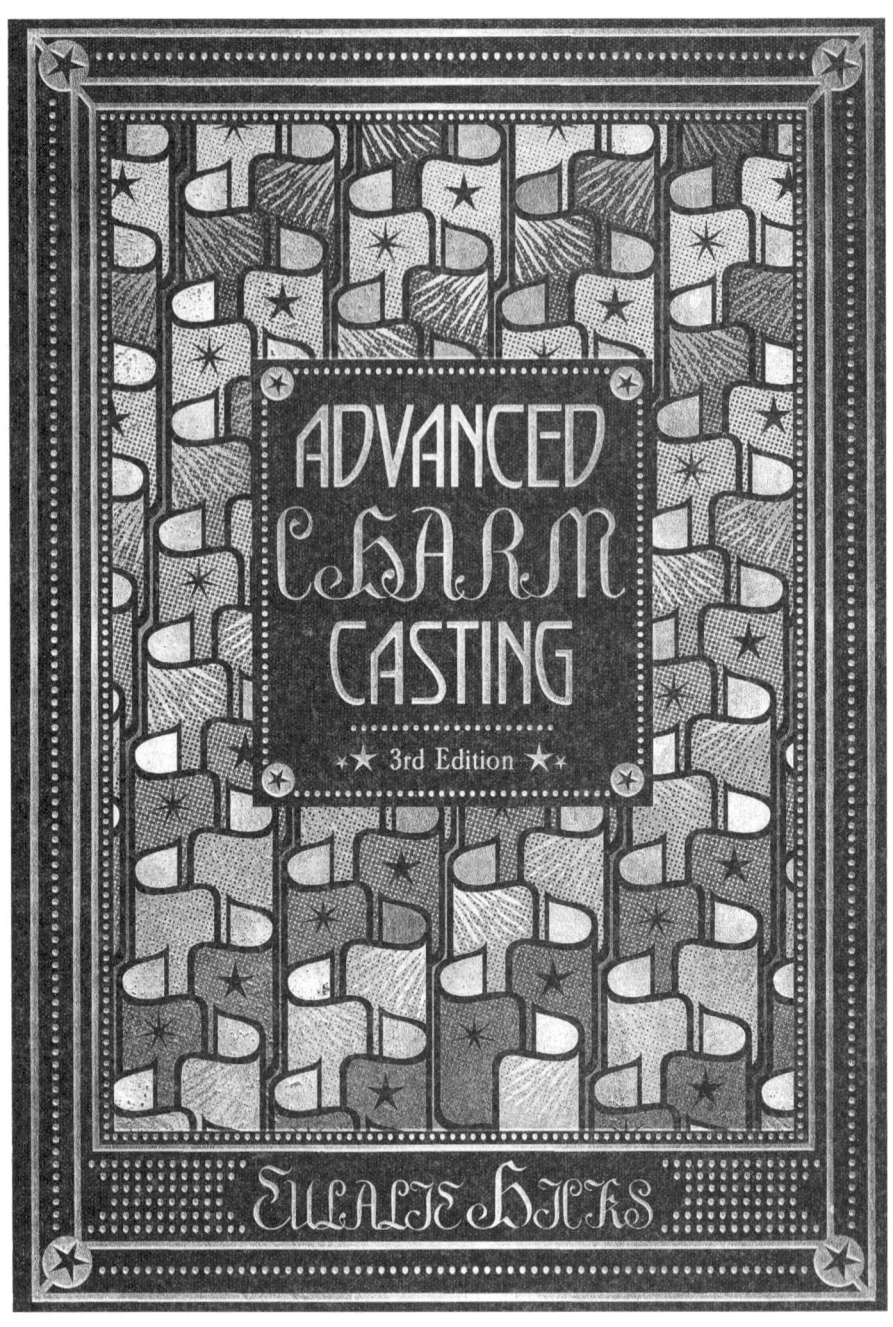

ADVANCED CHARM CASTING

★ 3rd Edition ★

EULALIE HICKS

DISEÑO DE LA CUBIERTA DE *ENCANTAMIENTOS AVANZADOS*
DE EULALIE HICKS

ASIA   EUROPE   AFRICA   OCEANIA

BOREALIS

NW   N   NE

NEWT
SCAMANDER
FANTASTIC
BEASTS
AND WHERE TO
FIND THEM

2nd Edition

W   E

S

AUSTRALIS

ANTARCTICA   S. AMERICA   N. AMERICA   N. POLE

DISEÑO DE LA CUBIERTA DE *ANIMALES FANTÁSTICOS Y DÓNDE ENCONTRARLOS*
DE NEWT SCAMANDER

NEWT

Lo dicho: indispensable. Y él es...

KAMA

Yusuf Kama. Encantado.

NEWT

Y, obviamente, ya conoce a Jacob.

Theseus CARRASPEA. Newt se queda mirándolo. Theseus arquea las cejas.

THESEUS

Newt.

NEWT

Ah, sí, perdón. Éste es mi hermano,
Theseus. Y trabaja para el ministerio.

THESEUS

Soy director de la Oficina de Aurores
británica.

LALLY

Vaya. Tendré que asegurarme de tener
en regla mi varita.

Lally sonríe.

THESEUS

Sí. Aunque, rigurosamente hablando,
eso no es competencia mía...

Newt se da la vuelta rápidamente y se dirige hasta el fondo del vagón. Los otros lo siguen.

NEWT

Muy bien, imagino que estaréis todos
preguntándoos qué hacéis aquí.

Consenso general entre los demás.

NEWT (CONT'D)

Así que, anticipándose, Dumbledore
me ha pedido que os transmita un
mensaje. Bien, Grindelwald tiene la
habilidad de ver fragmentos del futuro,
por lo que debemos suponer que será
capaz de adelantarse a nuestros actos.
Así que, si queremos derrotarlo... para
salvar nuestro mundo y el tuyo, Jacob...
nuestra mejor baza es confundirlo.

Cuando Newt termina de hablar, lo recibe un... silencio.

JACOB

Perdón. Lo siento. ¿Cómo se confunde
a alguien que puede ver el futuro?

KAMA

Contraplanificación.

NEWT

Exacto. El mejor plan es que no haya plan.

LALLY

O muchos planes que se solapen.

NEWT

Es decir, confusión.

JACOB

Conmigo está funcionando.

NEWT

De hecho, Dumbledore me ha pedido que te dé una cosa, Jacob.

Los otros esperan mientras Newt (con el estilo de un mago aficionado) se saca una VARITA de la manga.

NEWT (CONT'D)

Es de colubrina. Es... poco común.

JACOB

¿Estás bromeando? ¿Es de verdad?

NEWT

Sí. Bueno, no tiene núcleo, así que más
o menos, pero sí.

JACOB

¿Más o menos de verdad?

NEWT

Lo más importante es que donde vamos
la vas a necesitar.

Jacob coge la varita y la contempla impresionado. Newt empieza a buscar en sus bolsillos.

NEWT (CONT'D)

También tengo algo para ti, creo,
Theseus...

Los otros vuelven a esperar, intrigados. Newt (esta vez como un verdadero mago) intenta sacar una cosa del interior de su abrigo, pero algo se lo impide. Newt forcejea un momento, vuelve a dar un tirón y le habla a un bolsillo interior de su abrigo...

NEWT (CONT'D)

Teddy, por favor, suelta. Teddy, por
favor, suelta. No. Teddy, pórtate bien.
Es para Theseus...

Tras un fuerte tirón, Teddy rueda por el vagón hasta que Jacob lo atrapa. Vemos caer un trozo de tela al suelo.

Jacob y Teddy se miran.

Newt se agacha y recoge el trozo de tela. Es una corbata ROJA con un RELUCIENTE FÉNIX estampado. Newt se incorpora y se la entrega a Theseus, que la coge y la examina.

> **THESEUS**
> Claro, cómo no. Ahora todo tiene
> sentido.

> **NEWT**
> Lally. Lally, creo que a ti ya te han dado
> material de lectura.

> **LALLY**
> Ya sabes lo que dicen. «Un libro puede
> transportarte a cualquier lugar del
> mundo, sólo tienes que abrirlo.»

> **JACOB**
> *(soltando a TEDDY)*
> No bromea.

NEWT

Bunty. Esto es para ti. Me han dicho
que sólo puedes verlo tú.

Newt saca una HOJITA DE PAPEL doblada y se la da a Bunty. Ella la despliega y la sorpresa se refleja en su rostro, pero, antes de que pueda releer la nota, la hoja arde y se desintegra.

NEWT (CONT'D)

Kama...

KAMA

Yo tengo cuanto necesito.

JACOB

¿Qué hay de Tina? ¿Tina viene?

NEWT

Tina... no puede venir. A Tina... la han
ascendido. Está muy ocupada.
(pausa)
Bueno, por lo que tengo entendido.

LALLY

A Tina la han nombrado directora de
la Oficina de Aurores estadounidense.
Nos conocemos bien. Es una mujer
extraordinaria.

Newt se queda un momento mirando a Lally, y entonces:

NEWT

Lo es.

THESEUS

¿Así que éste es el equipo que va a acabar con el mago más poderoso al que nos hemos enfrentado en más de un siglo? Un magizoólogo, su indispensable ayudante, una profesora, un mago descendiente de una dinastía francesa muy antigua... y un pastelero muggle con una varita falsa.

JACOB

Eh, y también estás tú, amigo. Y su varita funciona.

Jacob se bebe una copa de un trago y...

THESEUS

Cierto. ¿Quién no querría estar en nuestro lugar?

... ríe. Entonces CORTE A:

DUMBLEDORE escoge a personas que tienen buen corazón y a personas con un ta-
lento muy específico. Lally es una reputada
profesora de Encantamientos y es muy admirada
en el mundo mágico. Theseus es el hermano de
Newt, el mejor en su campo y director de la Oficina
de Aurores del Ministerio Británico. Kama, por sus
raíces, tiene un pasado familiar que podría serle útil.
Pero ¿por qué elige Dumbledore a Jacob? ¿Por qué
añade a un muggle a su banda? Porque Jacob tiene
una moral sólida, es un hombre decente y tiene un
gran corazón.

—DAVID HEYMAN

(Productor)

25 EXT. ESTACIÓN DE FERROCARRIL – BERLÍN – NOCHE

En el andén, los berlineses, muertos de frío, ven llegar el tren a la estación con gran ESTRUENDO.

26 INT. VAGÓN DE TREN MÁGICO – NOCHE

Newt, arrodillado junto a su maleta, acaba de dar de comer al qilin y, con cuidado, cierra la tapa.

> NEWT
> Tranquilo, pequeñín.

> LALLY
> Berlín. Qué bien.

Newt se da la vuelta y ve a Lally de pie junto a una de las ventanillas. Un hombre (AUROR ALTO) destaca por su estatura y su actitud.

El tren se detiene y la locomotora emite un SILBIDO. Los otros empiezan a recoger sus cosas. Kama es el primero en acercarse a la puerta.

> THESEUS
> Kama, ten cuidado.

Kama se detiene, mira brevemente a Theseus y asiente. Cuando sale, un VIENTO GÉLIDO recorre el vagón. Bunty aparece al lado de Newt.

> BUNTY
> Yo también debo irme ya, Newt.

Newt va a responder, se interrumpe, mira hacia abajo, ve que la mano de Bunty está entrelazada con la suya, con la que sujeta el asa de la maleta.

> BUNTY (CONT'D)
> Nadie puede saberlo todo, ni siquiera tú.

Él la mira, pero ella no dice nada más. Finalmente, Newt suelta el asa.

Cuando ella se va, Newt ve que Theseus y Jacob lo observan. Newt se da la vuelta, mira por la ventanilla y ve a Kama y a Bunty marcharse en direcciones opuestas.

27 EXT. CALLE – BERLÍN – MOMENTOS MÁS TARDE – NOCHE

NIEVA DÉBILMENTE mientras Jacob, Newt, Lally y Theseus caminan por la calle.

> NEWT
> Bien. Aquí es.

Newt los guía por un callejón hacia una PARED DE LADRILLO con un BLASÓN. Mientras los otros caminan a grandes zancadas, Jacob mira a un lado y a otro, arriba y abajo, y entonces...

¡FIU!

... los cuatro han atravesado la pared y aparecen al otro lado. Jacob frunce el ceño, mira hacia atrás y ve la misma pared y el reverso del mismo blasón.

Jacob se encoge de hombros, mira hacia delante y ve, estampada en unos ENORMES ESTANDARTES colgados en la calle, la cara de un MAGO DE ASPECTO BONDADOSO (ANTON VOGEL). Más allá se alza un edificio rodeado de SEGUIDORES de Liu y Santos.

THESEUS

El Ministerio Alemán de Magia.

NEWT

Sí.

THESEUS

Entiendo que estamos aquí por algún
motivo.

NEWT

Sí, tenemos que asistir a una ceremonia del
té. Si no nos damos prisa, llegaremos tarde.

UNA cosa que siempre me encantó de las películas de Harry Potter y de todo el mundo de los magos es la idea de que nosotros vivimos en este mundo y, en la casa de al lado, detrás de nuestra pared, existe otro mundo fantástico y más emocionante. Ha sido fabuloso ver que pasa lo mismo en otros países, y no sólo en Londres y Gran Bretaña.

—EDDIE REDMAYNE
(Newt Scamander)

INSIGNIA DEL MINISTERIO ALEMÁN DE MAGIA

MONEDA MÁGICA ALEMANA

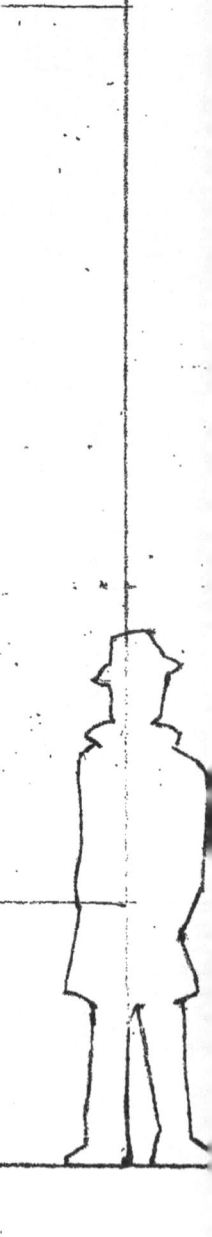

BOCETO DEL EXTERIOR DEL MINISTERIO ALEMÁN DE MAGIA

Newt sigue andando; Theseus y Lally se miran y lo siguen. Jacob va tras ellos dando traspiés y mirando alrededor embelesado.

> LALLY (FUERA DE CUADRO)
>
> ¡Jacob!

Él la busca y ve que Lally le está haciendo señas.

> LALLY (CONT'D)
>
> No te separes del grupo.

Jacob se apresura y pasa ante un cartel de SE BUSCA con la fotografía de Grindelwald, cuya mirada sigue todos sus movimientos.

Jacob no puede evitar sostenerle la mirada a Grindelwald, receloso.

28 EXT. ENTRADA – MINISTERIO ALEMÁN – MOMENTOS MÁS TARDE – NOCHE

Los SEGUIDORES de LIU y SANTOS GRITAN A CORO y enarbolan PANCARTAS en una exhibición de partidismo apasionada pero pacífica. NEWT y los demás se abren paso entre la multitud hacia la entrada del edificio.

Cuando Theseus guía a los otros entre el gentío hacia la entrada del ministerio, uno de los AURORES ALEMANES apostados a lo largo del perímetro intenta impedir que Newt, Lally y Jacob suban los escalones.

DISEÑO PRELIMINAR DEL CARTEL DE «SE BUSCA»,
CON ESPACIOS EN BLANCO PARA LAS FOTOGRAFÍAS MÓVILES DE GRINDELWALD

RENDER DEL EXTERIOR DEL MINISTERIO ALEMÁN DE MAGIA

THESEUS

Buenas, Helmut.

HELMUT

Theseus.

THESEUS

Eh, eh, vienen conmigo.

El auror desvía la mirada, ve a Theseus y lo reconoce. Mira al JEFE DE AURORES (HELMUT), que está en lo alto de los escalones, y éste le hace una señal afirmativa con la cabeza.

THESEUS empieza a subir los escalones y los otros lo siguen.

Justo entonces, la multitud se agita. Rosier y Carrow se abren paso entre un grupo de seguidores de Santos mientras suenan tambores.

Rosier le hace una señal a Carrow, que levanta la varita. Un chorro de fuego impacta contra una pancarta de Santos. La cara de Santos se convierte en cenizas, y de pronto la atmósfera se torna siniestra y hay golpes y empujones.

29 INT. GRAN SALÓN – MINISTERIO ALEMÁN – MOMENTOS MÁS TARDE – NOCHE

CIENTOS de DELEGADOS se arremolinan mientras unas TETERAS FLOTAN por el espléndido salón. Theseus camina

al lado de Newt, que mira alrededor sin disimulo, como si buscara a alguien.

THESEUS

Entiendo que no estamos aquí por los sándwiches.

NEWT

No. Tengo que dar un mensaje.

THESEUS

¿Un mensaje? ¿A quién?

Newt se detiene y mira. Theseus sigue la mirada de su hermano.

En el extremo opuesto de la sala, Anton Vogel, el mago de rostro benévolo al que hemos visto en las PANCARTAS DE LA CALLE, saluda a la gente mientras una falange de GUARDAESPALDAS lo sigue de cerca, y una AGREGADA (FISCHER) lo hace avanzar.

THESEUS (CONT'D)

Estarás de broma.

NEWT

No.

Newt se dirige hacia ellos y Theseus lo sigue, y entonces hay un CORTE A:

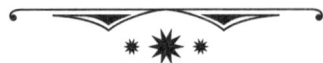

NUEVA TOMA — JACOB Y LALLY

JACOB

Pero ¿qué hago yo aquí? Vámonos. No
se me dan bien estas situaciones.

LALLY

¿Estas situaciones?

JACOB

Con tanta gente. Y de esta categoría.

EDITH

¡Hola!

*Jacob se sobresalta y ve que tiene al lado a una mujer mayor
(EDITH).*

EDITH (CONT'D)

Lo he visto entrar y me he dicho:
«Edith, qué hombre tan interesante.»

JACOB
(nervioso)

Jacob Kowalski. ¿Qué tal? Encantado de
conocerla.

EDITH

¿Y de dónde es usted, señor Kowalski?

                    JACOB
De Queens.

                    EDITH
Ahhh.

Edith asiente despacio y hay un CORTE A:

NUEVA TOMA

Newt, seguido por Theseus, se acerca a Vogel y a sus acompañantes.

                    NEWT
Disculpe, Herr Vogel, ¿podríamos
hablar un segundo?

Vogel se da la vuelta al oír la voz de Newt.

                    VOGEL
¡Por las barbas de Merlín! Pero si es el
señor Scamander, ¿no?

                    NEWT
Herr Vogel...

Los guardaespaldas se aproximan. Theseus se aproxima. Vogel mira fijamente a Newt; entonces levanta una mano para

*indicar a los guardaespaldas que se aparten. Cuando éstos
retroceden, Newt se inclina hacia delante.*

> **NEWT (CONT'D)**
> Tengo un mensaje de un amigo. Y no
> puede esperar. «Haga lo correcto, no lo
> fácil.»

Newt se endereza. Vogel permanece quieto.

> **NEWT (CONT'D)**
> Me dijo que era importante que lo
> viera esta noche y que usted oyera esas
> palabras. Esta noche.

Aparece Fischer.

> **FISCHER**
> Es la hora, señor.

> **VOGEL**
> *(sin hacerle caso)*
> ¿Está aquí? ¿En Berlín?

Newt titubea: no está seguro de cómo debe responder.

> **VOGEL (CONT'D)**
> No, claro que no, ¿por qué dejar
> Hogwarts cuando el resto del mundo

arde envuelto en llamas?
(frunce el ceño)
Le doy las gracias, señor Scamander.

Fischer se lleva a Vogel y gira la cabeza para mirar a Newt.

Por encima del barullo se oye el ruido de una CUCHARA que golpea una TAZA DE PORCELANA, y todas las miradas se dirigen hacia Fischer, que está de pie con una taza en la mano, y a Vogel, que está a su lado. Una vez que obtiene la atención de los presentes en la sala, Fischer se aparta y Vogel se coloca frente al público, que aplaude.

> VOGEL (CONT'D)
> Gracias, gracias. Veo muchas caras
> conocidas aquí esta noche, colegas,
> amigos, enemigos...

Los invitados RÍEN.

> VOGEL (CONT'D)
> En las siguientes cuarenta y ocho horas,
> junto al resto del mundo mágico,
> elegirán a nuestro próximo gran líder.
> Una elección que dará forma a nuestras
> vidas durante las generaciones venideras.
> No tengo ninguna duda de que, gane
> quien gane, la Confederación estará en
> buenas manos. Liu Tao. Vicência Santos.

DISEÑO DE PANCARTAS ELECTORALES DE LOS CANDIDATOS LIU Y SANTOS

Vogel señala a Liu Tao y a Vicência Santos, a la que recono-
cemos de El Profeta, *y el público APLAUDE.*

> VOGEL (CONT'D)
> Es en momentos como éste cuando se
> nos recuerda que este pacífico traspaso
> de poder marca nuestra humanidad
> y le demuestra al mundo que, a pesar
> de nuestras diferencias, todas las voces
> merecen ser escuchadas.

Vogel desvía la mirada. Theseus, que observa desde cierta dis-
tancia, mira en esa dirección. Unos AURORES VESTIDOS DE
NEGRO van colocándose uno a uno en las diferentes salidas.

> VOGEL (CONT'D)
> Incluso aquellas que para algunos
> puedan resultar desagradables.

Theseus observa a los acólitos, que cruzan la sala.

> THESEUS
> Newt, ¿te suena la cara de alguno?

Newt sigue la mirada de Theseus.

> NEWT
> París. La noche que Leta...

THESEUS
Estaban con Grindelwald.

Theseus ve a Rosier entre la gente. Ella lo mira como desafiándolo a seguirla. Él va tras ella con la intención de alcanzarla, y Newt lo sigue a cierta distancia.

VOGEL
Por consiguiente, y tras una exhaustiva investigación, la Confederación ha concluido que no hay suficientes pruebas para procesar a Gellert Grindelwald por los crímenes contra la comunidad muggle de los que se lo acusaba. Queda así absuelto de todos sus presuntos crímenes.

Newt registra las palabras de Vogel. De pronto, la sala estalla en reacciones diversas: indignación, algunos aplausos, confusión...

JACOB
¿Está de broma? ¿Van a soltarlo? ¡Yo estaba allí! ¡Mató a gente!

El rostro de Lally se ensombrece. Entonces:

THESEUS
¡Estáis detenidos! ¡Todos! ¡Bajad las varitas!

Theseus, con la varita en ristre, les planta cara a cinco aurores vestidos de negro.

Theseus recibe un HECHIZO en la nuca y cae al suelo. Aparece Helmut con la punta de la varita humeante.

> HELMUT
> *Nehmen Sie ihn weg.*

Dos aurores levantan a Theseus.

Newt echa a correr entre la gente, conmocionado, como si a él también lo hubiese alcanzado un hechizo.

> NEWT
> ¡Theseus! ¡Theseus!

Newt se abre paso por la sala y Lally y Jacob llegan junto a él.

> LALLY
> Newt, Newt. Aquí no. Newt, no
> tenemos ninguna posibilidad.

Helmut se vuelve con serenidad, y la falange de aurores de negro que tiene detrás lo imitan.

> LALLY (CONT'D)
> Vamos. Newt, se han hecho con el
> Ministerio Alemán. Tenemos que irnos.
> Vamos.

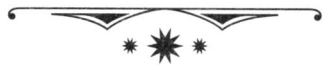

Jacob se vuelve hacia la sala y grita, pero queda atrapado en el éxodo masivo.

JACOB

¿Lo dice en serio? No puede ser.
¿Qué justicia es ésa? «Exhaustiva
investigación»... ¡Yo estaba allí! ¿Estaba
usted? ¿Estaba usted? ¡Yo estaba allí!
¡Ha soltado a un asesino!

Lally lo agarra.

LALLY

Jacob. Jacob. ¡Tenemos que irnos!
¡Tenemos que irnos!

El ESTRUENDO de la MULTITUD se INTENSIFICA. Se desenrolla el ESTANDARTE de Grindelwald por encima de la muchedumbre que rodea el ministerio. La gente empieza a COREAR el nombre de Grindelwald, las voces son cada vez más FUERTES, y CORTAMOS A:

SILENCIO ABSOLUTO

CAE UNA NIEVE QUE PARECE AZÚCAR

DESDE UN CIELO OSCURO

RENDER DEL EXTERIOR DE CABEZA DE PUERCO

30 EXT. HOGSMEADE – NOCHE

Los escaparates tienen las persianas echadas. La calle es una larga sábana blanca. Prístina.

31 INT. HABITACIÓN DEL PISO DE ARRIBA – CABEZA DE PUERCO – AL MISMO TIEMPO – NOCHE

Dumbledore está de pie ante el CUADRO DE ARIANA. Parece que ella esté observándolo.

32 INT. CABEZA DE PUERCO – AL MISMO TIEMPO – NOCHE

Dumbledore y Aberforth comen sentados uno frente a otro en la taberna vacía. Durante un rato, lo único que se oye es el ruido de las cucharas hundiéndose en los cuencos que cada uno tiene delante.

> **DUMBLEDORE**
> *(señala la sopa)*
> Está muy buena.

Aberforth sigue comiendo.

> **DUMBLEDORE (CONT'D)**
> Su favorita. ¿Recuerdas cómo le
> suplicaba a mamá que se la hiciera?
> Ariana. Mamá decía que la calmaba,
> pero creo que era más una ilusión que...

RETRATO DE ARIANA DUMBLEDORE

ABERFORTH

Albus.

Dumbledore se detiene y ve que su hermano lo mira fijamente.

ABERFORTH (CONT'D)
Yo estaba allí, crecí en la misma casa.
Todo lo que viste tú, lo vi yo.
(pausa)
Todo.

Aberforth sigue tomándose la sopa. Dumbledore observa a su hermano, abrumado por la distancia que los separa, y luego vuelve a concentrarse en su cuenco... Pero de repente se oyen unos GOLPES. Aberforth GRITA MALHUMORADO:

ABERFORTH (CONT'D)
¡Lee el letrero, imbécil!

Dumbledore mira la SILUETA que hay detrás de la puerta, que le resulta FAMILIAR. Se levanta.

33 INT./EXT. ENTRADA DE LA TABERNA – MOMENTOS MÁS TARDE – NOCHE

Dumbledore abre la puerta: es MINERVA McGONAGALL.

MINERVA McGONAGALL
Siento molestarte, Albus.

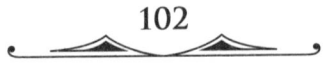

DUMBLEDORE
Dime, ¿qué pasa?

MINERVA McGONAGALL
Berlín.

34 INT. CABEZA DE PUERCO – CONTINUO – NOCHE

Aberforth permanece sentado escuchando a McGonagall y a Dumbledore, que hablan en VOZ BAJA. Entonces, como si notara algo, vuelve la cabeza.

La SUPERFICIE del ESPEJO SUCIO que hay detrás de la barra RELUCE de FORMA EXTRAÑA.

Aberforth se levanta despacio, cruza la habitación y mira fijamente el espejo. Sobre su borroso REFLEJO APARECEN unas PALABRAS, como si hubiesen ascendido a la superficie de un estanque.

¿ACASO SABES LO QUE ES...?

Aberforth observa el mensaje un momento. Entonces coge un trapo sucio y limpia el espejo con él.

35 INT./EXT. ENTRADA DE LA TABERNA – MOMENTOS MÁS TARDE – NOCHE

McGonagall se frota las manos con nerviosismo. Dumbledore está muy serio, pensando en lo que acaba de contarle.

DUMBLEDORE

Voy a necesitar a alguien que me
sustituya en las clases de la mañana.
¿Puedo abusar de tu amabilidad?

MINERVA McGONAGALL

Por supuesto. Y, Albus, por favor, sé...

DUMBLEDORE

Sí, lo intentaré.

McGonagall se dispone a marcharse, pero se detiene y GRITA:

MINERVA McGONAGALL

¡Buenas noches, Aberforth!

ABERFORTH (FUERA DE CUADRO)

Buenas noches, Minerva. Discúlpame
por haberte llamado «imbécil».

MINERVA McGONAGALL

Disculpas aceptadas.

McGonagall se da la vuelta y Dumbledore cierra la puerta.

36 INT. CABEZA DE PUERCO – CONTINUO – NOCHE

*Al oír los pasos de su hermano, Aberforth se da la vuelta y ve
a Dumbledore con su abrigo y su sombrero.*

DUMBLEDORE
Me temo que voy a tener que poner fin
a nuestra velada.

ABERFORTH
A salvar el mundo, ¿no?

DUMBLEDORE
Haría falta alguien mejor que yo.

Dumbledore se pone el abrigo. Entonces se detiene con la mirada clavada en el espejo y ve cómo las palabras ¿ACASO SABES LO QUE ES ESTAR SOLO? aparecen poco a poco. Desvía la mirada y ve a Aberforth observándolo fijamente.

ABERFORTH
No preguntes.

Los dos hermanos se quedan así, mirándose el uno al otro, hasta que Dumbledore se marcha. Aberforth lo oye salir y mira una vez más las palabras del espejo.

37 EXT. PATIO '– CASTILLO DE NURMENGARD – AL MISMO
TIEMPO – NOCHE

El FÉNIX, reluciente, vuela para atrapar una corteza de pan. Credence lo observa, y su rostro refleja una serena alegría.

38 INT. SALÓN – CASTILLO DE NURMENGARD – AL MISMO TIEMPO – NOCHE

Grindelwald está de pie junto a una gran ventana. Mientras observa al fénix, la imagen de Dumbledore aparece en el cristal, y entonces, poco a poco, deja paso a la imagen de Kama. La mira fijamente y en ese momento aparece Rosier.

ROSIER
Miles en la calle corean tu nombre. Eres un hombre libre.

Grindelwald asiente con la cabeza.

GRINDELWALD
Diles a los otros que se preparen para partir.

ROSIER
¿Esta noche?

GRINDELWALD
Mañana. Tendremos una visita por la mañana.

Detrás de la ventana vemos pasar al fénix, que suelta ceniza tras él. Grindelwald mira hacia el patio, donde está Credence.

ROSIER
¿Por qué se queda cerca de él?

GRINDELWALD
Presentirá lo que está a punto de hacer.

ROSIER
¿Y estás seguro... de que puede matar a
Dumbledore?

GRINDELWALD
Su poder reside en su dolor.

Rosier mira a Grindelwald.

39 INT. DESPACHO DEL MINISTERIO ALEMÁN – CONTINUO –
MAÑANA

*Newt, Lally y Jacob persiguen a un FUNCIONARIO DEL MI-
NISTERIO por un pasillo.*

NEWT
¡El hombre por el que pregunto es
el director de la Oficina de Aurores
británica! ¿Cómo han podido perder
al director de la Oficina de Aurores
británica?

El funcionario se vuelve y mira imperturbable a Newt.

FUNCIONARIO DEL MINISTERIO
Nosotros sostenemos que, dado que
nunca ha estado bajo nuestra custodia,
no hemos podido perderlo.

LALLY
Señor, había decenas de personas allí,
cualquiera podría corroborar...

FUNCIONARIO DEL MINISTERIO
¿Y usted se llama...?

El funcionario mira a Lally a los ojos, y entonces:

JACOB
Salgamos de aquí. ¡Un momento! ¡Ése
es...!

Newt y Lally se dan la vuelta. A través de la pared de cristal del pasillo, vemos a Helmut salir de un despacho acompañado del auror alto que vimos por primera vez en el andén de la estación.

Jacob le hace señas al funcionario para que lo siga.

JACOB (CONT'D)
¡Venga aquí! ¡Venga aquí!

Jacob, Lally y Newt corren hacia la puerta.

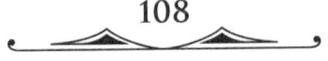

JACOB (CONT'D)
¡Perdone! ¡Eh! ¡Es él! Él sabe dónde está
Theseus. ¡Hola! ¿Dónde está Theseus?

Helmut sigue andando sin hacerles caso.

JACOB (CONT'D)
Es él. Él sabe dónde está Theseus.

*De repente, una hoja de cristal se desliza desde el techo como
una guillotina.*

40 EXT. MINISTERIO ALEMÁN – MOMENTOS MÁS TARDE – MAÑANA

*Newt, Jacob y Lally salen por una puerta lateral, y Lally
se detiene.*

LALLY
Newt.

*Newt y Jacob miran hacia atrás y ven un GUANTE que flota
en el aire. El GUANTE señala hacia la esquina. Entonces
Newt avanza y lo coge, pero ve otro guante, lo sigue y se acerca
a una figura que está detrás de una columna. Es Dumbledore.*

41 EXT. MINISTERIO ALEMÁN – MOMENTOS MÁS TARDE – MAÑANA

*Dumbledore atrapa el guante que flota en el aire y coge el que
tiene Newt. Entonces guía a los otros a buen paso por una*

avenida muy concurrida. No deja de mirar a un lado y a otro, como si tras cada sombra se ocultara una amenaza.

NEWT

Albus...

DUMBLEDORE

A Theseus se lo han llevado a Erkstag.

NEWT

Pero Erkstag cerró hace años.

DUMBLEDORE

Sí, bueno, ahora es... el *bed and breakfast*
secreto del ministerio. Necesitarás
esto... para verlo. Y uno de éstos. Y esto.

Dumbledore mete los dos guantes dentro de su sombrero, del que saca unos DOCUMENTOS que le entrega a Newt mientras escudriña su mirada.

Dumbledore los lleva hasta una pared y la atraviesan. Lally empuja a Jacob, que parece reacio.

JACOB

¡Un momento, un momento, un
momento!

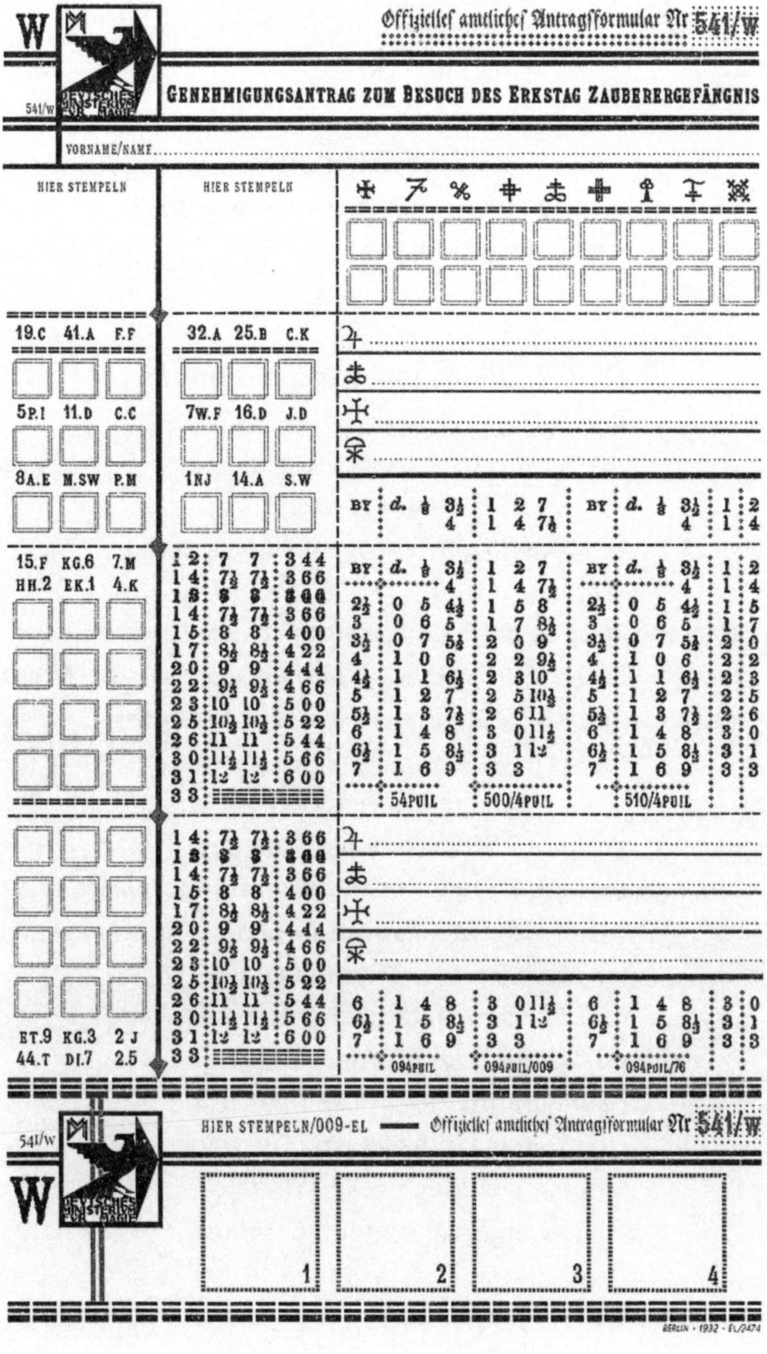

GENEHMIGUNGSANTRAG ZUM BESUCH DES ERKSTAG ZAUBERERGEFÄNGNIS

VORNAME/NAME.................

HIER STEMPELN	HIER STEMPELN

19.C 41.A F.F	32.A 25.B C.K
5P.I 11.D C.C	7W.F 16.D J.D
8A.E M.SW P.M	1NJ 14.A S.W
15.F KG.6 7.M	
HH.2 EK.1 4.K	

BY	d.	⅛	3½	1	2	7	BY	d.	⅛	3½	1	2
		4		1	4	7½			4		1	4

12	7	7	3	4	4	BY	d.	⅛	3½	1	2	7	BY	d.	⅛	3½	1	2
14	7½	7½	3	6	6			4		1	4	7½			4		1	4
13	8	8	3	6	6	2½	0	5	4½	1	5	8	2½	0	5	4½	1	5
14	7½	7½	3	6	6	3	0	6	5	1	7	8½	3	0	6	5	1	7
15	8	8	4	0	0	3½	0	7	5½	2	0	9	3½	0	7	5½	2	0
17	8½	8½	4	2	2	4	1	0	6	2	2	9½	4	1	0	6	2	2
20	9	9	4	4	4	4½	1	1	6½	2	3	10	4½	1	1	6½	2	3
22	9½	9½	4	6	6	5	1	3	7	2	5	10½	5	1	3	7	2	5
23	10	10	5	0	0	5½	1	3	7½	2	6	11	5½	1	3	7½	2	6
25	10½	10½	5	2	2	6	1	4	8	3	0	11½	6	1	4	8	3	0
26	11	11	5	4	4	6½	1	5	8½	3	1	12	6½	1	5	8½	3	1
30	11½	11½	5	6	6	7	1	6	9	3	3		7	1	6	9	3	3
31	12	12	6	0	0													
33							54PUIL		500/4PUIL					510/4PUIL				

14	7½	7½	3	6	6
13	8	8	3	6	6
14	7½	7½	3	6	6
15	8	8	4	0	0
17	8½	8½	4	2	2
20	9	9	4	4	4
22	9½	9½	4	6	6
23	10	10	5	0	0
25	10½	10½	5	2	2
26	11	11	5	4	4
30	11½	11½	5	6	6
31	12	12	6	0	0
33					

6	1	4	8	3	0	11½	6	1	4	8	3	0
6½	1	5	8½	3	1	12	6½	1	5	8½	3	1
7	1	6	9	3	3		7	1	6	9	3	3
	094PUIL			094PUIL/009				094POIL/76				

ET.9 KG.3 2J	
44.T DI.7 2.5	

W 𝕸   541/w   HIER STEMPELN/009-EL —— Offizielles amtliches Antragsformular Nr 541/w

1	2	3	4

BERLIN · 1932 · EL/2474

FORMULARIO DE VISITA DE ERKSTAG

DUMBLEDORE (CONT'D)
Confío en que esté disfrutando de su
varita, señor Kowalski.

JACOB
¿Yo? Sí, gracias, señor Dumbledore. Es
la repera.

DUMBLEDORE
Le aconsejo que la tenga siempre a mano.

*Mientras Jacob se pregunta qué significa eso, Dumbledore se
saca un RELOJ DE BOLSILLO de la chaqueta y lo mira. Newt
ve a Credence REFLEJADO en el cristal de la esfera.*

DUMBLEDORE (CONT'D)
Profesora Hicks, suponiendo que
no tenga ningún otro compromiso,
y, francamente, aunque lo tuviera,
la animo a asistir a la cena de los
candidatos de esta noche. Llévese al
señor Kowalski. Estoy seguro de que
habrá un intento de asesinato. Todo
cuanto puedan hacer para frustrarlo
será bienvenido.

LALLY
Será un placer. Acepto con gusto el
desafío. Además, me acompañará Jacob.

Jacob, que ha estado muy atento a esta conversación, se muestra levemente alarmado. Dumbledore se da cuenta.

> **DUMBLEDORE**
> No se preocupe. La magia defensiva de la profesora Hicks es soberbia. Hasta la próxima.

Sonríe, se toca el sombrero y se marcha.

> **LALLY**
> Qué adulador.
> *(pausa)*
> Bueno, no. Es que es soberbia.

Newt se adelanta y lo llama.

> **NEWT**
> ¡Albus!

Dumbledore se da la vuelta.

> **NEWT (CONT'D)**
> Me preguntaba...

Newt hace como si sostuviera una maleta.

> **DUMBLEDORE**
> Ah, sí. La maleta.

NEWT

Sí.

DUMBLEDORE

(sigue caminando)

Estate tranquilo, está en buenas manos.

42 EXT. CALLES DE BERLÍN – MOMENTOS MÁS TARDE – ÚLTIMA HORA DE LA MAÑANA

Bunty, con la maleta de Newt en la mano, esquiva un taxi y cruza rápidamente la calle hacia una TIENDA DE MARRO-QUINERÍA.

43 INT. MARROQUINERÍA OTTO'S – AL MISMO TIEMPO – ÚLTIMA HORA DE LA MAÑANA

Se oye el tintineo de una CAMPANILLA y OTTO, un HOM-BRE alto de pelo ralo con delantal, levanta la vista de una mesa llena de tijeras, mazas y abrazaderas.

OTTO

¿En qué puedo ayudarla?

Bunty se acerca al mostrador y deja con cuidado la maleta de Newt sobre la superficie de cristal.

BUNTY

Necesitaría una réplica de esta maleta.

BOCETO DEL VESTUARIO DE BUNTY BROADACRE

OTTO

Cómo no.

Bunty observa nerviosa mientras Otto examina la maltrecha maleta desde todos los ángulos con sus manos callosas, hasta que intenta abrir uno de los cierres.

BUNTY

¡Ah, no! No puede abrirla. Quiero
decir... que... no es necesario. El interior
no es importante.

El hombre mira a Bunty con curiosidad y se encoge de hombros.

OTTO

No veo ningún inconveniente para
hacerle otra.

Cuando Otto se vuelve para coger papel y lápiz del estante que tiene detrás, la cría de qilin asoma la cabeza por la maleta y mira alrededor con curiosidad. Bunty se apresura a meterla dentro con cuidado, antes de que el hombre se dé la vuelta de nuevo.

OTTO (CONT'D)

Si la deja aquí...

BUNTY

Ah, no, no puedo... dejarla. Y voy a
necesitar más de una. Verá, mi marido

es un poco despistado. Siempre se le
olvida todo. El otro día olvidó que
estaba casado conmigo. ¿Se imagina?

Suelta una risita un poco histérica, se da cuenta y se recompone.

> BUNTY (CONT'D)
> Pero lo quiero.

> OTTO
> ¿Exactamente cuántas tenía en mente?

> BUNTY
> Unas seis. Y las necesitaré dentro de un
> par de días.

44 EXT. CALLES DE BERLÍN – MOMENTOS MÁS TARDE – ÚLTIMA
HORA DE LA MAÑANA

Bunty vuelve a cruzar la calle con la maleta de Newt en la mano.

45 INT. HABITACIÓN DE CREDENCE – CASTILLO DE NURMENGARD
– ÚLTIMA HORA DE LA MAÑANA

*Queenie mira hacia abajo. Ve a Zabini y a Carrow en acti-
tud defensiva.*

> ZABINI
> ¡Enseñe las manos!

Una FIGURA levanta despacio las manos y sigue andando...

46 EXT. PATIO – CASTILLO DE NURMENGARD – AL MISMO TIEMPO – ÚLTIMA HORA DE LA MAÑANA

La figura da unos pasos más. Se detiene. Es Kama. Zabini se separa de los otros y avanza hacia él.

> ZABINI
>
> ¿Quién es?

> KAMA
>
> Me llamo Yusuf Kama.

Grindelwald y Rosier salen del castillo.

> GRINDELWALD
>
> ¿Quién nos visita?

> KAMA
>
> Soy... un admirador.

> ROSIER
>
> Asesinaste a su hermana. Se llamaba Leta.

Grindelwald lo mira.

> KAMA
>
> Leta Lestrange.

BOCETO DEL VESTUARIO DE YUSUF KAMA

GRINDELWALD

Ah, sí. Su hermana y usted comparten un antiguo linaje.

KAMA

Compartíamos. Es lo único que compartíamos.

Grindelwald observa atentamente a Kama.

GRINDELWALD

Lo envía Dumbledore, ¿no es eso?

KAMA

Teme que esté en posesión de una criatura. Teme lo que pueda hacer con ella. Me ha enviado a espiarlo. ¿Qué le gustaría que le contara?

GRINDELWALD

Queenie. ¿Dice la verdad?

Queenie mira a Kama. Sus ojos delatan que hay algo que la inquieta.

Queenie asiente.

Grindelwald mira a Credence, que está entre las sombras. Grindelwald le hace una señal casi imperceptible con la

cabeza y Credence se marcha. Grindelwald vuelve a mirar a Kama.

GRINDELWALD

¿Qué más?

QUEENIE

Aunque cree en ti, te considera responsable de la muerte de su hermana. Siente su ausencia cada día. Cada respiración le recuerda que ella ya no respira.

Queenie ve que Kama la mira a los ojos. Grindelwald asiente como si reflexionara sobre esas palabras. A continuación, saca la varita.

GRINDELWALD

Entonces supongo que no le importará que lo libere del recuerdo de su hermana.

Grindelwald avanza y le pone la punta de la varita en la sien a Kama, sin dejar de observarlo, para ver si ofrece resistencia. Pero Kama permanece inmóvil, entregado.

GRINDELWALD (CONT'D)

¿Cierto?

KAMA

Cierto.

Poco a poco, Grindelwald retira la varita y extrae un HILO TRASLÚCIDO. Queenie intenta mantener la compostura cuando ve que, por un breve instante, la pena se refleja en el semblante de Kama.

Justo entonces, el hilo traslúcido se suelta de la sien de Kama. Revolotea como la cola de una cometa, enganchado al extremo de la varita de Grindelwald, hasta que se convierte en BRUMA.

GRINDELWALD

Ya está. ¿Mejor?

Kama se queda quieto con la mirada desenfocada. Al final asiente con la cabeza.

GRINDELWALD (CONT'D)

Me lo figuraba. Cuando permitimos que
nos consuma la ira, la única víctima
somos nosotros mismos.
                    (sonríe; entonces:)
Bien, estábamos a punto de irnos.
A lo mejor le gustaría unirse a nosotros.
Venga, seguiremos hablando de nuestro
común amigo, Dumbledore.

Queenie observa a Kama, que sigue a Grindelwald al interior del castillo y, al pasar por su lado, Kama la mira con sus ojos inexpresivos, que de pronto brillan brevemente, como si

estuvieran enviándole un mensaje. Cuando Kama entra por la puerta:

ROSIER

Tú primero.

Queenie levanta la cabeza y ve a Rosier observándola. Rosier le hace un gesto, cierra la puerta detrás de ella y CORTE A:

47 EXT. CALLE MUY CONCURRIDA – BERLÍN – DÍA

Dumbledore camina a buen paso por las calles de Berlín. Credence lo sigue.

Dumbledore cruza la calle y, poco a poco, se detiene delante de una tienda, donde ve a Credence reflejado en el cristal del escaparate, visible detrás de él y entre los coches que pasan.

Dumbledore sopla suavemente sobre un copo de nieve, que se transforma en una gota de agua.

Seguimos la trayectoria de la gota, que atraviesa el cristal como una bala traslúcida y sobrevuela la escena reflejada de los tranvías y los coches hasta que llega a Credence y le estalla en la frente. Cuando revienta, el ruido de la calle se atenúa y parece lejano.

DUMBLEDORE

Hola, Credence.

Dumbledore se da la vuelta y lo mira. Credence se pone en tensión, con la varita preparada, y Dumbledore baja de la acera a la calzada. A su alrededor todo parece distinto, más lento, como si hubiésemos entrado en una imagen especular de BERLÍN, en un reflejo de la ciudad.

Ambos se mueven en círculo, y parece que los transeúntes no los vean. Credence enarbola su varita.

CREDENCE
¿Acaso sabes lo que es... no tener a
nadie? ¿Estar siempre solo?

Dumbledore empieza a comprender.

DUMBLEDORE
¡Eras tú! El de los mensajes en el espejo.

CREDENCE
Soy un Dumbledore. Me abandonasteis.
La misma sangre que corre por mis
venas corre por las vuestras.

El FÉNIX pasa volando y Dumbledore lo mira. La energía oscura que emana del interior de Credence empieza a desbordarse y abre grietas en la calzada y levanta las vías del tranvía. Dumbledore examina esa energía, la reconoce, pero a su alrededor parece que la vida transcurra con normalidad.

CREDENCE (CONT'D)
No está aquí por ti. Está aquí por mí.

El suelo empieza a resquebrajarse y a abrirse alrededor de Credence. Dumbledore intuye lo que se avecina y se pone en tensión.

De la varita de Credence sale un RAYO VERDE. Dumbledore lo bloquea con movimientos fluidos y ágiles. Inmediatamente, Credence avanza y dispara otro hechizo con el que levanta el suelo y lo lanza contra Dumbledore, que se desaparece y se aparece para esquivar cada nueva arremetida.

Ahora Credence corre detrás de Dumbledore levantando coches, ladrillos, ventanas, y lanzando violentos y ondulantes temblores sísmicos hacia Dumbledore.

Dumbledore no puede seguir esquivándolo y Credence lo alcanza. Entrelazan los brazos y siguen batiéndose en duelo.

Detrás de ellos se acerca un TRANVÍA, y Dumbledore se desaparece hacia atrás. Credence lo sigue y SUBIMOS con ellos al TRANVÍA; Credence no cede en su arremetida y sigue persiguiendo a Dumbledore. Lanza otro potente hechizo que parte el TRANVÍA POR LA MITAD; viajamos a toda velocidad DESDE DENTRO HACIA FUERA y volvemos con ellos a la calle.

SILENCIO

Ahora, en la CALLE reina una misteriosa quietud, y Credence se percata por primera vez de que a su alrededor todo parece distinto.

Credence nota una varita en la nuca; se vuelve y ve a Dumbledore de pie detrás de él.

Dumbledore levanta el DESILUMINADOR.

> **DUMBLEDORE**
> Las cosas no son lo que parecen, Credence. Independientemente de lo que te hayan contado.

Con una sacudida, el aparato absorbe la CALLE en la que se encuentran, que se funde como un cuadro y deja una imagen en negativo del mundo real, una especie de recuerdo remoto.

> **CREDENCE**
> Me llamo Aurelius.

> **DUMBLEDORE**
> Te ha mentido. Para alimentar tu odio.

Credence, frustrado, ataca de nuevo, veloz, y por un instante Dumbledore y él se baten en duelo a una velocidad vertiginosa.

NORMALMENTE, si destrozamos una ciudad, luego tenemos que arreglarla. Pero aquí Dumbledore y Credence se mueven en un mundo especular, y eso nos ofrece una oportunidad única de exhibir las peculiares habilidades de Credence como mago e inventar nuevas formas de visualizar los hechizos, que básicamente son como hermosas esculturas en el aire. Una de las cosas que hicimos fue experimentar con los cambios de estado de la materia: lo que parece que debería ser sólido se vuelve líquido, o un tsunami de escombros descomunal se convierte en nieve con un simple movimiento de la varita. Y al final nos quedamos en un mundo que se ha vuelto completamente negro, pero en los charcos de nieve derretida que hay por el suelo se ve la luz del día y el tráfico del Berlín real, donde todo sigue como antes.

—CHRISTIAN MANZ

(Efectos especiales)

Dumbledore se defiende sin problemas cuando Credence le lanza una DESCARGA DE HECHIZOS EXPLOSIVOS que lo obligan a retroceder tambaleándose. Entonces, Dumbledore extiende un brazo y, con la mano, le lanza un hechizo a Credence, lo hace retroceder de nuevo y de su cuerpo surge una masa cinética negra.

La mano de Dumbledore empuja hacia abajo a Credence, que desciende despacio sobre la calle nevada y se queda mirando fijamente el turbulento cielo, donde el fénix vuela describiendo círculos.

Respirando entrecortadamente, Dumbledore baja la varita y, mientras un humo negro se arremolina detrás de Credence, ve descender al fénix, que se queda suspendido por un instante encima de él, bate las alas y se aleja volando.

NUEVA TOMA — CREDENCE

Dumbledore se acerca, se agacha despacio y se queda junto a Credence.

Credence mueve los ojos y fija la mirada en los de Dumbledore.

DUMBLEDORE (CONT'D)
Lo que te ha contado no es verdad. Pero
sí compartimos la misma sangre. Eres
un Dumbledore.

Al oír eso, Credence mira fijamente a Dumbledore. Se quedan así un momento, conectados, hasta que la masa flotante negra vuelve a meterse en Credence. Dumbledore posa con suavidad una mano en el pecho de Credence.

DUMBLEDORE (CONT'D)
Lamento tu dolor. No lo sabíamos, te lo prometo.

Dumbledore vuelve a levantar el DESILUMINADOR, lanza un hechizo y Credence y él están de nuevo en la calle. Ahora vemos el mundo en el que se han batido en duelo reflejado bajo ellos, en los charcos de nieve derretida.

Dumbledore le tiende la mano a Credence sin dejar de observarlo.

Como Credence no se la coge, Dumbledore lo levanta del suelo. Luego se pierde en la bulliciosa calle. Credence lo ve marchar.

48 EXT. ENTRADA DE METRO CERRADA – BERLÍN – AL MISMO TIEMPO – NOCHE

Vemos acercarse a Newt, que abre una REJA OXIDADA.

49 INT. CÁRCEL DE ERKSTAG – BERLÍN – MOMENTOS MÁS TARDE

Una VELA MEDIO CONSUMIDA ilumina con una luz siniestra a un desaliñado CARCELERO sentado ante una pared LLENA de CASILLAS.

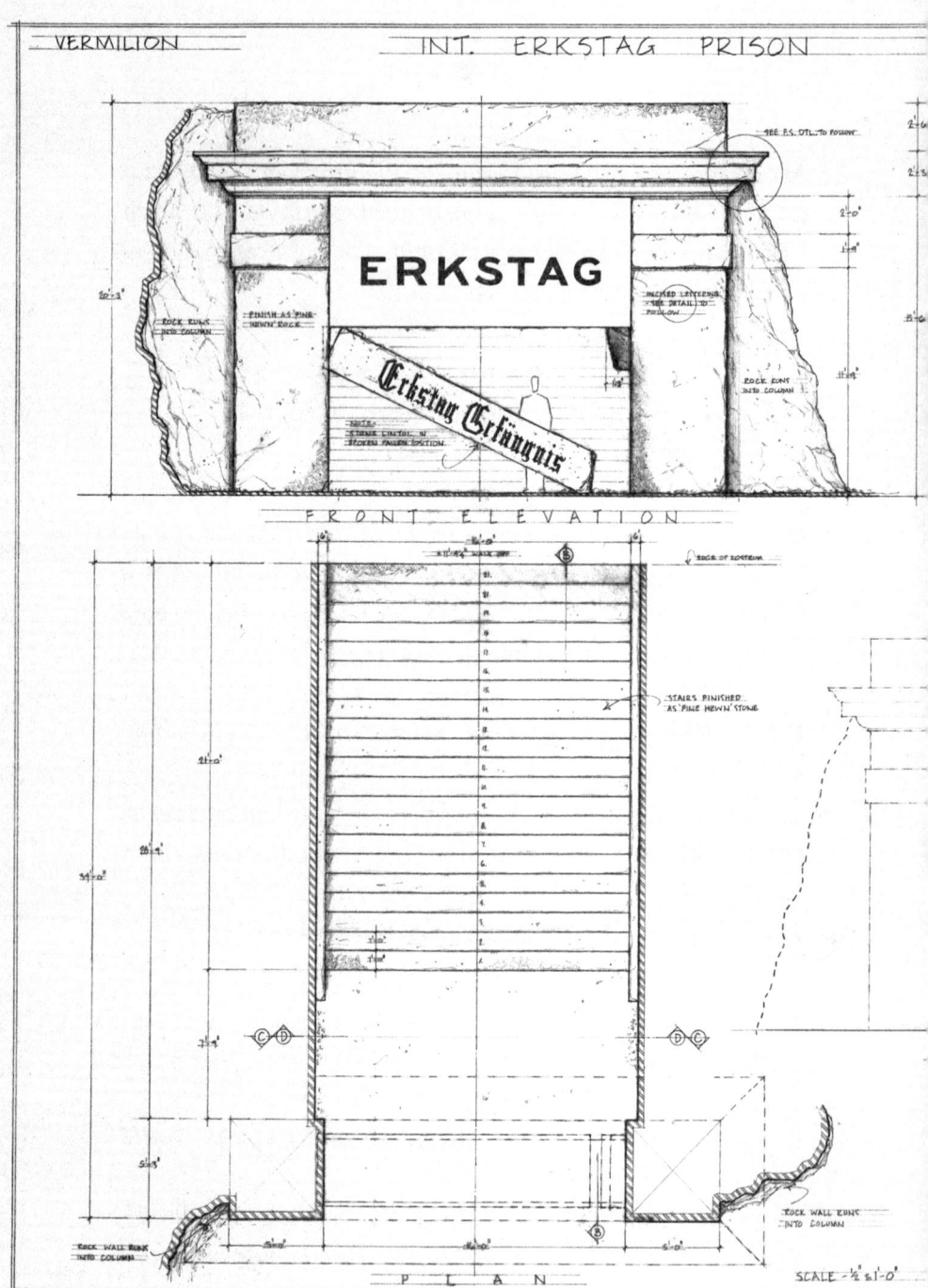

ALZADO DE LA CÁRCEL DE ERKSTAG

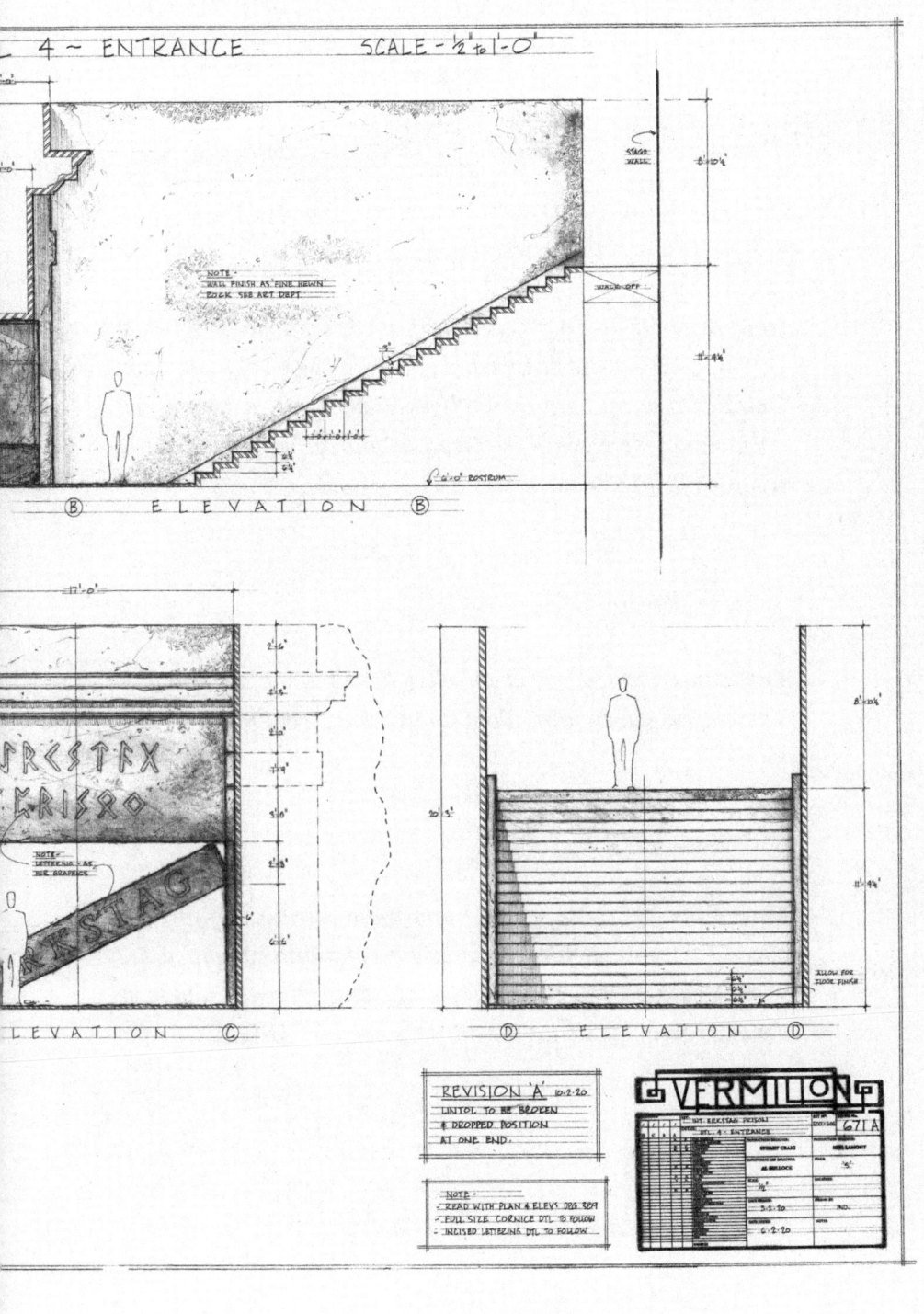

NEWT

Vengo a ver a mi hermano. Se llama
Theseus Scamander.

*Newt le tiende los DOCUMENTOS que le ha dado Dumbledo-
re, y una FOTOGRAFÍA gastada de Tina cae en el mostrador.
Un SELLO encantado extradiligente pasa por encima de los
documentos de Newt y va hacia la fotografía, pero Newt la
recupera justo a tiempo.*

NEWT (CONT'D)

Perdone. Es...

*En ese momento ve que el carcelero lleva puesta la corbata de
Theseus. Se queda mirándola un instante, y entonces:*

CARCELERO

La varita.

*Newt frunce el ceño, se mete una mano dentro del abrigo y
obedece a regañadientes. El carcelero se levanta con dificultad
y empieza a pasarle la varita por encima a Newt. Cuando se
detiene sobre uno de los bolsillos, se oye un CHILLIDO.*

NEWT

Ah, eso es... Soy magizoólogo...

El carcelero saca a Pickett del bolsillo.

NEWT (CONT'D)

Es totalmente inofensivo. En realidad...
sólo es una mascota.

Pickett estira el cuello y frunce el ceño.

NEWT (CONT'D)

Perdona.

Teddy saca la cabeza de otro bolsillo y bosteza.

NEWT (CONT'D)

Ah, éste es Teddy. No para quieto, la
verdad.

CARCELERO

Ellos se quedan aquí.

*Newt accede de mala gana y, con pesar, ve cómo el carcelero
mete a Pickett en una casilla, junto con la varita, y a Teddy
en otra, en la que su cuerpo regordete apenas cabe. Pickett
GIME SUPLICANTE.*

*Con un RUIDO de SUCCIÓN y CHAPOTEO repugnante, el
carcelero mete la mano en un CUBO LLENO DE LARVAS,
extrae una y la sacude dentro de la mano cerrada, donde la
larva se ESTREMECE brevemente y se transforma en una
LUCIÉRNAGA. El carcelero la introduce en un FAROLILLO
de latón, y la luciérnaga revolotea y empieza a emitir una*

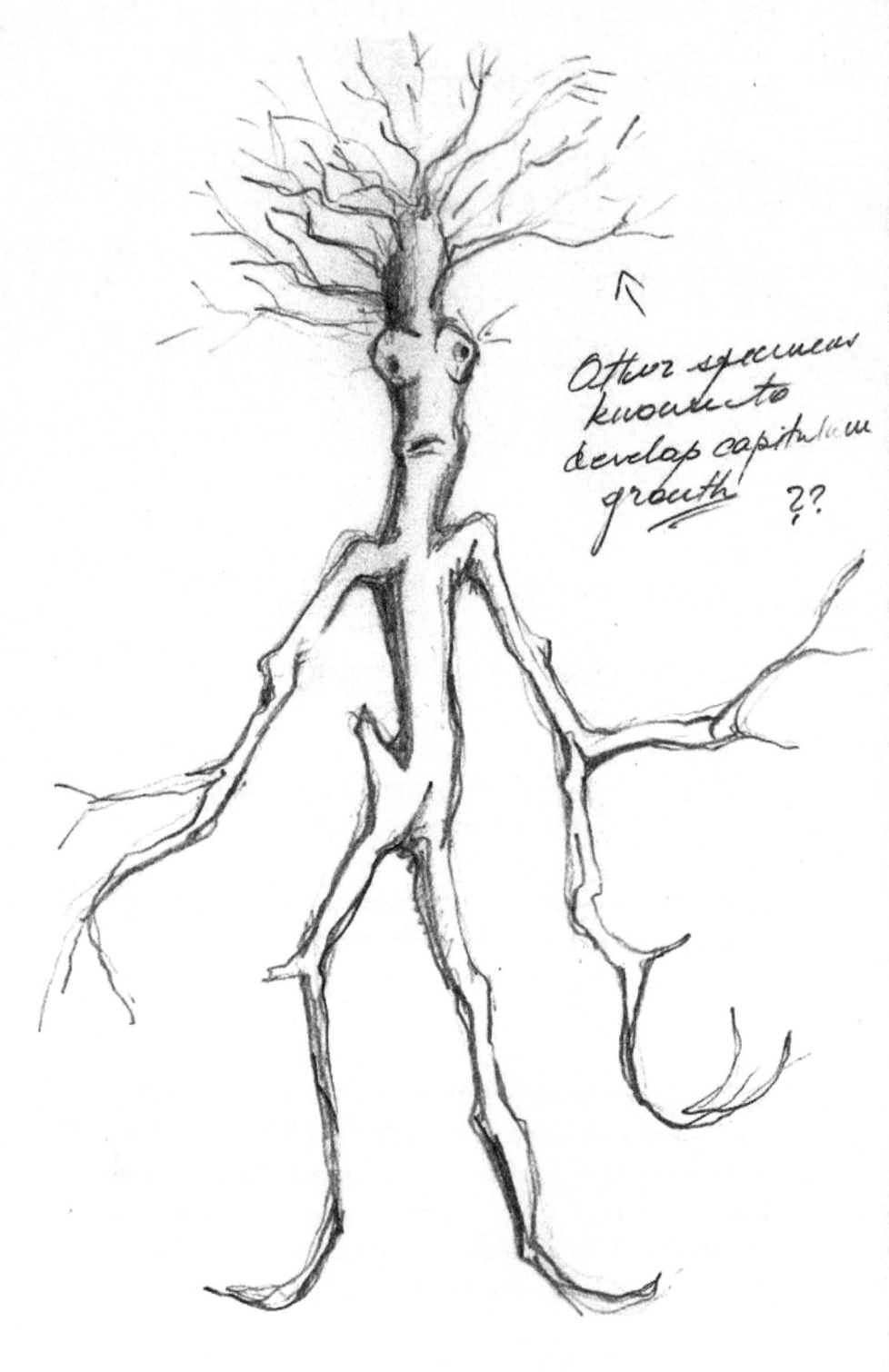

Other specimens
known to
develop capitulum
growth ??

should probably.
give these to B!

BOCETOS DEL CUADERNO DE NEWT SCAMANDER

débil y TRÉMULA LUZ. Newt coge el farolillo y se asoma a un pasillo oscuro.

NEWT

¿Y cómo sabré dónde encontrarlo?

CARCELERO

¿No es su hermano?

NEWT

Sí.

CARCELERO

Será el que se parezca a su hermano.

Newt se pone en marcha y Pickett se queda mirándolo.

NEWT

Volveré, Pick. Te lo prometo.

Justo antes de desaparecer en la oscuridad, Newt se da la vuelta.

CARCELERO

«Volveré, Pick. Te lo prometo.» Y yo
seré ministro de Magia. Algún día.

El carcelero SONRÍE con CRUELDAD. Teddy se asoma a mirar y ve que Pickett le saca la lengua.

50 EXT. MINISTERIO ALEMÁN – NOCHE

Las calles que rodean el ministerio están abarrotadas de segui-
dores de Grindelwald provistos de pancartas con su imagen.
Algunos llevan TAMBORES y los golpean con fuerza. Desde
lo alto de los escalones de la entrada, Helmut contempla la
escena impasible.

51 INT. COCHE DE GRINDELWALD – CONTINUO – NOCHE

Grindelwald observa con fría fascinación la CÓMICA MASA
DE CARAS que hay al otro lado del cristal tintado. Rosier va
sentada a su lado.

Las caras dejan de estar enfocadas. Aparece una IMAGEN en
el cristal, una imagen que sólo puede ver Grindelwald: Jacob
blandiendo una varita.

Rosier se ha inclinado hacia delante y habla con el chófer.

ROSIER

Llévenos por detrás. Esto no es seguro.

GRINDELWALD
(sale de su ensimismamiento)
No. Bájala.

ROSIER

¿Qué?

DISEÑO DEL MONOGRAMA ORNAMENTAL DEL CAPÓ
DEL COCHE DE GELLERT GRINDELWALD

GRINDELWALD
La ventanilla. Bájala.

Rosier extiende una mano temblorosa y BAJA un poco la ventanilla. Al instante, unos DEDOS empiezan a buscar a tientas en el interior oscuro del coche y SE OYEN GRITOS. Grindelwald permanece sereno, con los ojos cerrados. Entonces, sin previo aviso, TIRA de la manija de la puerta...

ROSIER

¡No! ¡No!

Grindelwald se lanza a la vorágine de fuera del coche. Rosier se queda paralizada en el asiento.

52 EXT. MINISTERIO ALEMÁN – CONTINUO – NOCHE

Saludando como un magistrado romano, Grindelwald deja que la marea de seguidores enardecidos lo suba por los escalones.

53 INT. BALCÓN – MINISTERIO ALEMÁN – AL MISMO TIEMPO – NOCHE

Una BRUJA BRITÁNICA ALTA está de pie al lado del MINISTRO FRANCÉS (VICTOR), Fischer y Vogel, contemplando a la exaltada multitud.

VOGEL

Esa gente no está sugiriéndonos que la escuchemos. No está pidiéndonos que la escuchemos. Nos lo está exigiendo.

BRUJA BRITÁNICA

No estarás proponiendo que ese hombre se presente...

VOGEL

Sí, sí, que se presente.

FOR THE GREATER GOOD

→→ VOTE ←←

Gellert GRINDELWALD

MATERIAL DE LA CAMPAÑA ELECTORAL DE GRINDELWALD

→VOTE←

Gellert

GRINDELWALD

FOR
SUPREME MUGWUMP

INTERNATIONAL
CONFEDERATION
OF WIZARDS

BEHOLD THE INSIGNIA OF THE GREATER GOOD

Abajo, Rosier, pálida como un fantasma, sale del coche y ve a Grindelwald abrirse paso entre la gente.

> BRUJA BRITÁNICA
> ¡Gellert Grindelwald quiere una guerra entre magos y muggles! Y si lo consigue, no sólo destruirá su mundo, sino también el nuestro.

> VOGEL
> ¡Por eso no puede ganar! Que figure como candidato. Que la gente vote. Cuando pierda, la gente se habrá pronunciado. Pero, si silenciamos su voz, las calles serán un reguero de sangre.

Los otros miran hacia abajo y ven a Grindelwald llevado en volandas por sus seguidores, que lo suben por los escalones de la entrada del ministerio.

54 INT. PASILLO – CÁRCEL DE ERKSTAG – NOCHE

Vemos aparecer una lucecita parpadeante. Cuando se acerca, distinguimos a Newt, que se detiene.

> NEWT
> ¡Theseus!

Se oyen pequeños movimientos en la oscuridad circundante.

Newt se agacha y hace oscilar el farolillo. Un animal diminuto, parecido a un cangrejo —una CRÍA DE MANTÍCORA—, aparece correteando. Al ver a Newt, agita las antenas. No se puede negar que es adorable.

Newt no parece muy contento. Mientras observa, aparece otra cría de mantícora, y luego otra, y otra más. Una se acerca, lo mira, enseña los DIENTES. No tiene nada de adorable.

Newt retrocede hacia un atrio central y camina por el borde de una gran fosa. Mira hacia abajo y ve un enorme agujero oscuro. Al fondo, algo se remueve en la oscuridad.

De repente, Newt adopta una postura extraña, como si imitara la forma de andar de un cangrejo. Las crías de mantícora lo imitan.

55 INT. GRAN SALÓN – MINISTERIO ALEMÁN – NOCHE

Llevan bandejas de langosta a las mesas. Lally, que ahora está sentada, rastrea la sala con la mirada, se fija en las mesas donde están sentados Liu y Santos y evalúa el grado de amenaza que suponen los CAMAREROS y AYUDANTES DE CAMARERO que van de un lado para otro. Un CAMARERO DE OJOS OSCUROS pasa una y otra vez por el campo visual de Lally.

La COPA de Jacob se llena mágicamente de vino. Jacob la coge y, al ver que Edith lo saluda entusiasmada desde el otro ex-

tremo de la sala, la levanta y brinda con ella. Entonces se fija en un MAGO DISTINGUIDO con pelo de director de orquesta que está sentado a la izquierda de Edith.

JACOB

Lally, el del bigote que está sentado al lado de Edith. Parece capaz de matar a alguien. Y también se parece a mi tío Dominic.

LALLY
(lo mira)

¿Tu tío Dominic es el ministro noruego de Magia?

JACOB

No.

LALLY

Me lo figuraba.

Lally sonríe. Entonces, de golpe, Grindelwald y su séquito irrumpen en la sala pletóricos y la atmósfera cambia por completo. Despeinado y con la chaqueta arrugada, Grindelwald parece atrevidamente auténtico en esta sala llena de gente patética y pretenciosa. Se vuelve hacia el CUARTETO de ELFOS DOMÉSTICOS y les ordena seguir tocando.

BOCETO DEL VESTUARIO DE JACOB KOWALSKI

ANIMALES FANTÁSTICOS

Avanza por la sala, seguido por Rosier, Queenie, Kama, Carrow, Zabini y otros acólitos.

Cuando Queenie pasa ante él, Jacob se levanta.

JACOB

Queenie... Queenie.

Queenie sabe que Jacob está ahí, pero no le presta atención.

GRINDELWALD

(al ver a Santos)

Ah, madame Santos, un placer. Cuenta con un gran apoyo.

SANTOS

(con una sonrisa fría)

Como usted, señor Grindelwald.

Grindelwald compone una sonrisa forzada.

56 INT. PASILLO INTERIOR – ERKSTAG – NOCHE

Theseus cuelga por los tobillos en una pequeña celda. Se OYE un ESTRUENDO, y Theseus vuelve la cabeza hacia el pasillo y ve aparecer a Newt, que camina de lado haciendo un extraño movimiento de tijera, seguido de CIENTOS de CRÍAS DE MANTÍCORA que, aparentemente, lo imitan a él.

THESEUS

¿Has venido a rescatarme?

NEWT

Ésa es la idea.

THESEUS

*(mientras Newt sigue haciendo
sus extraños movimientos)*
Y deduzco que esto, lo que sea que estés
haciendo, es parte de la estrategia.

NEWT

Sí, es una técnica llamada «mimetismo
límbico». Disuade del uso de la
violencia, en teoría. Sólo la he puesto
en práctica una vez.

THESEUS

¿Y los resultados?

NEWT

No concluyentes. Claro que fue en
un laboratorio y bajo condiciones
estrictamente controladas, y... Bueno,
las condiciones actuales son más
inestables, lo cual hace que el resultado
sea menos predecible.

NEWT no es nada sociable. Sólo se siente realmente cómodo con los animales. No se le da bien formar parte del sistema, ni siquiera supo adaptarse al colegio. ¡Hasta tal punto que lo echaron! Theseus, en cambio, es el clásico líder de la clase que ha acabado consiguiendo un cargo en el ministerio; ha sido un héroe de guerra y tiene la autoridad física y el don de gentes que no tiene Newt. Así que son como el día y la noche, y sin embargo, en esta película, como tienen que trabajar juntos, empiezan a darse cuenta de que en realidad se complementan muy bien.

—EDDIE REDMAYNE

(Newt Scamander)

THESEUS
El resultado sería supuestamente...
nuestra supervivencia.

Newt se queda inmóvil y una ANTENA inmensa surge de la oscura fosa. Theseus y Newt se miran alarmados. Newt se vuelve con cuidado hacia la antena, que lo examina brevemente, y justo en ese momento el farolillo que hay en la celda adyacente a la de Theseus chisporrotea y se apaga.

La antena retrocede, y entonces una cola semejante a la de un escorpión se lanza contra la celda, ahora oscura, extrae el cuerpo envuelto como un capullo que hay dentro y se lo lleva a la fosa. Pausa. De pronto:

El cuerpo sale CATAPULTADO de la oscuridad y SE ESTRELLA a unos palmos de donde están ellos. Newt levanta su farolillo y vemos que el cuerpo está destripado y que servirá de alimento a la horda de manticoras que se acercan en tropel para zampárselo. Newt aprovecha la oportunidad, camina de lado hasta meterse en la celda y arranca a toda prisa la cuerda fibrosa que rodea los tobillos de Theseus.

Newt arranca lo que queda de cuerda y Theseus cae al suelo.

THESEUS (CONT'D)
Muy bien.

Los dos hermanos salen de la celda y se encuentran ante una masa de mantícoras aún mayor, que les cierra el paso.

THESEUS (CONT'D)

¿Y el plan es...?

NEWT

Sujeta esto.

Le pasa el farolillo a Theseus. Entonces junta las manos y lanza un SILBIDO EXTRAÑO que recuerda al del chotacabras.

57 INT. CÁRCEL DE ERKSTAG – AL MISMO TIEMPO – NOCHE

Mientras el carcelero RONCA con los pies encima del mostrador, Pickett abre el candado de su casilla y abre la puerta.

58 INT. ERKSTAG – AL MISMO TIEMPO – NOCHE

THESEUS

¿Para qué demonios has hecho eso?

NEWT

Vamos a necesitar ayuda.

Newt adopta una GRÁCIL pose de mimetismo límbico. Inmediatamente, las crías de mantícora lo imitan.

EN la secuencia de Erkstag, todo está iluminado por unos farolillos que contienen una luciérnaga. La cuestión es que a las mantícoras no les gustan esos bichos, así que están colgados fuera de cada una de las celdas. Cuando se apaga un farolillo, las mantícoras atacan. Por eso, en cuanto ves que tu luciérnaga muere, sabes que estás perdido, porque las mantícoras vendrán a por ti.

—CHRISTIAN MANZ
(Efectos especiales)

ANIMALES FANTÁSTICOS

NEWT (CONT'D)

Haz lo mismo que yo.

(pausa)

Vamos.

Theseus adopta la misma pose y Newt y Theseus empiezan a avanzar de lado.

NEWT (CONT'D)

No te estás balanceando bien.
Balancéate... Balancéate, pero con
delicadeza.

THESEUS

Me estoy balanceando como tú, Newt.

NEWT

Discrepo.

Entre ellos dos, otro FAROLILLO que está colgado en la puerta de una celda se apaga, y la cola asciende y se lleva otro cuerpo.

Tras una pausa, ese otro cuerpo también va a parar justo a sus pies. Theseus y Newt se miran.

THESEUS

Me balanceo.

59 INT. GRAN SALÓN – MINISTERIO ALEMÁN – NOCHE

Queenie está sentada en silencio. Una LÁGRIMA resbala por el lado de su cara que ninguno de los que están sentados a su mesa puede ver.

En el otro extremo de la sala, Jacob la mira fijamente. LA CÁMARA SE MANTIENE en ellos, absortos el uno en el otro; todo lo que los rodea parece irrelevante y se vuelve borroso hasta que...

> GRINDELWALD
> Ve con él.

Queenie se sobresalta y ve a Grindelwald inclinado hacia ella. Grindelwald señala con la cabeza más allá de Queenie, y vemos a Credence junto a la puerta. Queenie se levanta.

> GRINDELWALD (CONT'D)
> Queenie. Dile que no pasa nada. Sé que
> ha fracasado. Tendrá otra oportunidad.
> Es su lealtad lo que más valoro.

Grindelwald la mira fijamente. Ella asiente, se separa de él y se va.

NUEVA TOMA — LALLY

Lally ve que Queenie cruza la sala. Jacob se levanta cuando Queenie pasa por su mesa, pero ella, sobreponiéndose —aho-

ra nos damos cuenta de que le cuesta—, vuelve a ignorarlo. Jacob, destrozado, se sienta de nuevo.

Lally mira a Grindelwald. Rosier entra en la sala con el camarero de ojos oscuros. Le habla al oído. El camarero de ojos oscuros se detiene y mira hacia la mesa de Santos.

Lally sigue con la mirada al camarero de ojos oscuros, que recorre la sala con una copa llena de un líquido de color rojo rubí. Lally tira su servilleta, se levanta y se dirige a Jacob antes de alejarse de la mesa.

LALLY

Quédate aquí.

Jacob se bebe otra copa de vino de un trago.

Lally se abre paso entre los ayudantes de camarero.

LALLY (CONT'D)

Perdón.

Lally ve que el camarero de ojos oscuros se acerca a Santos...

... se inclina hacia Santos y le pone la copa delante. Lally se acerca, pero dos guardaespaldas le cierran el paso.

JACOB

¡Oh, vaya!

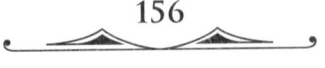

Jacob se acerca a la mesa de Grindelwald tambaleándose, como si caminara por un barco.

Cuando Santos levanta su copa, el líquido de color rojo rubí asciende amenazadoramente en el aire. Lally lanza un hechizo con disimulo, y el líquido suspendido sobre la copa de Santos sale despedido por encima de la mesa, se estrella contra una puerta y corroe la madera.

Cuando Jacob llega a la mesa, Grindelwald, que acaba de fijarse en él, lo mira con desdén.

> **JACOB (CONT'D)**
> Deje que se vaya.

> **GRINDELWALD**
> ¿Cómo dice?

Jacob saca su varita.

> **MINISTRO NORUEGO**
> ¡Asesino!

Lally se da la vuelta y mira incrédula a Jacob, que ahora levanta ambas manos.

¡FIU! Lally vuelve a agitar su varita y la mano con la que Jacob sostiene la suya asciende verticalmente. Un REMOLINO

similar a un tornado se apodera de la sala, como si todo lo que hay en ella estuviera dentro de una batidora.

Lally lanza rápidamente otro hechizo y ata los cordones de los zapatos de los dos guardaespaldas.

Los invitados huyen, las arañas de luces TIEMBLAN, los tapices se agitan a lo largo de la pared, los manteles se inflan y las servilletas vuelan como palomas.

Entrevemos una FIGURA, una forma BORROSA a lo lejos. Cuando Jacob consigue ENFOCARLA, vemos que la FIGURA es...

Queenie.

Queenie está como Jacob, inmóvil en medio del caos, y lo mira fijamente. Sus ojos se encuentran...

... y Queenie empieza a desaparecer de la escena, porque Kama tira de ella.

Helmut y sus aurores entran en la sala.

Antes de salir, Queenie SACUDE su varita y lanza una silla contra Helmut, impidiéndole momentáneamente ver a Jacob.

Lally saca su libro y lo lanza al aire. Con otro hechizo hace caer una araña de luces sobre Helmut y sus aurores. Enton-

ces las hojas del libro se desprenden y descienden en cascada formando unos escalones. Jacob los sube a toda prisa, seguido de Lally, que no para de lanzar hechizos contra los aurores.

Helmut lanza un fogonazo que hace que las hojas empiecen a arder y Jacob corre hacia Lally. ¡FIU! El libro los engulle.

60 INT. CÁRCEL DE ERKSTAG – AL MISMO TIEMPO – NOCHE

El carcelero RONCA y su silla se inclina hacia atrás. Teddy, que sujeta con la boca un extremo de la corbata, resbala hacia delante, y sus pequeñas patas CHIRRÍAN en la superficie del mostrador.

En lo alto, Pickett se asoma peligrosamente al borde de su casilla mientras trata de sacar la varita de Newt.

ABAJO, el carcelero se despierta y la silla se endereza. Entonces...

Cuando por fin el nudo de la corbata se deshace del todo, la silla cae hacia atrás, el carcelero SE ESTRELLA como un árbol talado contra las casillas y Pickett sale lanzado hacia delante.

Teddy salta hacia arriba, se cruza con Pickett en el aire, pero lo ignora por completo y, antes de caer al suelo, atrapa unas monedas que han salido despedidas de las casillas.

Vuelve a resonar el SILBIDO de Newt.

61 INT. CELDAS – ERKSTAG – AL MISMO TIEMPO – NOCHE

El farolillo que Theseus lleva en la mano amenaza con apagarse. De repente oímos un crujido, y Theseus se detiene.

De pronto, las crías de mantícora se paran. Theseus mira hacia abajo y, lentamente, con cuidado, levanta el pie derecho, bajo el que vemos una cría de mantícora aplastada.

Theseus mira a Newt.

Y en ese preciso instante, la luz del farolillo de Theseus parpadea, se apaga y los deja a los dos a oscuras. Las crías de mantícora echan a correr.

La ENORME cola asciende y se da impulso para atacar.

Los dos hermanos echan a correr a la vez y la cola se estrella contra la pared de las celdas a sólo unos palmos de ellos.

Newt y Theseus corren por los pasillos; la cola y las antenas de la mantícora van CULEBREANDO, azotando a diestro y siniestro, aplastándolo todo y lanzándoles fogonazos, seguidas por la MANTÍCORA GIGANTE, que los persigue metiéndose por las grietas.

Theseus tuerce a la derecha y corre con dificultad por una cornisa mientras la mantícora se abalanza feroz sobre él. Los ojos, las garras y las extremidades de la bestia se le echan

encima, pero *Theseus tuerce a la izquierda y esquiva por los pelos la extremidad que se disponía a atravesarlo.*

Newt y Theseus vuelven a encontrarse y corren a la desesperada, y justo en ese momento el techo se derrumba detrás de ellos y atrapa a la mantícora gigante.

Theseus suspira aliviado, pero entonces una de las antenas de la mantícora le rodea la cintura y tira de él. Newt los sigue con desesperación y agarra a su hermano.

Teddy corre hacia ellos con la corbata de Theseus entre los dientes. Pickett va montado en su lomo como un vaquero y sujeta la varita de Newt. El carcelero les va lanzando hechizos, y cuando uno de ellos alcanza a Teddy, Pickett sale despedido hacia delante con la varita de Newt.

Newt no suelta a su hermano, al que la mantícora gigante arrastra hacia el borde de la fosa. Pickett aterriza a sus pies con la varita.

Newt lo ve y recupera su varita, y Pickett se agarra a ella. Newt le lanza un hechizo a Teddy...

NEWT

¡Accio!

... que salta por los aires y va dando volteretas hacia ellos.

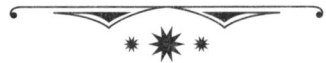
NEWT (CONT'D)
¡Coge la corbata!

Empiezan a precipitarse en la fosa.

... Y desaparecen.

El carcelero se ríe hasta que su farolillo empieza a parpadear y se apaga. Mira a su alrededor, alarmado, pero está completamente a oscuras.

62 EXT. ZONA BOSCOSA – CONTINUO – A LA MAÑANA SIGUIENTE

Newt y Theseus caen a través de un matorral y van a parar a un suelo cubierto de musgo. Se levantan recubiertos de hojas; todavía van cogidos de la mano.

Theseus se quita la antena de la mantícora que aún lleva alrededor de la cintura. La antena culebrea hacia el lago.

NEWT
Era un traslador.

Theseus le da a Teddy, que todavía está agarrado a la corbata.

THESEUS
Sí.

> **NEWT**
> *(a Pickett y a Teddy)*
> Lo habéis hecho fenomenal.

Newt y Theseus salen del bosque y contemplan un lago resplandeciente. Más allá se alza un CASTILLO. Teddy y Pickett asoman por el bolsillo de Newt. Pickett SUSURRA con admiración.

Hogwarts.

Sobrevolando el castillo, un JUGADOR DE QUIDDITCH persigue una SNITCH DORADA.

63 INT. GRAN COMEDOR – HOGWARTS – MOMENTOS MÁS TARDE – MAÑANA

Lally está acabando de desayunar con unos cuantos alumnos.

> **LALLY**
> Ya sé que no me lo habéis preguntado,
> pero os recomiendo la asignatura de
> Encantamientos.

Entran Newt y Theseus.

> **NEWT**
> Lally.

RENDER DE LOS EXTERIORES DE HOGWARTS

LALLY

¿Dónde estabais?

NEWT

Hemos tenido algunas complicaciones.
¿Y vosotros?

LALLY

Hemos tenido algunas complicaciones.

Le pasa El Profeta *a Newt. Theseus se asoma por encima del hombro de Newt. En la primera plana hay una FOTOGRAFÍA de Jacob bajo un GRAN TITULAR:*

¡MUGGLE ASESINO!

THESEUS

¿Jacob ha intentado matar a
Grindelwald?

LALLY

Es... una larga historia.

Jacob está sentado con un grupo de alumnos a la mesa de una de las casas. Les está mostrando su varita.

RAVENCLAW PELIRROJO

¿De verdad es de colubrina?

DISEÑO PRELIMINAR DE *EL PROFETA* CON ESPACIO EN BLANCO
PARA LA FOTOGRAFÍA MÓVIL DE JACOB KOWALSKI

JACOB

Claro que es de colubrina.

Una BRUJA MENUDA de SEGUNDO AÑO se inclina hacia él.

BRUJA MENUDA

¿Puedo...?

La bruja menuda alarga un mano hacia la varita.

JACOB

No. Es muy peligrosa. Muy poderosa.
Y singular. En las manos equivocadas,
menuda se lía.

BRUJA MENUDA

¿De dónde la ha sacado?

JACOB

Me la ha traído Papá Noel.

LALLY (FUERA DE CUADRO)

¡Jacob, mira quién está aquí!

Jacob se vuelve y ve a Lally, Newt y Theseus.

JACOB

¡Anda, son mis amigos magos!

HOGWARTS
SCHOOL OF
WITCHCRAFT & WIZARDRY

NAME: ....

CLASS: .... YEAR: ....

DISEÑO DE LA CUBIERTA DE UN CUADERNO DE HUFFLEPUFF

(a los niños)
Newt y Theseus. Estamos así.

Jacob cruza el dedo medio y el índice, separando al mismo tiempo el pulgar.

JACOB (CONT'D)
Y éste soy yo. Tengo que irme. Bueno, que os divirtáis. No hagáis nada que no haría yo.

Cuando Jacob se reúne con los demás:

JACOB (CONT'D)
Menudo sitio. Hay brujas y magos diminutos correteando por aquí.

THESEUS
No me digas.

JACOB
(a Newt)
El asesino era yo.

LALLY
Newt y Theseus estudiaron en Hogwarts.

JACOB

Ah, ya lo sabía. Han sido muy
simpáticos conmigo. Los chicos esos
de Slytherin me han dado esto. Están
riquísimos. ¿Queréis uno?

*Jacob se saca un paquete del bolsillo y se mete un trozo de
UNA COSA OSCURA en la boca. Se la ofrece a los demás.*

NEWT

Nunca me han gustado mucho los
cucuruchos de cucarachas, aunque los
de Honeydukes son supuestamente
los mejores.

*Jacob palidece, y se oyen RISAS de los de Slytherin. Siguen has-
ta el fondo del Gran Comedor. Los demás ven a McGonagall,
que se lleva a unos alumnos. Dumbledore se acerca.*

THESEUS

McGonagall. Albus.

DUMBLEDORE

Muy bien. Muy bien todos.
Enhorabuena.

THESEUS

¿Enhorabuena?

CREO que Hogwarts es el lugar donde Dumbledore se siente realmente a gusto. Es su refugio del mundo.

—JUDE LAW

(Albus Dumbledore)

EN esta película, vemos a un Dumbledore un poco más elegante que en las anteriores, sobre todo en cuanto a telas y materiales. Sus trajes de tweed transmiten una idea de refinamiento y comodidad, y los grises claros recuerdan a los tonos lavanda que más adelante lleva en las películas de Harry Potter.

—COLLEEN ATWOOD

(Vestuario)

BOCETO DEL VESTUARIO DE ALBUS DUMBLEDORE

TRANSFIGURATION

2/6

=== TODAY ===

EDITION
5948

THE MAGAZINE THAT CHANGES LIVES ←←

TRANSFIGURATION MASTER-MINDS OF TOMORROW ←—←←

A LOOK AT THE TOP WIZARDING STUDENTS OF HOGWARTS AND BEYOND...

Aliquam felis tellus, lobortis eget ante sit amet, pharetra fermentum massa. Pellentesque bibendum mi a erat eleifend, non interdum nisi pharetra. Etiam pretium odio nec malesuada consectetur. Nullam sed gravida enim in eleifend augue. Quisque sit amet lorem feugiat, mollis mauris in, ultrices velit. Nullam luctus facilisis purus et egestas. Pellentesque mattis egestas lectus, vel viverra lectus vulputate vitae. Aenean ipsum diam, convallis ac porttitor vel, luctus ut lectus. Proin sagittis sagittis purus, sed vehicula urna tempus cul. Ut porta risus dolor, sit amet porta felis lobortis eu. Aliquam erat volutpat. Suspendisse laoreet

Sed mauris velit, dignissim ac sollicitudin tincidunt, varius ut metus. Suspendisse purus sem, sollicitudin vitae ante ut, eleifend mattis magna. Maecenas luctus odio nec arcu ullamcorper, eget mollis ligula dictum. In ultricies velit iaculis porta tincidunt, lectus enim posuere purus, ut congue est metus sed velit. Sed bibendum at mi vel congue. Integer vel nisl vitae odio pretium feugiat. Nunc hendrerit arcu sit amet leo pretium, nec vestibulum lorem elementum. as vel vestibulum elit vitae nibh. Duis turpis neque, egestas congue diam eu, iaculis convallis lacus. Nunc laoreet ullamcorper sapien

Quam in purus auctor dapibus. Maecenas in elit dignissim, pulvinar dui et imperdiet est. Aenean facilisis urna el dolor euismod. Donec velit urna, vestibulum et consectetur id, porttitor pellentesque justo. Cras placerat quam vehicula vulputate auctor. Nulla porta augue sit amet justo interdum egestas. Ut hendrerit tortor et leo scelerisque, porta tincidunt leo blandit. Quisque aliquam, orci et fringilla consequat nibh tristan faucibus ex, sed dapibus dui orci at nibh. Integer pretium nisl vel nunc blandit, ut posuere nunc ornare. Suspendisse et lacus massa. Morbi sodales sem vestibulum est condimentum.

CONTINUES ON............................... PG. 4

►'OUT OF◄ THIN AIR'
DISCOURSE IN
CONJURATION

In cursus dapibus mattis. Duis consequat id urna vitae ornare. Etiam tellus urna, hendrerit a tellus eros, semper pretium nulla. In hac habitasse platea dictumst. Praesent viverra a purus ut cursus. Suspendisse id tincidunt libero, at dictum nisl. Phasellus non neque imperdiet, fermentum ipsum sit amet interdum quam. Etiam vehicula eleifend nibh. Quisque sit amet eros a velit cursus dapibus. Nulla turpis elit, blandit id ullamcorper sed, placerat ac ipsum. Pellentesque facilisis lectus at euismod vehicula, eros ligula fringilla ligula, sed varius dolor orci ut nibh. Vestibulum sem lacus, pellentesque ac euismod eget, facilisis maximus orci. In id tristique lacus, a viverra mauris. Ut convallis, nisi sit amet blandit feugiat, magna arcu aliquet enim, vel tempor orci est quis erat. Donec ac vulputate ante. In et nisl nisl. Vestibulum congue ex in sagittis posuere. Nullam posuere tortor et diam porta gravida.

CONTINUES ON..... PG. 14

JOIN THE DISCUSSION:
GAMP'S LAW TO BE LOOSENED ?

Sed mauris velit, dignissim ac sollicitudin tincidunt, varius eu metus. Suspendisse purus sem, sollicitudin vitae ante ut, eleifend mattis magna. Maecenas luctus odio nec arcu ullamcorper, eget mollis ligula dictum. In ultricies velit iaculis porta tincidunt, lectus enim posuere purus, ut congue est metus sed velit. Sed bibendum at mi vel congue. Integer vel nisl vitae odio pretium feugiat. Nunc hendrerit arcu sit amet leo pretium, nec vestibulum lorem elementum. as vel vestibulum elit, vitae nibh. Duis turpis neque, egestas congue diam eu, iaculis convallis lacus. Nunc laoreet ullamcorper sapien

Aliquam felis tellus, lobortis eget ante sit amet, pharetra fermentum massa. Pellentesque bibendum mi a erat eleifend, non interdum nisi pharetra. Etiam pretium odio nec malesuada consectetur. Nullam sed gravida enim in eleifend augue. Quisque sit amet lorem feugiat, mollis mauris in, ultrices velit. Pellentesque mattis egestas lectus, vel viverra lectus vulputate vitae. Aenean ipsum diam, convallis ac porttitor vel, luctus ut lectus. Proin sagittis sagittis purus, sed vehicula urna tempus cul. Ut porta risus dolor, sit amet porta felis lobortis eu.

CONTINUES ON............................... PG. 9

ESSAYS on REPARIFARGE

ALBUS DUMBLEDORE
»»» PRESENTS ←←←

THEORY & PRACTICE IN 20ᵀᴴ CENTURY TRANSFIGURATION

Print
By M. Pres...
Ed. 5948/08

DUMBLEDORE

Por supuesto. La profesora Hicks ha logrado frustrar un asesinato. Y estáis todos sanos y salvos. El hecho de que todo no haya salido exactamente como estaba planeado era exactamente el plan.

LALLY

Contraplanificación nivel uno.

THESEUS

Albus, disculpa, pero ¿no estamos tal y como empezamos?

DUMBLEDORE

En realidad, yo diría que estamos mucho peor.
(a Lally)
No se lo has contado, ¿no?

Theseus y Newt miran a Lally.

LALLY

Han permitido a Grindelwald presentarse a las elecciones.

THESEUS/NEWT

¿Qué? Pero ¿cómo?

DUMBLEDORE

Porque Vogel ha antepuesto lo fácil a lo
correcto.

*Dumbledore agita la varita y traza IMÁGENES de MONTA-
ÑAS y VALLES dibujados a mano, como si fuera un pintor
callejero. Las imágenes empiezan a MATERIALIZARSE y,
poco a poco, componen un hermoso paisaje. Los demás lo
contemplan maravillados.*

Jacob mira a su alrededor, desorientado.

THESEUS

Tranquilo.

NEWT

Bután.

DUMBLEDORE

Correcto. Tres puntos para Hufflepuff.
El reino de Bután se encuentra en el
borde oriental del Himalaya. Es un
lugar... de una belleza indescriptible.
Parte de nuestra mejor magia procede
de allí. Y dicen que, si escuchas con
atención, el pasado te susurra. También
es donde se elegirá al candidato.

Se forman NUBES bajo el techo del Gran Comedor. Entre ellas se distingue la TORRE de una especie de templo, que sólo se ve un momento y luego desaparece.

THESEUS
No puede ganar, ¿verdad?

DUMBLEDORE
Hace sólo unos días era un prófugo de
la justicia. Ahora es un candidato oficial
de la Confederación Internacional de
Magos. Los tiempos peligrosos
favorecen a los hombres peligrosos.

Dumbledore se da la vuelta y echa a andar hacia el otro lado del Gran Comedor. La imagen de Bután empieza a esfumarse detrás de él.

Todos se quedan mirando a Dumbledore.

DUMBLEDORE (CONT'D)
Por cierto, cenaremos con mi hermano
en el pueblo. Si necesitáis algo antes,
avisad a Minerva.

Cuando Dumbledore se marcha, Lally se adelanta y habla en voz baja.

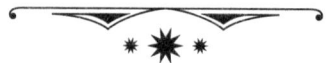

LALLY

¿Dumbledore tiene un hermano?

64 INT. CABEZA DE PUERCO – MÁS TARDE – NOCHE

Aberforth le ofrece un platillo de leche al qilin. El qilin se levanta al instante y emite una serie de ruiditos de felicidad al inclinarse sobre el platillo y empezar a sorber. Bunty lo observa.

Justo entonces SE OYE la puerta de la calle, y una ráfaga de viento y copos de nieve se cuela en la taberna. Se oyen VOCES y PISADAS DE BOTAS, y al cabo de un momento entran Dumbledore, Newt, Theseus, Lally y Jacob.

NEWT

¡Bunty! ¡Estás aquí!

BUNTY

Sí.

NEWT

¿Cómo está?

BUNTY

Ah, está bien.

Newt se agacha al ver que un escarbato corre hacia él.

NEWT

¿Qué ha hecho Alfie ahora? Oye, no habrás vuelto a morderle en el culo a Timothy, ¿verdad?

DUMBLEDORE

Señorita Broadacre, espero que mi hermano haya sido un amable anfitrión.

BUNTY

Sí, amabilísimo.

Dumbledore mira a su hermano.

DUMBLEDORE

Me alegra oírlo. Ah... Tenéis preparadas habitaciones en el pueblo, y aquí Aberforth os hará una deliciosa cena, una de sus recetas.

CORTE A:

65   INT. CABEZA DE PUERCO – MÁS TARDE – NOCHE

¡PAF! Aberforth, con un cazo grasiento en la mano, SIRVE un ESTOFADO espeso y grisáceo en los cuencos desportillados que tienen delante los miembros del grupo, que están sentados a una mesa alargada.

ABERFORTH

Hay más... si gustan.

Los otros miran sus cuencos con asco mientras Aberforth se dirige a la escalera.

BUNTY

Gracias. Gracias.

Aberforth se detiene y mira con el ceño fruncido a Bunty, que sonríe; asiente brevemente y sigue subiendo.

THESEUS

Impresionante. Nunca una comida
con un aspecto tan repugnante me ha
sabido tan deliciosa.

El qilin da un BALIDO de placer. Los demás empiezan a comer.

JACOB

¿Quién es la criaturita? ¿Oye, te
importa...?

Newt ve a Jacob compitiendo con el qilin por el estofado de su cuenco.

NEWT

Es un qilin, Jacob. Son increíblemente
singulares. Una de las criaturas más
adoradas en el mundo mágico.

JACOB

¿Por qué?

NEWT

Porque pueden ver tu alma.

JACOB

Me tomas el pelo.

NEWT

(niega con la cabeza)
No. Si eres bueno y noble, lo verá. Y si
eres cruel y deshonesto, también lo
verá.

JACOB

¿Ah, sí? ¿Y te lo... dice?

NEWT

No lo dice exactamente.

LALLY

Bueno, se inclina, pero sólo ante alguien verdaderamente puro de corazón.

Jacob mira a Lally embelesado.

LALLY (CONT'D)

En fin, casi nadie lo es, con independencia de que uno intente ser buena persona. Hubo un tiempo, hace muchos muchos años, en el que el qilin elegía a nuestro líder.

Jacob coge su cuenco y va con él a donde el qilin tiene su platillo de leche. El qilin danza a su alrededor. Jacob pone un poco de su estofado en el cuenco del qilin.

Newt sonríe satisfecho, pero entonces se fija en el espejo, donde están apareciendo una a una estas palabras:

QUIERO IR A CASA.

66 INT. HABITACIÓN DEL PISO DE ARRIBA – CABEZA DE PUERCO – MOMENTOS MÁS TARDE – NOCHE

Dentro, Dumbledore y Aberforth están de pie uno frente a otro. Hablan en voz baja, pero su postura indica que mantienen una discusión tensa.

> **DUMBLEDORE**
> Ven conmigo. Te ayudaré. Es tu hijo,
> Aberforth. Te necesita.

Es un PLANO SUBJETIVO de Newt. Va a darse la vuelta, pero entonces ve que Aberforth tiene algo en la mano: una PLUMA cubierta de CENIZA que le está manchando los dedos. Es una PLUMA DE FÉNIX.

Newt llama a la puerta...

> **DUMBLEDORE (CONT'D)**
> Newt.

Aberforth pasa al lado de Newt sin decir nada. Todavía lleva la pluma en la mano.

> **DUMBLEDORE (CONT'D)**
> *(a Newt)*
> Pasa.

Newt entra.

> **NEWT**
> Albus, en el espejo de abajo hay un
> mensaje.

DUMBLEDORE

Cierra la puerta.

Newt cierra la puerta y mira a Dumbledore.

DUMBLEDORE (CONT'D)

Es de Credence, Newt. El verano en el que Gellert y yo nos enamoramos, mi hermano también se enamoró, de una chica de Godric's Hollow. Se la llevaron de allí. Hubo rumores... de un bebé.

NEWT

¿Credence...?

DUMBLEDORE

Es un Dumbledore. Si me hubiera llevado mejor con Aberforth, si hubiera sido mejor hermano, tal vez habría confiado en mí. Tal vez las cosas habrían sido diferentes, y ese niño podría haber formado parte de nuestras vidas, de nuestra familia.

(pausa)

Credence ya no tiene salvación, sé que lo sabes, pero a lo mejor él sí puede salvarnos... a nosotros.

Mientras Newt asimila esas palabras, Dumbledore levanta una mano. Tiene los dedos manchados de hollín.

DUMBLEDORE (CONT'D)
Ceniza de fénix. El ave va hacia él porque se muere, Newt. Conozco las señales.
(sin mirar a Newt)
Verás, mi hermana era una obscurial.

Newt mira perplejo a Dumbledore.

DUMBLEDORE (CONT'D)
Y, como Credence, nunca aprendió a expresar su magia. Con el tiempo se volvió más oscura y empezó a envenenarla.

Dumbledore observa el cuadro.

DUMBLEDORE (CONT'D)
Lo peor de todo es que ninguno fuimos capaces de aliviar su dolor.

NEWT
¿Puedes decirme cómo... cómo fue su final?

THE
DUMBLEDORE
FAMILY
TREE

The Dumbledores originally lived in Mould-on-the-Wold, but moved to Godric's Hollow after Percival Dumbledore was sent to Azkaban for attacking Muggles he did not inform the authorities that his actions were in retaliation for the Muggles' traumatising attack on his daughter, Ariana. The Dumbledores were the subject of much gossip, since Ariana was rarely seen, and a fist fight broke out at her funeral between her older brothers.

PERCIVAL
DUMBLEDORE
ꟾVꟾꟾꟾꟾXꟾ

KENDRA
(DUMBLEDORE)
ꟾVꟾꟾꟾVX - ꟾVꟾꟾꟾꟾXꟾX

ALBUS
DUMBLEDORE
ꟾVꟾꟾꟾVꟾꟾꟾꟾ

ABERFORTH
DUMBLEDORE
ꟾVꟾꟾꟾVꟾꟾꟾꟾꟾ

ARIANA
DUMBLEDORE
ꟾVꟾꟾꟾVꟾꟾꟾꟾV - ꟾVꟾꟾꟾꟾXꟾX

The Dumbledores Nullam lobortis ullamcorper purus eget semper purus dignissim quis. Proin et tortor nisl. Sed nec massa volutpat diam tempus hendrerit. Donec vitae nisl ligula. Curabitur sit amet lacus lacinia, ultrices enim quis ornare nisl. Ut nec tincidunt ipsum, vel ultricies tortor. Sed feugiat consectetur ultrices. Aenean nibh massa, ultricies id odio sit amet placerat tristique est. Cras tincidunt sit amet nibh sit amet consequat. Pellentesque sollicitudin dignissim lacus sed sagittis est molestie vel. Sed sodales convallis neque. Vitae molestie mi feugiat venenatis. Ut id aliquet erat, a aliquet tortor.

Mauris accumsan, ligula sit amet eleifend suscipit diam lacus tempus enim. nec luctus dolor velit, sit amet lacus. Sed in pellentesque dui. Praesent lacus tellus, semper non lacus at dictum condimentum massa. The Dumbledores venenatis sem a bibendum eleifend. lacus metus commodo erat ut con-

consequat odio brem nec nisl. Proin vitae volutpat felis. Nulla et dolor consequat erat iaculis viverra vel sit amet tortor. Nam metus justo, semper sed consectetur at convallis at. The Dumbledores mi. Duis in odio sagittis vestibulum odio ut ullamcorper ante. Nullam in rutrum risus et ullamcorper quam. Vestibulum sit amet egestas elit a mattis quam.

The Dumbledores vehicola elementum. Donec feugiat justo ac tempor scelerisque. Proin tincidunt et ipsum non lacinia. Suspendisse venenatis libero quis efficitur placerat velit ipsum convallis velit quis egestas felis erat eu justo. The Dumbledores Vestibulum at finibus nunc. Nam sed facilisis dui vel dictum ipsum Curabitur nec fermentum sapien. Phasellus tortor. The Dumbledores leo facilisis quis eros in. interdum placerat tortor. Duis in odio sagittis vestibulum odio ut ullamcorper ante. Nullam in rutrum risus et ullamcorper quam. ed facilisis dui.

(*arriba*) **BLASÓN DE LA FAMILIA DUMBLEDORE**

(*pág. anterior*) **ÁRBOL GENEALÓGICO DE LA FAMILIA DUMBLEDORE**

> **DUMBLEDORE**
> Gellert y yo habíamos hecho planes
> para irnos juntos. Mi hermano no
> lo aprobaba. Una noche se enfrentó
> a nosotros, hubo gritos y amenazas.
> Aberforth sacó su varita, una estupidez.
> Yo saqué la mía, otra estupidez mayor.
> Gellert se rió. Nadie oyó a Ariana bajar
> las escaleras.

A Dumbledore le brillan los ojos mientras contempla el cuadro.

> **DUMBLEDORE (CONT'D)**
> No sé con seguridad si fue mi
> encantamiento. Tampoco importa ya.
> Estaba allí y de repente desapareció...

Su voz se apaga.

> **NEWT**
> Lo siento mucho, Albus. Si te sirve de
> consuelo, tal vez se le ahorró sufrir...

> **DUMBLEDORE**
> No, no me decepciones, Newt. Tú no.
> Tu sinceridad es un don, aunque a
> veces resulte doloroso.

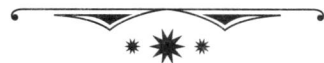

Newt observa a Dumbledore, que contempla el cuadro una vez más.

DUMBLEDORE (CONT'D)
Nuestros amigos estarán cansados y querrán retirarse. Deberías irte.

Newt asiente y hace ademán de salir, pero se detiene en el umbral.

NEWT
Albus, Lally ha dicho algo antes sobre que... casi todos somos en el fondo imperfectos. Aunque cometamos errores, y graves, podemos intentar hacer las cosas bien. Y eso es lo que importa: que lo intentemos.

Dumbledore no se da la vuelta: sigue contemplando el cuadro.

67 EXT. CASTILLO DE NURMENGARD – ÚLTIMA HORA DEL DÍA

La cámara describe círculos en un cielo gris pizarra, sobre el castillo. Abajo vemos congregado a un EJÉRCITO DE FIGURAS VESTIDAS DE NEGRO. Cuando Grindelwald y Credence caminan hacia el castillo, las figuras se apartan. Al llegar a la entrada, Grindelwald se da la vuelta y las observa.

GRINDELWALD

Se aproxima el momento, hermanos. Se
acabó tener que escondernos. El mundo
oirá nuestra voz. Y será ensordecedora.

*Un RUGIDO se eleva de la multitud. Grindelwald esboza una
sonrisa y entonces clava la mirada en Kama, que está de pie
a un lado, frente a los entusiastas acólitos; está con ellos y, al
mismo tiempo, separado. Grindelwald se acerca a él y, para
gran sorpresa de Kama, le coge la cara con ambas manos.*

GRINDELWALD (CONT'D)

No ha venido a traicionar a
Dumbledore. Sabe, en su corazón de
Sangre limpia, que su sitio está aquí.
Creer en mí es creer en usted.

*Grindelwald lo mira fijamente a los ojos un momento y luego
lo guía hacia la multitud, empujándolo con suavidad hacia
los soldados que están allí congregados.*

GRINDELWALD (CONT'D)

Demuestre su lealtad, señor Kama.

Entonces lo suelta y se vuelve hacia el castillo.

L A gente nunca ha tratado bien a los magos y las brujas. Y tengo la corazonada (sólo es mi impresión personal sobre su pasado) de que Grindelwald fue víctima de algo imperdonable o incluso sumamente cruel a edad muy temprana, y que fue entonces cuando nació el odio que siente por los muggles. Ese odio fue creciendo más y más, y a medida que pasaba el tiempo se reafirmaba su convicción de que los muggles eran repugnantes.

—MADS MIKKELSEN
(Gellert Grindelwald)

68 INT. SÓTANO – CASTILLO DE NURMENGARD – MOMENTOS MÁS TARDE – ÚLTIMA HORA DEL DÍA

PLANO DETALLE — EL QILIN MUERTO

Cuando la cabeza del animal inerte cae hacia un lado, se revela el corte que tiene en el cuello.

... BAJO EL AGUA, mirando hacia arriba a través de una superficie que ondula de forma extraña. Reina un SILENCIO inquietante, como en un sueño, y entonces aparece una FIGURA —irreconocible a través del agua— que lleva algo en los brazos. La figura SUMERGE las manos y la cara del QILIN MUERTO se vuelve hacia nosotros. Brota sangre del corte que tiene en el cuello.

NUEVA TOMA — GRINDELWALD

Está de pie en una piscina, con el agua por la cintura y las mangas de la camisa arremangadas por los codos, y mantiene al qilin bajo el agua mientras murmura algo ininteligible. Espera a que el agua se quede quieta y entonces SUSURRA:

GRINDELWALD
Rennervate...

Credence, Vogel y Rosier observan desde las sombras.

Con gran ternura, Grindelwald desliza los dedos sobre la garganta del qilin, curándole la herida. Del fondo de la piscina

ascienden BURBUJAS. El qilin asoma la cabeza a la superficie y CHILLA. Grindelwald lo saca del agua.

> GRINDELWALD (CONT'D)
> Vulnera Sanentur...

Cuando la cicatriz desaparece bajo los dedos de Grindelwald, el qilin tuerce la cabeza hacia él; tiene la mirada ausente, pero por lo demás parece vivo y sano.

Grindelwald sonríe y lo acaricia.

> GRINDELWALD (CONT'D)
> Eso es, eso es, eso es...
> *(sin volverse)*
> Ven, mira.

Vogel desvía la mirada y no se mueve de donde está, pero Credence sale de las sombras y se acerca al borde de la piscina.

> GRINDELWALD (CONT'D)
> Por eso somos especiales. Ocultar
> nuestros poderes no es tan sólo una
> afrenta a nosotros mismos, es un pecado.

Grindelwald deja al qilin al borde de la piscina, y el animal se queda de pie. Credence examina al qilin embrujado. Satisfecho con la reacción de Credence, Grindelwald vuelve a mirar al qilin... y entonces se detiene y su sonrisa vacila. Una

SOMBRA PÁLIDA, idéntica al qilin que tiene en los brazos, aparece brevemente en las agitadas aguas. La mirada de Grindelwald se endurece.

GRINDELWALD (CONT'D)
¿Había otro?

CREDENCE
¿Otro?

GRINDELWALD
Aquella noche. ¿Había otro qilin?

En el rincón en sombras, Vogel se da la vuelta y mira hacia la piscina. Grindelwald, furioso, entorna los ojos. Credence, de rostro pálido y liso, parece de pronto angustiado.

CREDENCE
No lo creo...

A una velocidad espeluznante, Grindelwald aparta a Credence del borde de la piscina con un potente chorro de agua y lo inmoviliza contra la pared. Grindelwald se desaparece del agua y y cuando se aparece lo hace sujetando a Credence por el cuello y la cara. La cólera brilla en sus ojos.

GRINDELWALD
Es la segunda vez que me fallas. ¿No
entiendes el peligro que me haces correr?

Credence se estremece como un crío asustado.

GRINDELWALD (CONT'D)
Es tu última oportunidad. ¿Entendido?
Encuéntralo.

69   INT. CABEZA DE PUERCO – MAÑANA

Newt está dentro de su maleta.

Theseus tiene al qilin en brazos, como si sujetara a un recién nacido.

Theseus le pasa el qilin a Newt; parecen dos padrazos. Theseus y Bunty miran a Newt, que deja suavemente al qilin en su maleta.

70   EXT. HOGWARTS – AL MISMO TIEMPO – MAÑANA

La bruma se extiende sobre los terrenos de Hogwarts. El puente y el castillo brillan débilmente bajo la luz matutina.

71   INT. PASILLO DEL 7.º PISO – HOGWARTS – AL MISMO TIEMPO – MAÑANA

Seguimos a Lally, Newt, Theseus y Jacob hacia una puerta ornamentada que surge en la pared del fondo del pasillo.

RENDER DE LOS EXTERIORES DE HOGWARTS

72 INT. SALA DE LOS MENESTERES – MOMENTOS MÁS TARDE – MAÑANA

De repente, Newt, Theseus, Lally y Jacob aparecen en una sala escasamente amueblada.

Jacob, totalmente desconcertado, sigue la mirada de Newt y, al fondo de la sala, ve CINCO MALETAS idénticas a la de Newt dispuestas en círculo ante una enorme y ornamentada RUEDA DE PLEGARIA DE BUTÁN. Bunty está junto a las maletas.

JACOB
Eh, Newt. ¿Qué es este sitio?

NEWT
La Sala de los Menesteres.

Dumbledore entra en el plano.

DUMBLEDORE
Confío en que todos tenéis las entradas
que Bunty os dio.

Todos asienten. Jacob, obediente, levanta la suya para que todos la vean.

DUMBLEDORE (CONT'D)
Las necesitaréis para acceder a la
ceremonia.

DISEÑO DE LA ENTRADA «EL PASEO DEL QILIN»

Dumbledore desvía la mirada y observa a Newt, que está mirando fijamente el círculo de maletas.

> DUMBLEDORE (CONT'D)
> ¿Qué te parece, Newt? ¿Sabrías cuál es
> la tuya?

Newt las mira un momento más y luego niega con la cabeza.

> NEWT
> No.

> DUMBLEDORE
> Bien. Me preocuparía lo contrario.

> LALLY
> Deduzco que el qilin está en una de
> estas maletas.

> DUMBLEDORE
> Sí.

> LALLY
> ¿Y en cuál?

> DUMBLEDORE
> A saber.

JACOB

Ah, es como el juego de las tres cartas.

(mientras los otros lo miran)

O lo de adivinar dónde está la bolita. Es
un timo.

(se rinde)

Ni caso, cosas de muggles.

DUMBLEDORE

Grindelwald hará todo lo que pueda
para hacerse con nuestro singular
amigo. Es esencial que despistemos
a quien sea que envíe para que el
qilin pueda llegar sano y salvo a la
ceremonia. Si para la hora del té el
qilin, por no hablar de nosotros, sigue
vivo, podremos considerar que hemos
tenido éxito.

*Dumbledore se cala el sombrero y se enrolla una bufanda
al cuello.*

JACOB

Que yo sepa, nadie ha muerto por jugar
a las tres cartas.

DUMBLEDORE

Un detalle importante. Está bien, que
cada uno elija una maleta y en marcha.

LA MALETA DE NEWT Y SUS RÉPLICAS

Señor Kowalski, usted y yo seremos los
primeros.

JACOB

¿Yo? Muy bien...

Jacob se adelanta y escoge una maleta; pero Dumbledore
carraspea y niega con la cabeza de forma casi imperceptible.
Entonces Jacob elige otra y la señala. Dumbledore asiente y
se da la vuelta.

Jacob coge la maleta. Asiente. Mira a su alrededor. Frunce el
ceño. No ve ninguna salida.

La rueda de plegaria de Bután reluce ante Dumbledore. Dum-
bledore extiende un brazo y la toca, y un hermoso resplandor
baña la sala.

DUMBLEDORE

Estoy impaciente por que me ilustre
acerca del juego de las tres cartas.

Mira a Jacob y le tiende una mano.

JACOB

Será un placer.

Jacob le da la mano y, juntos, desaparecen dentro de la rueda,
que gira a gran velocidad.

Cuando Dumbledore y Jacob desaparecen, los otros miran las maletas restantes.

BUNTY
¡Bueno! Buena suerte a todos.

Newt se adelanta y elige una maleta.

NEWT
Buena suerte.

Newt desaparece.

LALLY
Lo mismo digo, Bunty.

Lally se adelanta, coge otra maleta y desaparece.

THESEUS
Hasta pronto, Bunty.

Theseus se adelanta, coge otra maleta y también desaparece dentro de la rueda.

Bunty inspira hondo y coge la última maleta. Va hacia la rueda de plegaria y desaparece.

73 EXT. BASE DE LA TORRE – BUTÁN – DÍA

A lo lejos se alzan montañas cubiertas de vegetación y, en lo alto, casi tocando el cielo, entrevemos la torre.

Hay una multitud congregada en la base de una escalinata enorme que asciende hacia las alturas, donde atisbamos una magnífica torre. Una figura se acerca a la jaula dorada que hay bajo la escalinata.

> VOGEL
>
> No es ningún secreto para nosotros, los líderes, que actualmente somos un mundo dividido. Cada día sabemos de una nueva conspiración.

El discurso de Vogel se proyecta en los Ministerios de Magia de todo el mundo.

> VOGEL (CONT'D)
>
> Cada hora que pasa, hay otro oscuro rumor. Estos rumores no han hecho más que intensificarse estos últimos días con la incorporación de un tercer candidato. Sólo hay una manera de que no haya la mínima duda de que hay un candidato digno entre los tres que se postulan.

RENDER DE LA TORRE

(arriba) ETIQUETAS DE CERVEZA DE MANTEQUILLA
Y TIPOGRAFÍA PERSONALIZADA

(pág. siguiente) PANCARTA CEREMONIAL, «EL PASEO DEL QILIN»

THE WALK OF THE WILD

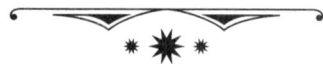

Vogel entra en la jaula dorada y sale con algo en los brazos. Cuando vuelve a su sitio y, poco a poco, muestra lo que sostiene, los presentes EXCLAMAN asombrados.

Es un qilin.

> VOGEL (CONT'D)
> Como todo estudiante sabe, el qilin
> es la criatura más pura de nuestro
> maravilloso mundo mágico. No se le
> puede engañar.
> *(lo sostiene ante sí)*
> ¡Que el qilin nos una!

74 EXT. AZOTEAS – BUTÁN – DÍA

A través de varias capas de nubes, descendemos hasta una ciudad y recorremos una serie de azoteas, donde aparecen unas figuras vestidas de negro. Rosier está de pie a la cabeza de un grupo, Helmut de otro. Observan las calles desde arriba y buscan entre la multitud que se está congregando.

75 EXT. CALLE – BUTÁN – AL MISMO TIEMPO – DÍA

Jacob va caminando con un grupo de seguidores de Santos. Lleva la maleta en la mano, y a su lado vemos a Dumbledore. Más adelante, el viento agita una gran PANCARTA con la imagen de Santos, que se retuerce en los palos que la sostienen

mientras los seguidores desfilan hacia las montañas que se ven a lo lejos.

Justo entonces, Dumbledore se fija en un grupo de aurores de negro que lo siguen. Guía a Jacob y se meten los dos en un callejón. Se aparecen por un umbral y dan esquinazo a sus perseguidores.

DUMBLEDORE

Vamos.

JACOB

¿Y ahora adónde?

DUMBLEDORE

Ah. Aquí es donde nos separamos.

JACOB

¿Cómo? ¿Que nos separamos?

Dumbledore se quita la bufanda.

DUMBLEDORE

Tengo que encontrarme con alguien, señor Kowalski. No se preocupe, estará perfectamente a salvo.

Dumbledore lanza su bufanda, que al volar se transforma en una cortina. Dumbledore vuelve a mirar a Jacob.

RENDER DE BUTÁN

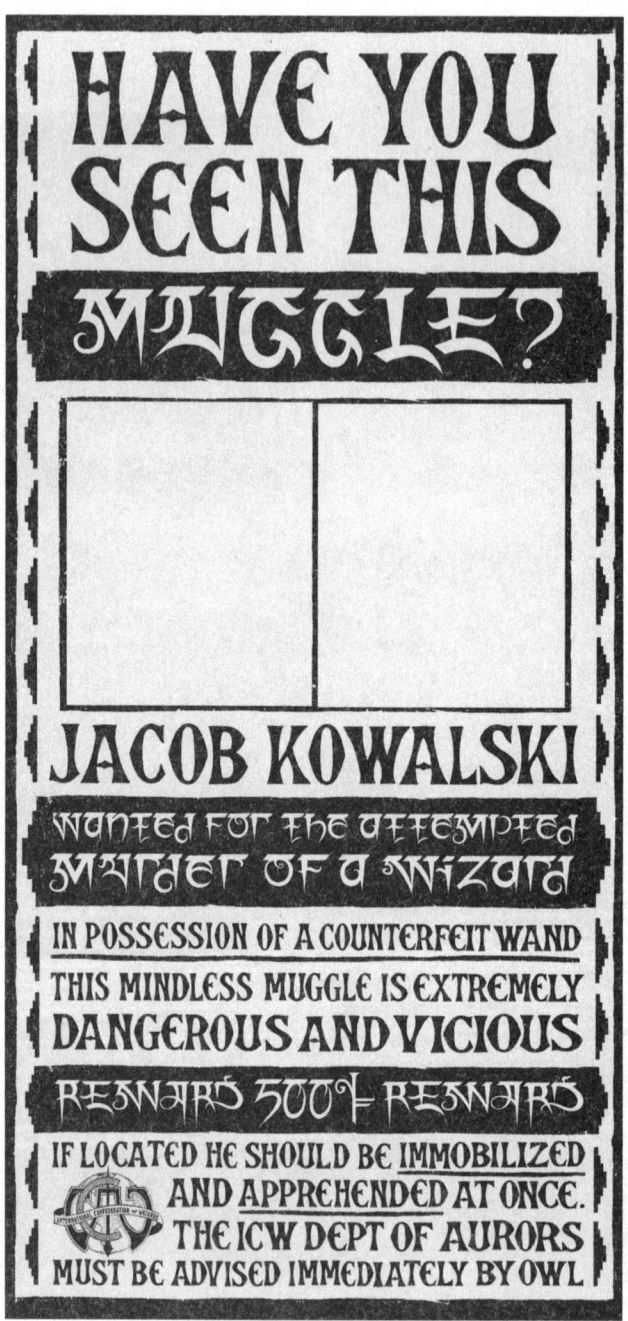

DUMBLEDORE (CONT'D)

Usted no tiene el qilin. No dude en tirar
la maleta a la primera señal de peligro.

(se detiene)

Y otra cosa, si me lo permite. Deje de
dudar de sí mismo. Tiene algo de lo que
muchos hombres carecen toda su vida,
¿sabe lo que es?

Jacob niega con la cabeza.

DUMBLEDORE (CONT'D)

Un corazón rebosante. Sólo un
verdadero valiente puede abrirse de una
forma tan sincera y plena. Como usted.

Dicho eso, Dumbledore se toca el sombrero y se marcha.

76 EXT. CALLE – BUTÁN – AL MISMO TIEMPO – DÍA

*Newt camina a toda prisa intentando no levantar sospechas.
Nota algo y se detiene. Se da la vuelta.*

Nadie.

RENDER DE BUTÁN

77 EXT. CALLE ESTRECHA – BUTÁN – AL MISMO TIEMPO – DÍA

Theseus avanza con cautela, sujetando la maleta con fuerza.

78 EXT. CALLE ESTRECHA – BUTÁN – AL MISMO TIEMPO – DÍA

Newt sigue recorriendo la ciudad. Una FIGURA CON TÚNICA VERDE entra en el plano.

79 EXT. CALLE – BUTÁN – AL MISMO TIEMPO – DÍA

Seguimos otra maleta, la de Lally, que avanza a buen paso. Mira hacia delante y ve a unos aurores. Se mete por un callejón y la perdemos de vista.

80 EXT. CALLE – BUTÁN – AL MISMO TIEMPO – DÍA

Theseus camina con precaución por una calleja estrecha. Vemos figuras que se mueven por los tejados. Más allá, ve a dos aurores y saca su varita.

81 EXT. CALLEJONES – BUTÁN – AL MISMO TIEMPO – DÍA

Lally camina deprisa, volviendo de vez en cuando la cabeza, y entonces...

82 EXT. CRUCE – CALLEJONES – BUTÁN – AL MISMO TIEMPO – DÍA

... choca con Theseus, pues ambos han llegado al final de su respectivo callejón. Se dan la vuelta y levantan la varita... y entonces se reconocen. Los dos miran alrededor a la vez. Por todas partes hay AURORES DE NEGRO.

Lally y Theseus esquivan, bloquean y atacan a los aurores de negro que los abordan por todos los lados. Retroceden subiendo unos escalones mientras lanzan contrahechizos y contraencantamientos sin parar.

Lally aturde a tres aurores de negro y Theseus aturde a unos cuantos más. Lally hace levitar una docena de bolas de cristal y las lanza en cascada contra los aurores, mientras Theseus aturde a un auror de negro que está en un balcón. Lally se da la vuelta e incapacita a otro envolviéndolo con telas, y luego lanza a otro auror contra una pared y lo deja aprisionado allí como si estuviese atrapado en un retrato.

Los aurores quedan tirados por la calle frente a ellos. Sin embargo, la victoria de Lally y Theseus es breve, porque en ese momento vemos dos varitas apuntándolos en la nuca...

HELMUT
Las maletas, por favor.

Helmut está detrás de ellos, flanqueado por dos aurores de negro.

RENDER DE BUTÁN

83 EXT. CALLEJAS/ESCALONES DE PIEDRA – BUTÁN – AL MISMO TIEMPO – DÍA

Newt dobla una esquina y, a cierta distancia, ve aparecer a dos aurores.

Detrás de ellos ve a alguien más.

JACOB

¡Buenas!

Los aurores se dan la vuelta y ¡ZAS!, Jacob los derriba golpeándolos con su maleta y sale corriendo. Los aurores se recuperan y lo persiguen.

84 EXT. CALLEJÓN ESTRECHO EN PENDIENTE – AL MISMO TIEMPO – DÍA

Jacob dobla una esquina como puede y sube unos escalones empinados y estrechos. Al cabo de un momento aparecen sus perseguidores, que se detienen y miran hacia arriba.

No hay nadie.

Sólo está la maleta de Jacob.

85 EXT. CALLEJONES – BUTÁN – AL MISMO TIEMPO – DÍA

Helmut y sus hombres cogen las maletas de Lally y Theseus y las ponen en el suelo. Un auror de negro apunta hacia ellas con su varita. Helmut levanta una mano.

> **HELMUT**
> Esperad. Abridlas y aseguraos de que
> está ahí antes. Idiotas.

El auror atrapado en la fachada la golpea con los puños para que lo ayuden a salir. Helmut suspira, levanta la varita y lo libera, y el auror se cae al suelo con un batacazo.

Lally y Theseus miran las maletas.

86 EXT. CALLEJONES – BUTÁN – AL MISMO TIEMPO – DÍA

Uno de los perseguidores de Jacob se acerca con precaución a la maleta abandonada.

Lally y Theseus ven cómo dos de los aurores de negro de Helmut se arrodillan junto a sus maletas.

¡PAF! La maleta de Jacob se abre y REVELA... un montón de PASTELES POLACOS.

Las maletas de Lally y Theseus se abren y revelan... LIBROS y la SNITCH DORADA.

RENDER DE BUTÁN

El auror de negro que contempla la maleta de Jacob coge un paczki y lo examina.

La snitch dorada empieza a ZUMBAR, y Helmut la ve elevarse y alejarse más allá de los tejados circundantes. Entonces...

¡FIU!

Los libros salen volando de la maleta de Lally y engullen a los aurores de negro, momificándolos en un vendaval de papel.

De la maleta de Jacob salen miles de pasteles que caen en cascada y forman una ola que tira a los aurores de negro por los empinados escalones.

El monstruoso libro de los monstruos *ataca mientras unas bludgers salen volando de la maleta de Theseus y se lanzan contra los aurores de negro que están en el callejón y subidos a los tejados.*

Helmut se arranca una hoja de papel de la cara, furioso, y descubre que Lally y Theseus han aprovechado para escapar en medio del caos.

87 EXT. CALLES/CALLEJONES – BUTÁN – AL MISMO TIEMPO – DÍA

Dumbledore camina veloz; alza la vista hacia un tejado cercano y ve cómo las bludgers caen sobre los aurores y los tiran al suelo. Una snitch va zumbando hacia él, y Dumbledore la

atrapa al vuelo y se la guarda en el bolsillo. De pronto, una fi-
gura sale de un callejón y se sitúa a su lado sin romper el paso.

Es Aberforth.

ABERFORTH
¿Cuánto tiempo le queda?

EL FÉNIX SOBREVUELA LA ESCENA...

88 EXT. CALLE – BUTÁN – DÍA

... deslizándose sobre el torrente de gente que llena la calle.

NUEVA TOMA — A NIVEL DE CALLE

Credence, más pálido que nunca, avanza dando tumbos entre
la masa de seguidores de Liu. Debilitado y dolorido, se detie-
ne y se apoya en un pilar para sobreponerse una vez más y
seguir andando.

89 EXT. CALLEJÓN ESTRECHO EN PENDIENTE – BUTÁN – DÍA

Jacob, ya sin maleta, recorre un callejón estrecho. Va a parar a una
calle. Pasa junto a la FIGURA CON TÚNICA VERDE, y enton-
ces otra figura se le acerca y lo agarra firmemente de la mano...

... y tira de él hacia otra callejuela, lejos de la calle principal.

CREDENCE, como muchos otros personajes de Jo, anhela encontrar su lugar. Sin embargo, en el fondo siente que su lugar no está junto a Grindelwald. Además, está muy enfermo: el obscurus cada vez lo deteriora más, así que, mientras se enfrenta a su mortalidad, Credence trata de averiguar cuál es su lugar en este momento de su vida.

—DAVID HEYMAN
(Productor)

QUEENIE

Aquí. Hola. Corres peligro. Tienes que irte.

JACOB

Bueno...

Jacob va a decir algo, pero ella le pone un dedo en los labios.

QUEENIE

No puedo. No puedo irme, ¿de
acuerdo? No puedo volver a casa. Es
demasiado tarde para mí. Algunos
errores son demasiado graves.

Jacob le aparta la mano.

JACOB

¿Me quieres escuchar?

QUEENIE

¡No hay tiempo! Me han seguido. Los
he despistado, pero no tardarán en
encontrarme.
          (se le quiebra la voz)
Y nos encontrarán.

JACOB

Me da igual. Eres lo único que tengo.
Sin ti nada tiene sentido.

QUEENIE

Jacob, ¿qué...? ¡Vamos! Ya no te quiero.
Vete de aquí.

JACOB

Eres la persona que peor miente del
mundo, Queenie Goldstein.

Justo entonces se oye un débil TAÑIDO DE CAMPANAS.

JACOB (CONT'D)

¿Has oído? Es una señal.

*Ella se queda mirándolo con gesto de severidad. Él le sostiene
la mirada.*

*Jacob coge una mano de Queenie entre las suyas y tira de
Queenie hacia él.*

JACOB (CONT'D)

Ven aquí, ven aquí. Cierra los ojos.
Por favor, cierra los ojos. ¿Sabes qué
me ha dicho Dumbledore? Que tengo
un corazón rebosante. Se equivoca.
Siempre voy a tener sitio para ti.

QUEENIE

¿Sí?

JACOB

Sí. Y lo sabes. Mírame. Queenie Goldstein...

Una lágrima resbala por la mejilla de Queenie. Ambos levantan la vista y ven que están rodeados de FIGURAS.

90 EXT. PUENTE – BUTÁN – AL MISMO TIEMPO – DÍA

Newt ve que los seguidores de Santos cruzan un PUENTE que se eleva hacia el cielo; luego desaparecen por un portal que hay en mitad del puente. Newt agarra su maleta con más fuerza y echa a andar, mezclándose con la multitud.

Desde esta perspectiva, la montaña se alza imponente, con la cumbre envuelta en densas nubes.

Newt avanza por el puente y se dirige hacia el portal. Lo atraviesa y desaparece con un ¡fiu!

91 EXT. BASE DE LA TORRE – BUTÁN – DÍA

En la base de la torre vemos una escalinata enorme que se eleva hacia las nubes y hacia lo alto del edificio. Abajo vemos a Newt, que camina con paso decidido hacia la escalinata.

Enfrente hay una figura solitaria e inmóvil: es Fischer, que se da la vuelta y mira a Newt. Su actitud no resulta en absoluto amenazadora.

RENDER DE LA TORRE

RENDER DE BUTÁN

Newt se plantea dar un rodeo, pero sólo hay una forma de subir, y entonces...

FISCHER

Señor Scamander, no nos han
presentado como es debido. Henrietta...
Fischer, la agregada de herr Vogel.

NEWT

Ah, sí... ¡Hola!

Ella señala hacia las nubes con la cabeza.

FISCHER

Puedo llevarlo. Hay una entrada
privada para los miembros del Consejo.
Si me acompaña...

Newt la mira con escepticismo y no se mueve.

NEWT

Disculpe, ¿por qué iba a hacer eso?
¿Llevarme?

FISCHER

¿No es obvio?

NEWT

No, francamente, no lo es.

FISCHER

Me envía Dumbledore.

(mira la maleta)

Sé lo que lleva en esa maleta, señor
Scamander.

Fischer entorna los ojos, y entonces una masa de entusiastas seguidores de Santos, Liu y Grindelwald entra en el plano. Rápida como una serpiente, Fischer intenta coger el asa de la maleta de Newt. Se miran a los ojos y Newt trata de apartarle la mano a Fischer mientras la muchedumbre se congrega a su alrededor. Siguen forcejeando por el control de la maleta mientras la multitud los empuja hasta el centro de la plaza, donde se ven rodeados de caras sonrientes y voces alegres.

¡FLASH! Un rayo de fuego golpea a Newt detrás de la oreja y lo tira al suelo. Aparece Zabini, de pie entre el gentío; lo mira mientras sostiene una varita HUMEANTE. Fischer sonríe, se da la vuelta y se marcha con la maleta.

92 EXT. PUENTE – BUTÁN – AL MISMO TIEMPO

Theseus espera nervioso; a su lado está Lally. El puente ya está casi desierto. El sonido de un CUERNO, parecido a un TOQUE DE CLARÍN, se eleva sobre la ciudad.

LALLY

Estará a punto de llegar.

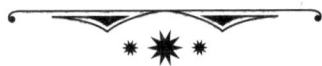

Justo enfrente aparecen Kama y un grupo de aurores de negro dirigiéndose hacia ellos. Los aurores de negro alzan las varitas. Kama pasa entre los aurores.

De pronto, Kama se agacha y golpea el suelo con la varita, liberando una oleada de magia que aturde a los aurores. Todos caen al suelo al instante.

> **THESEUS**
> ¿Dónde estabas?

Theseus, Lally y Kama van hacia el puente y desaparecen.

93 **EXT. BASE DE LA TORRE – BUTÁN – DÍA**

Newt recobra el conocimiento y se ve rodeado por la muchedumbre. Mira a su alrededor acongojado.

Ve a Fischer subiendo la escalinata.

Por encima de las cabezas de los seguidores y votantes hay unas PANCARTAS enormes que se sostienen solas y que hacen las veces de PANTALLAS en las que se proyecta la ceremonia que se desarrolla arriba. Newt contempla una de esas pancartas y ve a Vogel reflejado en ella.

> **VOGEL**
> Agradezco a los candidatos sus
> palabras...

94 EXT. TORRE – BUTÁN – CONTINUO – DÍA

Liu, Santos y Grindelwald están de pie uno al lado de otro.

>   VOGEL
> Cada uno representa una visión
> diferente de cómo se dará forma no
> sólo a nuestro mundo, sino al no
> mágico también. Lo que nos lleva a
> la parte más importante de nuestra
> ceremonia. El paseo del qilin.

Le llevan un qilin.

CORTE A:

95 EXT. TORRE – BUTÁN – AL MISMO TIEMPO – DÍA

Newt llega hasta la escalinata que conduce a la torre y, a lo lejos, ve a una figura diminuta con su maleta: Fischer.

Mientras sube la escalinata a toda prisa, mira más allá de las pancartas y ve que están poniendo al qilin ante Grindelwald, Liu y Santos.

Hacemos UN RÁPIDO TOUR ALREDEDOR DEL MUNDO. Los dignatarios de los MINISTERIOS DE MAGIA de EUROPA y de otros lugares están viendo la ceremonia.

En la pantalla, el qilin avanza con paso vacilante hacia los candidatos... Mientras va hacia ellos, Grindelwald, Liu y Santos se miran.

Newt corre hacia Fischer, que se da la vuelta y lo mira impasible.

El qilin se planta delante de Grindelwald y lo mira.

Fischer le tiende la maleta a Newt. Newt mira a Fischer, desconcertado por su actitud, y finalmente coge la maleta. Cuando sus dedos se tocan, la maleta empieza a desintegrarse. Presa del pánico, Newt ve cómo el viento arrastra las partículas por el aire. Vuelve a mirar a Fischer, que sigue sonriendo.

Cuando el polvo se dispersa, las pancartas muestran a Grindelwald y al qilin.

El qilin le hace una reverencia a Grindelwald. Durante unos instantes se produce un largo silencio.

> VOGEL
> El qilin ha visto. Ha visto bondad, fuerza,
> cualidades esenciales para liderarnos y
> guiarnos. ¿A quién ven ustedes?

Los magos y las brujas allí congregados alzan sus varitas y lanzan HECHIZOS. Los TRES COLORES de Liu, Santos y Grindelwald surcan el cielo y luego se reducen a uno solo: el verde de Grindelwald.

Newt contempla la escena perplejo.

Grindelwald se deleita con tantas adulaciones.

> **VOGEL (CONT'D)**
> Gellert Grindelwald es el nuevo líder
> del mundo mágico por aclamación.

Mientras el público BRAMA, dos acólitos aparecen a ambos lados de Newt y lo suben por la escalinata. Grindelwald mira a Rosier y asiente, y ella se acerca a Queenie y a Jacob.

Newt intenta interponerse, pero los dos acólitos se lo impiden.

Rosier hace subir a Jacob por la escalinata y le da su varita de colubrina a Grindelwald.

Grindelwald contempla a la muchedumbre, que se mantiene expectante sin apartar la vista de él, y entonces señala a Jacob.

> **GRINDELWALD**
> Éste es el hombre que intentó
> arrebatarme la vida. Este hombre, un
> no mago dispuesto a casarse con una
> bruja y contaminar nuestra sangre.
> Crear una unión prohibida nos volvería
> inferiores, débiles, como ellos. Y no
> está solo, amigos míos. Hay miles que
> quieren hacer lo mismo. Sólo puede

haber una respuesta ante semejante
plaga.

Grindelwald tira la varita de Jacob y levanta la suya.

Jacob se vuelve para mirarlo y Grindelwald le lanza un hechizo que lo tira por la escalinata y lo deja tendido boca arriba a los pies de Queenie.

> **GRINDELWALD (CONT'D)**
> *¡Crucio!*

Jacob recibe el impacto del rayo luminoso del hechizo y se retuerce de dolor a los pies de Queenie.

> **NEWT**
> ¡No!

> **QUEENIE**
> ¡Hagan que pare!

> **GRINDELWALD**
> ¡Nuestra guerra contra los muggles
> comienza hoy!

Los SEGUIDORES de Grindelwald JALEAN enardecidos.

Vemos a Lally, a Theseus y a Kama caminando conmocionados entre la muchedumbre.

Jacob sigue retorciéndose de dolor en el suelo hasta que Santos levanta la varita y anula la maldición cruciatus *que está torturándolo. Aliviado, Jacob se recuesta en los brazos de Queenie.*

Grindelwald levanta la mirada hacia el cielo y disfruta de su momento de esplendor.

Permanece así, deleitándose, y entonces...

... ve al fénix describiendo círculos en lo alto. Una solitaria mota de CENIZA desciende en zigzag y se le adhiere a la mejilla. Grindelwald se la quita y pone cara de consternación.

Grindelwald se da la vuelta, entorna los ojos y ve una FIGURA que sube por la escalinata.

Es Credence.

Grindelwald observa con interés a Credence, que parece debilitado pero desafiante. Cuando Credence se detiene delante de Grindelwald, extiende la mano como si fuera a acariciarle la cara, pero desliza un dedo por su mejilla y le deja una mancha de ceniza. Aberforth y Dumbledore salen del fondo de la multitud cuando Credence se da la vuelta y se dirige a los dignatarios.

CREDENCE

Les está mintiendo. Esa criatura está
muerta.

ANIMALES FANTÁSTICOS

Newt contempla con tristeza al qilin hechizado.

Ya al límite de sus fuerzas, Credence cae de rodillas.

Aberforth quiere ir a ayudarlo, pero Dumbledore se lo impide sujetándolo con suavidad.

DUMBLEDORE
Ahora no. Espera.

Newt se libera de sus captores.

NEWT
Lo ha hecho para engañarlos. Lo ha matado y hechizado para que crean que él es digno de liderarlos. Pero no quiere liderarlos, quiere manipularlos.

GRINDELWALD
Palabras. Palabras ideadas para engañarlos. Para hacerles dudar de lo que han visto con sus propios ojos.

NEWT
Aquella noche nacieron dos qilin. Gemelos. Y lo sé... Lo sé porque...

GRINDELWALD

¿Por qué...? Porque no tiene pruebas.
Porque no hubo un segundo qilin. ¿Me
equivoco?

NEWT

A su madre la mataron.

GRINDELWALD

¿Y dónde está ahora, señor Scamander?

Grindelwald mira a Newt triunfante, y entonces se fija en una dignataria con túnica verde...

La mujer avanza hasta salir a la luz; lleva una MALETA en la mano y se la entrega a Newt, que se queda mirándola atónito.

La figura de la túnica levanta la cabeza y descubrimos que es... Bunty.

BUNTY

Nadie puede saberlo todo, Newt.
¿Recuerdas?

Mira a su alrededor y de pronto se da cuenta de que está rodeada de gente importante; entonces se aparta y Newt abre la maleta.

De la maleta asoma una cabecita que mira con curiosidad.

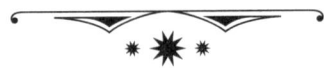

Es el qilin.

Vogel lo mira incrédulo, y luego mira con nerviosismo a Grindelwald, que también parece inquieto. Theseus y Lally se miran sorprendidos. Tina observa desde el MINISTERIO ESTADOUNIDENSE. Newt, más atónito que nadie, sonríe aliviado y agradecido.

Ante la atenta mirada de todos los presentes, el qilin sale de la maleta y se pone en pie; parpadea aturdido e intenta orientarse. Entonces percibe algo, se da la vuelta y ve:

Al qilin hechizado, que está de pie al lado de Grindelwald.

Inmediatamente, el qilin emite un DÉBIL LAMENTO, una llamada, un sonido emotivo y desgarrador, pero su gemelo hechizado no muda la expresión: sus ojos permanecen inexpresivos.

Newt se arrodilla junto al qilin, que está aturdido.

NEWT
(en voz baja)

No puede oírte, pequeñín. Aquí no,
pero a lo mejor te está escuchando
desde otro lugar.

VOGEL

¡Éste es el auténtico qilin!

Vogel agarra al qilin hechizado, se da la vuelta y observa a los presentes.

VOGEL (CONT'D)
Mírenlo, pueden verlo con sus ojos.
Éste es el auténtico...

Titubea al ver que el qilin que sostiene se cae hacia un lado, y vemos que el animal tiene los ojos negros y sin brillo.

La bruja británica a la que vimos por última vez en Berlín da unos pasos adelante.

BRUJA BRITÁNICA
¡Esto es inaceptable! Hay que votar de
nuevo. Vamos, Anton. ¡Haz algo!

Vogel parece confundido y asustado.

El qilin vivo camina poco a poco hacia Dumbledore.

DUMBLEDORE
No. No, no, no, no, por favor.

El qilin lo observa atentamente y su mirada inquisitiva hace callar a Dumbledore. El qilin empieza a resplandecer y entonces, despacio, hace una reverencia.

Newt observa con curiosidad y cariño.

DUMBLEDORE (CONT'D)

Es un honor.

(turbado, hace una pausa)

Pero, igual que nacisteis dos aquella noche, aquí hay otra persona igual de digna. Estoy seguro.

Dumbledore acaricia al qilin con suavidad.

DUMBLEDORE (CONT'D)

Gracias.

El qilin mira a Dumbledore con curiosidad y luego va a hacerle una reverencia a Santos, mientras Grindelwald observa la escena con repugnancia.

Grindelwald mira a Dumbledore cada vez más turbado y levanta la varita. Credence, al ver que Grindelwald apunta con ella al qilin, reúne las escasas fuerzas que le quedan y se planta delante de él.

Sin dudar ni un instante, Grindelwald mueve la varita y le lanza un hechizo a CREDENCE, y ENTONCES...

... UN ESCUDO DE LUZ CEGADORA se materializa delante de Credence, cortesía de...

... Dumbledore y Aberforth, que instintivamente, cada uno por su lado, han lanzado sendos hechizos protectores.

El hechizo de Grindelwald se estrella contra el ESCUDO RE-LUCIENTE. Seguimos la dirección de su mirada, que recorre el camino trazado por el hechizo, y descubrimos...

... que su hechizo y el de Dumbledore se han conectado.

Se miran a los ojos, ambos perplejos al encontrarse encadenados el uno al otro. Por un instante permanecen así, conectados, absorbiendo el uno el poder del otro, como si el mundo se hubiese detenido. Entonces:

La cadena del PACTO DE SANGRE se rompe y el FRASCO DE CRISTAL cae girando lentamente hacia el suelo. Grindelwald y Dumbledore ven que la luz que sale del frasco empieza a PARPADEAR hasta que emite un DESTELLO y de pronto todo queda en silencio. Todo se queda QUIETO, como si hasta la rotación de la tierra se estuviese ralentizando.

El frasco sigue girando despacio en el aire y su centro se resquebraja.

Los hechizos de ambos se evaporan. Grindelwald y Dumbledore se miran a los ojos, y ambos se dan cuenta al mismo tiempo de que han quedado liberados.

Al instante, levantan la varita y DISPARAN con ellas una y otra vez (atacan y se defienden, atacan y se defienden) en una vertiginosa y catártica exhibición de poder. Mientras siguen peleando, se van acercando más y más, pues ninguno de los

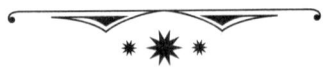

dos consigue vencer al otro, ninguno quiere darse por vencido, hasta que, por fin, cuando ya están casi cara a cara, sus brazos se entrelazan un momento, y entonces...

Pausa. Respiración entrecortada. La mirada de uno clavada en la del otro. Dumbledore extiende un brazo y apoya delicadamente la mano sobre el corazón de Grindelwald. Grindelwald hace lo mismo y pone la mano sobre el corazón de Dumbledore.

Dumbledore baja ligeramente la cabeza y mira a los ojos a Grindelwald.

Justo entonces, un FINO HILO de LUZ AMARILLA que surge de la multitud que está abajo se abre camino por el cielo. Al cabo de un momento, se le suma otro HILO de LUZ AMARILLA. Y luego otro.

Grindelwald los observa, y su semblante delata un temor latente.

Dumbledore ve cómo más hilos luminosos van abriéndose paso por el cielo y, extrañamente conmovido, se da la vuelta y se dispone a entrar de nuevo en el mundo que ha dejado congelado.

Grindelwald se queda donde está.

GRINDELWALD
¿Quién te querrá ahora, Dumbledore?

El frasco de sangre cae al suelo.

CRAC.

Se parte en dos y de su centro sale humo... La tierra empieza a rotar de nuevo sobre su eje, las figuras que rodean a Grindelwald y a Dumbledore vuelven a la vida.

Dumbledore se aleja de Grindelwald sin mirar atrás y Grindelwald se queda solo.

GRINDELWALD (CONT'D)
Estás solo.

Al cabo de un instante, MILES DE HILOS AMARILLOS SE ENTRELAZAN EN EL CIELO y todos los presentes quedan bañados en una suave luz amarilla. Los MINISTERIOS DE MAGIA de todo el mundo, incluidos los de Brasil y Francia, vitorean a Santos y también envían al cielo hechizos explosivos amarillos. Grindelwald lo contempla todo, derrotado.

Mira a sus oponentes, que ahora se han unido y avanzan hacia él apuntándolo con la varita, encabezados por Santos y el qilin.

Grindelwald se desaparece, se materializa en el borde del enorme precipicio y se queda de pie, de espaldas al vacío. Rápidamente crea un escudo a su alrededor, porque todos empiezan a lanzarle hechizos.

Pero a él sólo le importa una persona: Dumbledore.

GRINDELWALD (CONT'D)

Nunca he sido tu enemigo, ni antes ni ahora.

TODOS le lanzan hechizos a Grindelwald casi a la vez, y entonces, tras dedicarle una última mirada a Dumbledore... cae hacia atrás y se desaparece.

Theseus, Lally y Kama, seguidos por muchos otros, corren hacia el borde del precipicio y ven...

... que Grindelwald ya no está.

Dumbledore desvía la mirada y ve a Aberforth abrazando a Credence. Credence ya está muy débil y mira a Aberforth con curiosidad. Una luz amarilla baña su rostro.

CREDENCE

¿Alguna vez has pensado en mí?

ABERFORTH

Siempre. Ven a casa.

Aberforth levanta a su hijo del suelo. Cuando comienzan a bajar por la escalinata, Dumbledore ve que el fénix echa a volar tras ellos mientras desciende lentamente de la montaña.

Newt contempla aquel paisaje dorado y, más allá, el reino de Bután. De pronto parece cansado.

LO que me encanta de los personajes de Jo es que no son planos. Grindelwald es realmente siniestro, pero, a diferencia de Voldemort, el amor no es lo único que falta en su vida. Creo que lo entristece que Dumbledore, su gran amor, no se haya unido a él en este viaje. Por lo tanto, sí, Grindelwald es un ser cruel, siniestro y ansioso de poder, un ser que no se detendría ante nada para conseguir sus objetivos. Pero debajo de todo eso hay un sentimiento de pérdida, de melancolía.

—DAVID HEYMAN

(Productor)

BUNTY

Aquí está.

Newt se da la vuelta y ve a Bunty con el qilin en brazos.

NEWT

Buen trabajo, Bunty.

Bunty niega con la cabeza y sonríe.

NEWT (CONT'D)

Vamos, pequeñín.

Newt abre la maleta para introducir en ella al qilin.

BUNTY

Lo siento. Te habré dado un susto de
muerte.

Newt coge al qilin y niega con la cabeza.

NEWT

No. A veces, hasta que no pierdes algo
no te das cuenta de lo mucho que
significa para ti.

*Bunty mira la maleta de Newt mientras éste sigue abrazando
al qilin. Ve la fotografía de Tina y esboza una sonrisa.*

BUNTY
Y otras... no hace falta...

Titubea. Newt la observa.

Bunty se da la vuelta y va a reunirse con los demás.

NEWT
Vale, adentro.

Cuando Newt mete al qilin en la maleta, CORTE A:

Dumbledore, que mira a Jacob desde cierta distancia.

DUMBLEDORE
Señor Kowalski, le debo una disculpa.

Jacob, que se da la vuelta y ve a Dumbledore.

DUMBLEDORE (CONT'D)
No era mi intención que fuera víctima
de la maldición *cruciatus*.

JACOB
Sí, bueno, hemos recuperado a
Queenie, así que estamos en paz.
(*pausa*)
Oiga, una pregunta...

Jacob mira a su alrededor, se inclina hacia Dumbledore y le dice en VOZ BAJA:

JACOB (CONT'D)
¿Puedo quedármela? Ya sabe, por los viejos tiempos, ¿mmm?

Dumbledore mira hacia abajo, ve la varita de colubrina que Jacob tiene en la mano; luego levanta la cabeza y vuelve a mirar a Jacob.

DUMBLEDORE
No se me ocurre nadie más digno de ella.

JACOB
Gracias, profesor.

Jacob sonríe contento y se la guarda en el bolsillo. Dumbledore lo ve ir hacia Queenie y luego va a reunirse con Newt.

Dumbledore examina el borde del precipicio; entonces se saca el pacto de sangre roto del bolsillo y se lo muestra a Newt.

DUMBLEDORE
Extraordinario.

NEWT
Pero ¿cómo? Creía que no podíais enfrentaros el uno al otro.

> **DUMBLEDORE**
> Y no lo hemos hecho. Él quería matar,
> y yo, proteger. Nuestros hechizos se
> han cruzado.

Dumbledore sonríe con pesar.

> **DUMBLEDORE (CONT'D)**
> Llamémoslo «destino». Al fin y al
> cabo, ¿cómo, si no, escribimos nuestro
> destino?

Newt lo observa con curiosidad, y entonces se les une Theseus.

> **THESEUS**
> Albus. Prométemelo. Lo encontrarás y
> lo detendrás.

Dumbledore asiente.

El horizonte dorado empieza a DIFUMINARSE, y hay un FUNDIDO A NEGRO.

96 **EXT. LOWER EAST SIDE – NUEVA YORK – NOCHE**

Una calle del Lower East Side. Una luz cálida se ve detrás de las VENTANAS de la PASTELERÍA KOWALSKI.

RENDER DE LA PASTELERÍA KOWALSKI

97 INT. PASTELERÍA KOWALSKI – CONTINUO – NOCHE

Varias PERSONAS entran y salen de cuadro, tanto muggles como magos. El pastel de boda de Jacob se muestra ahora con orgullo, con los novios reunidos en lo alto.

JACOB
¡Albert, no te olvides de los *pierogis*!

ALBERT
Sí, señor.

Jacob y Newt van vestidos con CHAQUÉS. Jacob se pelea con su corbata.

JACOB
¡Albert! Los *kolaczkis*, no más de ocho minutos.

ALBERT
Sí, señor.

JACOB
(a Newt)
Es un buen chico, pero no sabría diferenciar un *paszteciki* de un *golabki*.

Entonces entra Queenie con un PRECIOSO VESTIDO DE BLONDA.

QUEENIE

Cariño...

JACOB

¡¿Qué?!

QUEENIE

Newt no sabe de qué estás hablando.
Yo tampoco. Y hoy no trabajas,
¿recuerdas?
            (mirando a Newt)
¿Estás bien, cielo?
            (a Newt)
Ah, estás nervioso por el discurso. No
estés nervioso.
            (a Jacob)
Díselo, tesoro.

JACOB

No estés nervioso por el discurso.

NEWT

No estoy nervioso.

JACOB

¿Y ese olor? ¿Qué se está quemando?
¡Albert!

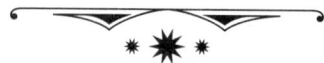

Jacob sale corriendo. Queenie pone los ojos en blanco.

QUEENIE
A lo mejor estás nervioso por otra cosa,
¿eh?

NEWT
No sé de qué estás hablando.

Queenie sonríe con complicidad y se marcha.

98 EXT. PASTELERÍA KOWALSKI – MOMENTOS MÁS TARDE – NOCHE

Newt sale de la tienda, se queda bajo el toldo de la entrada y se saca un trozo de PAPEL del bolsillo. Lo despliega. Empieza a RECITAR su discurso.

NEWT
El día que conocí a Jacob, eh... El día
que conocí a Jacob... estábamos los dos
en el Steen National Bank. Jamás me
habría...

NEWT frunce el ceño y levanta la cabeza. Ve a una FIGURA en el banco de la parada de autobús del otro lado de la calle, sentada bajo la nieve.

Justo entonces, Newt percibe algo en la periferia de su campo de visión y se da lentamente la vuelta. Una MUJER se acerca por la calle nevada. No necesita mirarla dos veces. Sabe quién es.

Tina.

> **NEWT (CONT'D)**
> La dama de honor, supongo.

> **TINA**
> El padrino, entiendo.

> **NEWT**
> ¿Te has hecho algo en el pelo?

> **TINA**
> No. Ah... Bueno, sí, sólo para esta
> noche.

> **NEWT**
> Te queda bien.

> **TINA**
> Gracias, Newt.

Se miran sin decir nada más y entonces...

... aparecen Lally y Theseus.

THESEUS

Hola.

NEWT

Mirad quién...

THESEUS

¿Cómo estás?

NEWT

Estás muy guapa, Lally.

LALLY

Gracias, Newt. Eres un encanto. Buena
suerte.

(a Tina)

Tina, vamos. Tienes que ponerme al día
del MACUSA.

Entran en la pastelería.

*Theseus hace ademán de seguirlas, pero entonces se detiene y
mira hacia atrás, hacia la calle. Tras un momento:*

THESEUS

¿Y yo qué? ¿Cómo me ves? ¿Estás bien?

NEWT

Muy guapo.

THESEUS

¿Te encuentras bien?

NEWT

Sí, claro.

THESEUS

No estarás nervioso, ¿no? No puedes
ponerte nervioso por un discurso
después de salvar el mundo.

*Se miran, y entonces Newt desvía la mirada hacia la otra
acera y ve a Dumbledore sentado en el banco de la parada
de autobús.*

Newt cruza la calle nevada y se detiene delante del banco.

DUMBLEDORE

Es un día histórico. Donde hubo un
ayer, habrá un mañana. Es curioso
cómo los días históricos parecen
ordinarios cuando los estás viviendo.

NEWT

A lo mejor eso es lo que pasa cuando las
cosas salen bien.

DUMBLEDORE
Es maravilloso saber que de vez en cuando es así.

Newt lo mira.

NEWT
No sabía si vendrías.

DUMBLEDORE
Yo tampoco lo sabía.

Se miran, y entonces Dumbledore desvía la mirada. Se abre la puerta de la pastelería y aparece Queenie. Está radiante.

QUEENIE
¡Eh, Newt! Jacob cree que ha perdido el anillo. Dime que lo tienes tú.

Newt se da la vuelta y Pickett se asoma por el bolsillo con un SENCILLO ANILLO con un DIAMANTE pequeño pero precioso.

NEWT
Lo tengo, tranquila. Sí.

Ella sonríe y vuelve a entrar en la tienda. Newt mira a Pickett.

NEWT (CONT'D)

Muy bien, Pick.

(mirando a Dumbledore)

Creo que debería...

Dumbledore no dice nada y sigue mirando hacia otro lado.

DUMBLEDORE

Gracias, Newt.

NEWT

¿Por qué?

DUMBLEDORE

Tienes donde elegir.

Newt asiente con la cabeza.

DUMBLEDORE (CONT'D)

No habría podido hacerlo sin ti.

Newt esboza una sonrisa. Dumbledore hace un gesto afirma- tivo con la cabeza. Newt empieza a alejarse, pero entonces se detiene.

NEWT

Volvería a hacerlo, por cierto. Si me lo pidieras.

Newt lo mira con curiosidad, se da la vuelta, se dirige a la pastelería y entra.

Cuando cierra la puerta, una JOVEN con un VESTIDO ESTAMPADO DE ROSAS ROJAS entra corriendo en el plano.

Aturdida, mira a su alrededor y entonces ve la pastelería.

Es Bunty.

Dumbledore la ve entrar a toda prisa.

Se queda sentado un momento más, observando la calle, y entonces se levanta.

99 INT. PASTELERÍA KOWALSKI – CONTINUO – NOCHE

Queenie avanza para ponerse al lado de Jacob ante un CLÉRIGO MÁGICO. Queenie se vuelve y mira a Jacob. Detrás de ellos, Newt, Tina, Lally, Theseus, Bunty y Albert observan emocionados.

JACOB
¡Vaya, estás preciosa!

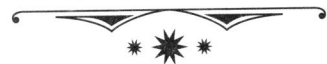

100 EXT. PASTELERÍA KOWALSKI – CONTINUO – NOCHE

Dumbledore mira a través del escaparate y sonríe. Se ciñe el cuello del abrigo y se pone en marcha, caminando solo por la calle cubierta de nieve hacia el lejano horizonte invernal.

RENDER DEL LOWER EAST SIDE, NUEVA YORK

J. K. ROWLING es la autora de los siete libros de la famosísima saga de Harry Potter, que ha marcado una época, así como de varias novelas independientes tanto para niños como para adultos y de la famosa serie protagonizada por el detective Strike, que firma con el seudónimo de Robert Galbraith. Muchos de sus libros se han adaptado al cine y a la televisión. Ha colaborado también en una obra de teatro que continúa la historia de Harry, *Harry Potter y el legado maldito*, y en una nueva serie de películas inspiradas en el libro complementario *Animales fantásticos y dónde encontrarlos*.

STEVE KLOVES escribió los guiones de siete de las películas de Harry Potter, basados en los libros de J. K. Rowling. También hizo de productor en *Animales fantásticos y dónde encontrarlos* y en *Animales fantásticos: los crímenes de Grindelwald*. Más recientemente, ha producido *Mowgli: La leyenda de la selva*. También ha trabajado en *Adiós a la inocencia, Jóvenes prodigiosos, Como uña y carne* y *Los fabulosos Baker Boys*. Además, ha dirigido estas dos últimas películas.

OTRAS OBRAS DE J. K. ROWLING

Harry Potter y la piedra filosofal
Harry Potter y la cámara secreta
Harry Potter y el prisionero de Azkaban
Harry Potter y el cáliz de fuego
Harry Potter y la Orden del Fénix
Harry Potter y el misterio del príncipe
Harry Potter y las Reliquias de la Muerte

Animales fantásticos y dónde encontrarlos
Quidditch a través de los tiempos
(Publicados a beneficio de Comic Relief y Lumos)

Los cuentos de Beedle el Bardo
(Publicado a beneficio de Lumos)

Harry Potter y el legado maldito
(Basada en una idea original de J. K. Rowling, John Tiffany
y Jack Thorne. Una obra de teatro de Jack Thorne)

Animales fantásticos y dónde encontrarlos
(Guión original de la película)
Animales fantásticos: los crímenes de Grindelwald
(Guión original de la película)

El ickabog
El cerdito de Navidad

Un agradecimiento especial al elenco y al equipo técnico y artístico de *Animales fantásticos: los secretos de Dumbledore*, cuyo trabajo queda reflejado en los renders de producción, los bocetos y los diseños gráficos incluidos en este libro.

El diseño de este libro es obra de Paul Kepple y Alex Bruce, de Headcase Design. Se ha usado la tipografía ITC Stone Serif, diseñada por Sumner Stone.